Free stuff notice

Buyers of the physical book are entitled to a free digital pdf, kindle and kobo versions. Scan the QR code below or go to smartworkbeatshardwork.com/claim on your phone.

Acknowledgements

There are many people who contributed to the creation of this book. Some of them are close to me and some I have never even met. Special thanks to those who kept me motivated by checking up on my work every Monday for almost a year, particularly those who commented with suggestions and words of encouragement: Martín, Sue, Tom, Lionel, Elaine, Andrew, JJ, Magalie, Rituparna, Mylene and Mikel. Extra gratitude to Fran, Liesbeth, Tom and Sasha who proofread the draft at multiple stages.

Table of Contents

How to read this book

Treat this book as a buffet. Find the things you like, consume them and skip what doesn't appeal to you.

To help you navigate effectively this book:

- uses of lists, headings and tables in favor of paragraphs
- shows **links** like this (smartworkbeatshardwork.com") as
  - clickable elements in the (free for physical book buyers) digital version
  - underlined words with the source domain after it in brackets

You will find **sidenotes** that look like this[1] and are inserted right after the paragraph in which they are used.

> [1] *This is a sidenote* ↵

I use these sidenotes both for comments and references. You can skip them while reading and still get the main points.

Structure of the sections

The book is separated into 4 sections:

1. Productivity & learning
2. Health & body recomposition
3. Finance & investment
4. My specific implementations of the information in this book

Each section ends with a shopping list of recommended items (no affiliate links).

Structure of the chapters

The chapters in the first 3 sections follow the same format. Each chapter is written so as to have a 'how to' approach. Every chapter has 5 sections:

1. The principles in this chapter
2. What you can expect in this chapter
3. Explanation of each principle
4. Getting started suggestions
5. My personal story in learning

Free digital versions

As mentioned on page 1, buyers of the physical book are entitled to a free digital pdf, kindle and kobo versions. Scan the QR code below or go to smartworkbeatshardwork.com/claim on your phone.

I **highly** recommend claiming the digital versions since they are updated periodically, and you get them for free.

Free digital copy claim

Chapter

Form new habits

Principles for forming new habits

1. Have a clear game plan
2. Set up motivational structures
3. Stack the environment in your favour
4. Have specific triggers
5. Commit for 30-days

In this chapter

- How one guy hired an assistant to slap him in the face
- Using human nature in your favour
- Leveraging technology to increase your odds of success

Have a clear game plan

Your plan of action is what will shape your actual behaviour. To increase your chances of success make sure that the plan:

1. is clear about what you are going to do
2. is within realistic bounds
3. incorporates clear triggers

A vague plan like 'I will exercise more' can never succeed because the goal is not defined. A plan like 'I will do 5 push-ups per day' works much better. Ideally, you formulate a trigger as well, like 'I will do 5 push-ups per day right before my daily shower'.

The above plan checks all boxes:

1. The plan (5 push-ups a day) is clear
2. You are capable of 5 push-ups a day (if not, lower the number)
3. There is a clear trigger for your intended habit

Another example may be saving money. The goal 'I want to save more money' could be formulated as 'I will transfer 10% of my paycheck to my savings account the day after I receive my wages'.

Set up motivational structures

After a clear game plan, you need to make sure that you have the right internal and external pressures to keep you going. For detailed strategies please read the chapter on motivation. The most important elements for habit formation are:

- Writing down the cost of failure
- Writing down the benefit of success
- Set up accountability
- Create a path of least resistance

The motivational elements are as important as setting well-defined goals with well-defined triggers. In particular, closely read the section on accountability, which is for most people the most powerful driver.

Stack the environment in your favour

The space around us and the things we are exposed to influence our decisions. Putting yourself in the right physical space and exposing yourself more to the things you want and less to the things you do not want is extremely powerful. Imagine how hard it would be to avoid eating sugar when you are in Willy Wonka's chocolate factory. Or how much easier it is to have a daily workout if there is a gym within walking distance. Your environment matters.

The idea here is to influence two variables:

- Making sticking to your habit easy and fun
- Making deviating from your habit difficult and painful

Your environment in the very physical sense should be conducive to sticking to your new habit.

- Consider what you need to stick to your new habit and have it around.
- Remove things that will tempt you to break your new habit.

If you are trying to drink more water, make sure you always have a bottle of water with you. If you are trying to eat less candy, make sure there is no candy in the house.

For many habits it pays off to have cues and reminders. Personally, I find Post-its very helpful. Stick reminders for your new habits in places you see often. I personally favour doors into rooms I am bound to visit multiple times a day like the bathroom/shower. You may opt for very direct triggers. An example of that is hanging a pull-up bar in a doorpost you walk through often. You may also opt for digital cues. I, for example, have a 'go to bed' alarm that rings at night. Likewise, when I open apps on my phone that tend to turn into time-sinks (email, Reddit, Instagram) I get a popup asking 'are you sure you want to spend time and focus on this?' for 5 seconds.

Make sticking to new habits more fun

To make sticking to your habit more fun, make sure to have a conducive environment and equipment set. For example, I find stretching far more enjoyable on a high-quality yoga mat, causing me to stretch more consistently. Likewise, if you are trying to cook healthier food, make sure to have tools like good knives to make it easier and more enjoyable.

This is not just true for equipment but also for space, time and other environmental variables. If you are trying to take up meditation, for example, it pays off to explore what location in your house/office/school is most silent during the times you like to meditate. I used to use an empty room where people dumped whiteboards and unused chairs for my afternoon meditation session at work.

Make breaking habits painful

In the same way that you make desirable behaviour easier, you want to introduce pain for undesirable behaviour.

One form of pain is introducing extra effort. You would be surprised at the effectiveness of things like:

- Browser extensions that block social media
- Having the bulk of your money in an account without a card
- Putting the chocolate in a cupboard high enough that you need a chair to reach it

These obstacles are all easy to circumvent. Funnily enough that extra little effort is often what we humans need to decide it is not worth it.

Another very effective method is committing money to things. Consider two scenarios, one in which you pay for 10 sessions with a personal trainer in one payment, and one where you pay the trainer after each session. Which of those scenarios do you think would result in more sessions with your personal trainer?

You can do this with plenty of new habits. Sink some cost into it combined with the other techniques in this section and you are likely to increase your odds of success. The reason this works is that not sticking to your habit after you have sunk money into it feels like (and is) losing money.

If you give a person €10 they will be happy. If you give them €20 and later steal €10 from them they will be sad. Even though in both scenarios they end up with €10 [2] . Humans are more risk-averse than goal-oriented, use that to your benefit.

[2] *See Wikipedia entry on Loss Aversion (en.wikipedia.org)* ↵

Have specific triggers

Effective triggers for habit formation come in the form of:

- **Location:** e.g. doing five push-ups when you get home
- **Time:** e.g. going to bed at 22:00
- **Activity:** e.g. read a page of an interesting book when you go to the bathroom
- **Feeling:** e.g. when I feel like smoking I will go for a walk instead

Depending on the habit you are trying to institute you can implement one of multiple triggers of any kind. It is important to make sure that triggers are realistic and that the corresponding habit is easy to execute.

Triggers are most effective when there is an outside force reminding you of them. If you just decide to go to bed at 10 every day, there is a high likelihood that there will be times you will lose track of time and fail to stick to your habit.

Personally, I find the following reminder mechanisms most effective:

- Location-based reminders
- Digital reminders
- Social reminders

Location-based reminders can be the previously discussed Post-its, but also, for example, making sure there are interesting books in your bathroom or having a pull-up bar in one or multiple doorposts.

Digital reminders have many forms. The obvious choice is setting recurring alarms, for example, the bedtime alarm mentioned before. Smartphones can do a lot more though. For example, most Androids and iPhones can give location-based reminders (e.g. a notification when you get home). Likewise, your digital calendar can be used to plan in workouts or even daily meditation sessions.

Social reminders depend on other people. For a while, I combined this with digital reminders to institute a daily meditation practice. I would sit down to meditate at 12:00 every day together with my little brother who was in Australia at the time. We would have a quick exchange through a messaging app beforehand and would ask each other how it went after. Likewise, you can ask a co-worker to remind you to go for a walk at lunch, or have your significant other remind you that you haven't worked out today.

Commit for 30-days

There is nothing magical about the number 30. It just turns out we are socially conditioned to see 30-days as a standardised amount of time because of our calendar system.

The power behind this commitment technique starts with the fact that implementing a habit for the rest of your life sounds incredibly significant and difficult. Contrarily, most people are pretty sure they can stick to even difficult new habits for 30-days.

Once something has a clear end date, a 'light at the end of the tunnel', it becomes easier to stick to it. The key here is that you are allowed to stop the habit after these 30-days. It's kind of like a 30-day free trial on a habit.

The funny thing about doing something for 30-days is that after they are over, many people find out that a habit has now become exactly that, a habit. This means that after the initial 30-days, most people find it trivially easy to keep the habit going.

To make your chances of success higher, you will, of course, have to combine this with the above techniques. But for many people using this technique makes it significantly easier to institute a new habit.

Getting started

Habit formation is a very powerful skill. To prove to yourself that you are capable of engineering your routines, I suggest starting with a 30-day experiment. To set it up:

1. Pick a clear & measurable goal
2. Pick a measuring device
3. Get others on board

For example, you may resolve to:

1. Do 5 push-ups a day
2. You strike an x on your calendar for every day you complete
3. You convince a sibling/friend/colleague to do the same and you keep track of each other

You may use some of the other measures in this chapter to make success more likely, but when getting started, simplicity makes it more likely you will actually get started.

If you are not sure what habit to start with, here are some of my favourite ones from easy to hard:

- Drink 2 large glasses of water within 10 minutes of getting up
- Meditate for 5 minutes (or more)
- Do x push-ups (5, 10, 20 depending on your fitness)
- Listen to productive podcasts on your way to work
- Don't use screens (TV, phone, computer) in the hour before sleeping
- End your showers with 1 minute of cold water
- Sleep for 8-9 hours a day
- Eat no added sugar

I'm sure that when you think for a few minutes, you can think of a habit that will make your life significantly better. As you can see above, it doesn't have to be a big or complex habit, start simple.

More time in a day

I, like many people, used to wish there were more than 24 hours in a day. It lead me to consider things like polyphasic sleep [3] to increase my waking hours. After a while, I realised that less time is not all that useful if you don't effectively utilise it. I concluded that there is no difference between an extra hour and increasing the utility of one hour. Similarly a lot of the things I wanted the extra time for were things that really only required proper management of time and discipline.

[3] *This is sleeping in small increments throughout the day rather than one monolithic block at night. You can use it to sleep hours less per day, at least short-term.* ↵

This caused me to go through a different process, one where I was not trying to optimise the amount of time I had but the quality of usage. There were all sorts of things I wanted to do. Reading more books, listening to podcasts, spending less time on social media and so on. Likewise, there were things about myself I wanted to change, like having high energy levels and a fit body.

Looking at things from a habits perspective was a big shift for me. I had all sorts of activities in the day that when used as a trigger for another behaviour had big impacts. One of those is listening to audiobooks and podcasts while biking to school, university and later to work. In the beginning, this was a difficult ordeal involving (legally) pirated audiobooks, wires and mp3 players without a screen. As the tech progressed this evolved into a simple app on my phone. This one habit singlehandedly shaped the ways in which I think about self-development (thanks, Tony Robbins), business (thanks, Blinkist) and pretty much everything else (thanks, Tim Ferriss & guests).

While I discovered the power of habits relatively early, it has taken me years to institute the ones that work best for me. Much of life is trial and error, and for me that meant trying out habits for a few weeks and then either sticking with them or discarding them. I now actually have a relatively unplanned pattern where I re-do my morning routine every few weeks to modify it with the new things I have found and my needs at the time. The process usually involves writing some things down in a notebook, and then translating that to Post-its that go on my bathroom door or scribbles that I write on my hand as a reminder.

The most extreme usage I have ever made of habits for the sake of productivity is the year that I juggled a full-time job with a full-time masters degree (which insisted on physical presence for all classes). Before starting it I knew it would be the biggest challenge I had taken up to that point with regards to time commitment. The preparation process for that year involved a lot of Post-its, see How I Survive Multiple Full Time Engagements (skillcollector.com). Eventually, the main habits that kept me in business/sane that year were to:

- Treat my body well with exercise and food
- Treat my mind well with sleep and meditation
- Take day/week planning seriously
- Work/study whenever and wherever I have 10+ minutes

In practice, that meant I would get up early and first thing spend half an hour planning the most important things that were on my to-do list that day. If I was staying in Amsterdam that morning I would go to the gym and, if not, then I'd be power walking to the train (while listening to inspiring podcasts). The 10 minutes spent waiting were dedicated to work and study, as were the train and tram rides to my client out of town. The advantage of this taking place in the Netherlands was that the trains were comfortable and usually on time. The train line I took was the same as many politicians take (since it went to The Hague) and I used to joke that the train operator took extra effort to make sure that the trains were never delayed (happened once in the entire year).

The ride to my client was spent prepping for that day's work, whereas the way back consisted of preparing for the class I'd be taking when I got back to Amsterdam. On an average day, I'd absorb the learnings from books through audio summaries, prepare and do work, prepare and participate in class, work out, meditate and cook good food. It was a rollercoaster that I wouldn't choose to repeat any time soon. But like a good rollercoaster, it was exciting and intense. The whole experience illustrated to me how powerful the right habits can be and the things they can facilitate in your life.

Chapter
Motivate yourself

Principles for self-motivation

- Motivation is not a feeling
- Inspiration is temporary
- Step 1: quantify your goals
- Step 2: write down the reward & punishment
- Step 3: create a path of least resistance
- Step 4: set up accountability
- Defeat procrastination

In this chapter

- Why you can't rely on 'feeling motivated'
- How to use your emotions in your favour
- Creating trackable goals
- Making it fun to keep going and painful to stop
- How I used a local spa as a study room

Motivation is not a feeling

Motivation is the expression of one simple question: why are you doing this? Consider an extreme thought experiment where a psychopath holds a gun to your head and tells you to burn down your house. Assuming you are sane and choose your life over your house, what motivated you to comply? Did you simply "feel motivated to burn down the house that day"? No, there was a cue in the outside world that gave you a reason — a motivation — to do something. This motivation was not a randomly arising feeling. It was the result of many factors, including the gun to your head.

More realistic scenarios like getting work done are no different. You can't rely on motivation to strike you, it is up to you to engineer the environment that will help you stick to your goals.

Motivation can take many forms. Many people split these into intrinsic and extrinsic motivation. Where:

- intrinsic motivation is 'I want to do this because I like it'
- extrinsic motivation is 'my friend will give me a cookie if I do this'.

I don't care much for that distinction. It's quite arbitrary. In my view, both are a case of "if I do X I am rewarded with Y". In the case of intrinsic motivation, the Y is simply a feeling instead of a thing. So what I've found a more effective perspective is emotional versus material motivation:

- Emotional motivation is a form where you do something to gain or avoid a feeling. Like working out because it makes you feel better about yourself.
- Material motivation is a form where you will get an object in return for your action. For example, getting paid in cash for washing a car.

Emotional motivation is the most powerful type. It is the desire to feel some things like pleasure, pride and satisfaction or to avoid feelings of pain, insecurity and fear. Motivation is not a feeling. It is a desire to create a certain outcome. Maybe the outcome you desire is not being shot by a psychopath like in the example above, maybe you want someone to respect you.

Either way, motivating yourself is about making clear to yourself what reward you seek and to keep in mind how badly you want that reward. In my opinion, that reward is most effective when it has a strong emotional component.

Inspiration is temporary

Inspiration is the spark you feel when watching an inspiring movie, listening to inspiring music or whatever gets you going. **Motivation** is a force that gets you to do something, regardless of what or how you feel.

If you feel inspired to lose weight, for example, that is not the time to go for a workout. That is the time to plan your workouts for the coming 3 weeks and set up accountability measures.

Inspiration is fickle and temporary. You can't rely on it. If you wake up tomorrow and don't feel inspired, that would mean you could get nothing done that day.

Self-motivating people don't feel inspired all the time. They get things done regardless of how they feel. Through discipline and self-management. This is easier than it sounds, especially if you harness feelings of inspiration to set up motivational structures.

Step 1: quantify your goals

Good goals can be measured in a clear way. The goal "I want more money" is not a good goal. If I give you a cent/penny it will be fulfilled. A good financial goal is "I want to have an investment portfolio worth €400,000".

Measurable goals are key for motivating yourself for 2 reasons:

- They make the finish line clear
- They allow you to track your progress

Depending on your nature, you can either gently track your progress or go nuts on it. Tracking your weight by the week, for example, is fine for some people who want to shed fat. I know of others who measure twice daily on a smart scale and use the resulting graph in the accompanying app as motivation.

Step 2: write down the reward & punishment

Regardless of what you want, there is great power in expressing why you want something as well as the price of not achieving it. Say, for example, you want to learn a new language.

You want this because:

- It will make you feel smart

- You know your friends will think highly of you
- The people in your favourite holiday country will appreciate you for speaking their language
- You will feel like you proved wrong your cousin who said you can't do it

If you fail to complete the challenge:

- You will feel mediocre
- Your friends will think you are a quitter
- The people in St. Holiday will think you are another dumb tourist
- Your cousin will hold this over your head

By expressing these things clearly and reminding yourself of them you can create motivation. Whenever it's the end of a long day and you don't want to do your daily language practice, imagine how you will feel when you achieve it, and imagine the face of your cousin as they will laugh at your failure.

Step 3: create a path of least resistance

Another step in motivating yourself is to make the right path the easiest path to choose. That involves two parts:

1. Making it pleasurable to do the task
2. Making it painful not to do the task

Take the writing of this book, for example. I took concrete steps to make writing it more pleasurable. For me, that meant writing it in a markup language called Markdown [4].

> [4] It's a text-only way of writing, favoured amongst programmers and engineers. It uses characters like #, ^ and - to indicate styling like headings and lists. ↵

Likewise, I took steps to make it painful not to progress. I sent my blog readers and friends an email asking them to join a mailing list that would remind them on a weekly basis to check whether I made 7 updates to my book that week (which was visible publicly). I specifically asked them to publicly shame me on social media if I didn't make it and to give me kind words if I managed.

This meant that writing this book was pleasurable and gave me a weekly boost of 'I made it!'. Likewise, not updating my book 7 times carried the pain of being judged by people I care about, my friends and readers.

There are many things to make your desired task easier, and not doing it too painful to consider. Find what makes you happy and make it a reward, find what makes you uncomfortable and make that a punishment.

Step 4: Set up accountability

An important key in the above is accountability. Humans are very sensitive to negative stimuli. By our nature, we fear loss more than gain appeals to us. This is the human tendency of loss aversion [5]. For example, consider two scenarios:

[5] *See Wikipedia entry on Loss Aversion (en.wikipedia.org)* ↵

- You receive €10 for no reason
- You receive €20 for no reason and later that day someone steals €10 from you

From experiments, we know that the first scenario makes people happy, whereas the second makes them very unhappy.

Likewise, consider:

- You avoid having to pay €5 for a meal
- You paid the meal earlier but someone gives you €5 later

In experiments on humans, the first one makes us much happier.

Of course, there are exceptions, but in most situations humans **hate losing** more than they **like winning**. For motivational purposes, it is often incredibly effective to set up monetary accountability like:

- **If you fail:** an automated donation to a charity you hate. See the Stickk website (stickk.com) where you appoint an honest but stern friend to keep track of your progress
- **A betting pool:** where a number of people commit money (small amount, but painful enough if you lose it) to sticking to a new habit and those who make the deadline get rewarded with the money of those who don't
- **Whatever works for you:** you could take the route of a blogger called Maneesh Sethi and hire someone to slap you in the face [6] if you don't stick to your intention.

[6] *See Why I Hired A Girl On Craigslist to Slap Me In The Face —*
And How It Quadrupled My Productivity (hackthesystem.com) ↵

Humans being social animals, one of the most powerful influences on us is the judgement of others. Embrace that part of our psychology and turn it to your advantage:

- For habits in groups. Get some friends together and hold each other accountable
- Have friends/family keep track of you and either shame/support you based on progress

Dealing with procrastination

When humans feel overwhelmed, we freeze. It's a fight-flight reaction which leads to procrastination. But postponing a task usually doesn't decrease how overwhelming it feels, often quite the oposite.

The keys to overcoming this are:

- Break the problem down into smaller goals
- Start for 5 minutes and allow yourself to quit
- Make common procrastination tools unavailable

Breaking the problem down sounds simple but is incredibly powerful. Wanting to learn conversational Spanish can seem very overwhelming, for example. But if you research your options you can find concrete ways of breaking down this problem. In this instance, you might break it down into doing 1 lesson from the Michel Thomas series on Spanish a day.

The second is the most ridiculous superpower. For most people, keeping going with a task is not all that hard, but starting is. If you find yourself shying away from a task, tell yourself:

> I will do it for 5 minutes. If I don't want to keep going after, I am allowed to stop.

Nine out of ten times those 5 minutes are all you need to get into a flow that will carry on for a good hour. This goes for work tasks, but also, for example, household tasks.

The last and final ingredient is to make procrastination tools unavailable. It is like the above paragraph on the path of least resistance. If you know that your house has too many distractions, go to work in a cafe. If you are on social media a lot, get a browser plugin that blocks them during certain hours. Make it easy to do the right thing and hard to do the wrong.

Getting started

Especially when you are used to low levels of motivation, getting started can seem quite daunting. The key to gaining momentum is to start small and snowball from there. The most important principles in this chapter with regard to getting started are:

1. Quantify a small but specific goal
2. Set up the path of least resistance
3. Start for 5 minutes

You can optimise much further using the other principles, but the above is enough for you to get started right now. Let's say you want to get better at studying:

1. Decide you want to spend 30 minutes a day deeply focussed on studying
2. Choose the right environment, for example, a library, and disable distractions like phone notifications and other things you know yourself to have a weakness for (social media? Netflix? News?)
3. Decide you will go for 5 minutes and if after those 5 minutes you can't do it, give yourself permission to go home

There is of course much more you can do, from a study buddy to betting money that you can do this. The above, however, should be enough of a start to help you develop your motivational structures further.

Another common example is doing exercise:

1. You want to do 30 minutes of exercise 2 times a week
2. You choose a sports facility close to your home and ask one of the employees there to hold on to €50 and that they can keep it if you don't show up on Tuesday and Thursday
3. On those two days, you show up and start your workout, with permission to go home if after 5 minutes you are not feeling it

Both of these instances have a very high chance of success. The key to getting started is to make the goals relatively small (this is specific to you) and to give yourself permission to stop. In practice, you will probably get in a flow and easily make your goal. If you sit down in a library and open a book for 5 minutes, you will easily lose track of time and spend 30 minutes. Likewise, being in a gym and doing your 5-minute warmup will put you in the mindset to keep going.

Using a spa as a study room

Throughout university, I would often find myself naked and sweating preparing for tests. 5 minutes from my house there was a new spa [7] that was usually empty during the day. I had negotiated a favourable unlimited access deal with the owner and would come there often with printed out summaries of my courses. Studying for tests was incredibly relaxing. I'd rotate between sessions of Finnish sauna, cold plunge baths, whirlpools and reading the study materials for whatever test I was taking.

[7] *Northern European spa/sauna complexes are per default fully nude.* ↵

I had come to the conclusion that motivation shouldn't be hard per se. Sure, there are mornings where you want to stay in bed, but progressing towards goals shouldn't be a struggle that makes you feel unhappy. Creating the path of least resistance for me meant eliminating distractions and making studying as easy as possible. To achieve that goal, I tried to construct:

1. A distraction-free study environment
2. Effective learning materials

The first came in the form of the sauna complex. No technology was allowed inside, so all I could bring were printed study materials. In addition, the ambience was one of silence and relaxation.

The learning materials was a different challenge. I knew I liked reading summaries but did not like creating them as much. This hurdle was solved by splitting the burden of summaries amongst my fellow students.

The years prior to university had been a struggle of trial and error. Some of the things I tried to motivate myself worked well. I still attribute my drive to graduate high school with good grades to a photoshopped copy of my diploma to be hanging in my room. Some things did not work as well, like taking a quick break to watch an episode of Doctor Who. Great show as it was, 10 minutes usually turned into an hour or more, and I didn't feel more motivated afterwards.

I soon learned that there were two aspects to motivating my personal psyche. Step 1 was getting started, step 2 was keeping going. I stopped looking at motivation as an external force, but rather saw it as a state you can create. It's like relaxation. Sure, sometimes it is easier to reach than other times but there are always actions you can take to reach that state.

This was for me the biggest turning point. Once I acknowledged that motivation was not a force that comes and goes but a choice, life became a lot easier. It also prompted me to read the writings of others who had written on the subject. Mostly this came down to bloggers and the odd book or two. Most of it was fluff, but the basic rules were similar in all of them.

At this point, I feel in control of my own motivated state. That is not to say that I always manage to motivate myself to do things. But when I fail, I can trace back the cause very clearly and choose to take steps to prevent it from happening again.

An example of this is my daily exercise routine. It works great when I'm at home, but is harder to maintain when I travel. Nine out of ten times this is due to it being harder to get started. The excuses are easy: There is no space, I have to get to the next event, I'll do it later.

The solution is to simply look back at the principles. Create a path of least resistance and then follow it. In hotels, that means that as soon as I get in I move around furniture so that there is space for push-ups and handstands. When I feel resistance to get started I decide to do only half the workout. In the worst case, some workout beats no workout, but usually I end up doing the full thing anyway once I get started.

You'd think that this is all quite a lot of work. But it doesn't take up all that much energy. It's actually the case that once you make sure you facilitate the right circumstances to get motivated, you expend less energy. Don't forget that failing to do what you want to do has an emotional price.

Chapter

Work productively and effectively

Principles to work productively

1. Have a system
2. Prioritise effectiveness over productivity
3. Assign no more time than you need
4. Prioritise based on urgency and importance
5. Collaborate and delegate where possible
6. Automate everything possible

In this chapter

- Automation tools you can use to let machines do your work
- Finding the 20% of tasks that generate 80% of output
- Why you never finish far ahead of a deadline
- "Everybody wins" scenarios in collaboration
- How I went from hating structure to thriving on it

Have a productivity system

The primary function of a productivity system is to reduce the time you spend thinking/worrying about your tasks.

Trust your mind to think, not to remember what to do [8]. Time spent thinking 'what should I do' or worse a generalised anxiety of 'am I forgetting something' detract from your ability to think at your best.

> [8] *The mind is a thought generation machine, not a remembering machine. A list of random numbers is hard to remember, thinking of a list of random numbers is easy.* ↵

To support a clean mind, your system should:

- be outside of your mind (so on an external medium)
- capture thoughts about what to do
- guide your actions to do what is most important
- have you trust it to let nothing fall through the cracks

There is no 'best' system, that depends on your life. Personally I use a 'Getting things done' [9] derivative that consists out of:

> [9] *See the book of that title by David Allen, it is a great way to get inspiration on how to set up your own productivity architecture.* ↵

1. An **inbox** where I dump any idea/task I want to spend time on
2. A **project list** that I assign the tasks to, every project should always have a next task scheduled
3. A **maybe** file where I put ideas/tasks that I might want to do later but not now
4. A **ticker** file where I put ideas/tasks I want to think about later (each ticker task gets a reminder attached to it)

This is combined with:

1. A daily check to make sure tasks are moved from the inbox to a project (preferably with a reminder date attached)
2. A weekly check to see whether all projects have a next action scheduled (otherwise they are not moving forward)
3. A monthly check to see if I want to spend time on any maybe/tickler tasks

Always remember that your todo system should *save time*, not cause you to spend extra time.

Prioritise effectiveness over productivity

Imagine you are on a little boat with a hole in it. You could:

- Find the best bucket to remove water from your vessel.
- Plug the hole in the boat

The first is analogous to productivity: finding the right tool/way to do a task quickly. The second is analogous to effectiveness: optimisation of an outcome by choosing the right task.

Many people are very good at optimising their productivity, but fail to spend time first deciding what tasks are effective to the extent that they deserve your attention. Even if you do them slower, choosing effective tasks will help you beat hyper-productive but ineffective people.

80/20 principle

A helpful principle to keep in mind is the Pareto principle, also known as the 80/20 rule. It observes that in many cases 20% of input is responsible for 80% of output. For example, with 20% of words in a language, you can have 80% of conversations. 20% of customers generate 80% of profits for a business. And indeed, 20% of tasks result in 80% of the effective outcome.

The following questions will help you prioritise doing the right things (effectiveness), rather than doing the wrong things more quickly (productivity).

- Is there any task that will make other tasks obsolete? Start there.
- Which of my tasks will affect me long term? Do them first.
- Can I drop any tasks without serious consequences? Excuse yourself from them.
- Are there any tasks that don't require my expertise? Outsource or delegate them.

5 Why's

An important element to choosing your tasks effectively is taking time to reflect what you are truly trying to achieve. Taiichi Ohno, who revolutionised the Toyota Production System back in the day, is attributed the technique of asking 'why' five times in order to get to the root of a problem. For example, let's say the problem you are diagnosing is that you spend too much time on managing emails:

- Why? Because I have emails to reply to.
- Why? Because I get a large volume of emails.
- Why? Because I am the only one in the company who knows how to do X.
- Why? Because there is no other person or resource that can solve X.
- Why? Because I haven't taken the time to either write down my knowledge or train someone else.

After the first why you might say "I need to spend more time on emails."

After the 5th your conclusion might be to either 1) hire another person or 2) write an internal document detailing the things you are often asked about.

Assign no more time than you need

Parkinson's Law states that "Work expands so as to fill the time available for its completion" [10]. While this principle started as part of a comedy piece, it rings true. If you give yourself a week to finish writing a piece, it will take a week. If you give yourself a month, it will only be done in a month.

> [10] Supposedly it is modelled after the fact that a gas will fill any space you allow it to, see the Wikipedia entry for Parkinson's law (en.wikipedia.org) ↵

Don't give tasks more time than they need. I recommend formulating how much time you allocate to a task based on how much time you:

- Think you need
- Are at most willing to spend

For example, set a 30-minute timer to process your email inbox, or setting yourself deadlines for larger assignments.

The counterbalance to this is to of course be realistic and build in buffer time. This law is not meant to make you miss deadlines.

Prioritise tasks based on importance and urgency

"I have two kinds of problems, the urgent and the important. The urgent are not important, and the important are never urgent." ~ Dwight Eisenhower

When it comes to tasks that have a significant impact on your life and happiness they tend to be important but not urgent. By using a matrix based on Eisenhower's quote you can prioritise the things that really matter.

This is the Eisenhower Matrix:

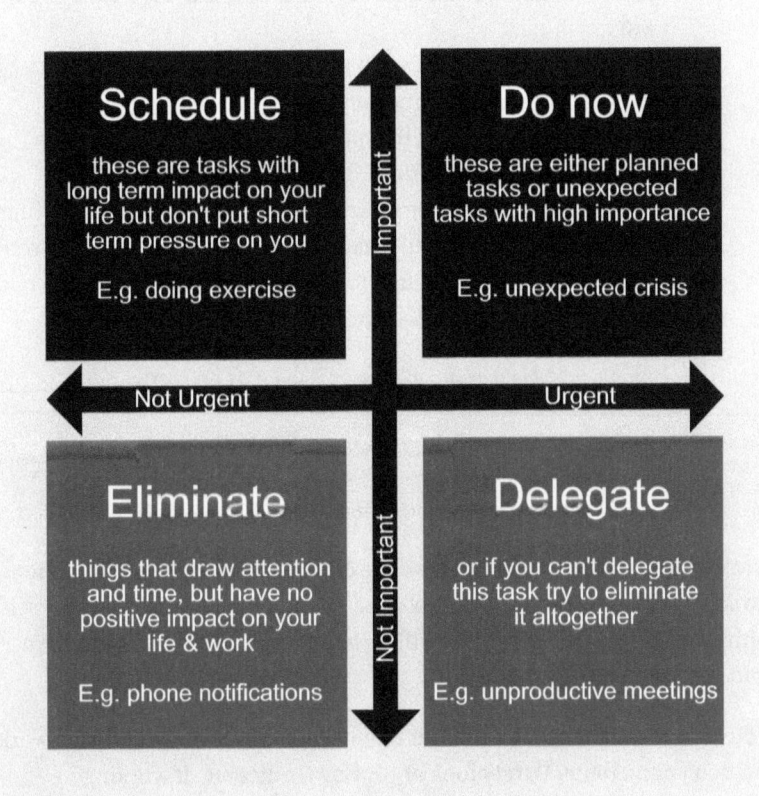

Eisenhower Matrix

It might take some time getting used to, but it pays off to take 5 minutes in the morning to look at your plans for that day and to apply the matrix.

Collaborate where possible

With every task, ask yourself: are more people doing this? If the answer is yes, organise a collaboration to eliminate duplicate work. It also pays off to check if someone else already started a collaboration, for example, online. No area of your life is off limits. Work, household, recreational clubs and so on. Approaches I like:

- **Find checklists:** no matter what kind of job you have, there is most likely someone out there on the internet who created a useful checklist. I personally find more than one checklist and combine them together. This technique works best for well-defined tasks like marketing a blog[11], travel [12] or planning a meeting[13]
- **Look for summaries:** you can check with people around you (colleagues/friends) but often the internet is a more reliable option. From book summaries to the second world war, there are summaries for almost anything.
- **Best practices:** is more common in professional spheres than personal. Regardless of your industry there is likely a person/company/government that published a best practices document. Examples include driving and programming.
- **Common mistakes:** doing something well is sometimes just avoiding messing up. You'd be surprised what people write about online. From cooking mistakes to losing weight to studying, it's out there. Just search for 'common cooking/weight loss/studying mistakes'

[11] *Search for 'blog marketing checklist': About 64.600.000 results* ↵
[12] *Search for 'travel checklist': About 9.880.000.000 results. You can narrow it down with 'travel to X* ↵
[13] *Search for 'meeting checklist': About 173.000.000 results* ↵

While collaboration might not have the exact outcome as you doing the work personally, often the result is good enough. If you surround yourself with fantastic people, the result will be better than what you could have made on your own.

Note that you shouldn't care about freeloaders who leech off of your work but don't contribute. Purely look at your own outcome. If working together saves you 50% of time, who cares that someone who didn't do anything benefits. You are better off now than before, that matters.

Consider a student who with 10 others writes summaries for their course. There are 90 freeloaders in the class using the summries too. Is this unfair?

That is the wrong question. The student now:

- Saved 90% of study time by sharing the workload of summarising
- Has high-quality study materials because 10 people reviewed each other's summaries
- Gained a reputation of being a helpful person

Note also what the large group of freeloaders did not:

- They didn't cost any time
- They didn't cause a decrease in outcome (good grade)

There are only upsides. Many of us have been trained to feel bad about freeloaders. Let go of this feeling. You will save time, build a reputation and build productive relationships.

Automate everything possible

Every task you complete should be subject to the question of whether you can automate it, or make it faster in the future. After a while, these automations will allow you to spend more time on things that matter.

When it comes to investments in equipment, do the math. For a €200 dishwasher for example:

- It saves you 20 minutes a day
- Over a year that is 121.67 hours
- Is your time worth more than $200 / 121.67 = €1.64$ an hour?

Look at the big picture. 5 minutes saved in a daily task is 30 hours per year or about 4 full-time work days.

Little things matter.

Getting started

The core of this chapter is to prioritise effectiveness, in other words, to choose your tasks well rather than doing them quickly/efficiently. A slow worker doing important things all day will outperform someone who replies to menial emails with superhuman speed. Combine this with an urgency and importance rating and you will do infinitely better.

The specifics below might not apply to your line of work, but the same principles apply. To get started:

1. Make a list of things you do on a daily/weekly basis or use Rescuetime (rescuetime.com") to automatically diagnose (at least your digital) behaviour.
2. Rate the things on that list as (un)important as defined by 'will this activity impact my life 2-8 weeks from now' and (not) urgent as defined by the deadline
3. Looking at this list, find the things that generate the best results (e.g. 2 hours of email resulted in nothing tangible, half an hour writing/programming/painting resulted in meaningful output)
4. Schedule a lot of time in your day to the things that are important and generate the most output

Many people fear that taking time away from unimportant things will break their day. "But I can't just ignore email!" and "these tasks are really urgent!" are common responses. The fact of the matter is that this is simply how you have been conditioned. Interestingly, when you stop focussing on urgent things you will come to realise that they don't matter as much.

For example, many people report great results from opening their email only once or twice a day at set times. Some (including me) even add a line in their email signature stating at what times they open their email so other people know what to expect.

Structurally important tasks always outperform urgent busywork.

After you get your priorities in order, start incorporating automation and collaboration into your routines. It is likely that you will notice the busywork you once found so urgent is often a ripe target for automation.

My journey to productivity

People who know me now would never guess how teenage me was. On multiple occasions, I showed up to trampolining competitions in a different country without my gear. Likewise, I never knew where to find school notes older than a week or so.

I remember my English teacher trying to persuade me to keep structured records and showcasing her cupboard filled with filing cabinets and folders. Back then the prospect of such a rigid structure horrified me.

Teenage me was cursed with fortunate circumstance. My genetics and parents had through no effort of my own instilled me with systems thinking (seeing the relation between things), though I didn't call it that at the time. This systems thinking meant I never memorised things (which is why I failed at languages) and instead built intuitive networks of principles in my mind. This created a reality where:

- I could function perfectly fine without structure
- Those who applauded structure didn't understand systems, so I dismissed them

Only later did I discover for myself that systems thinking and structured thinking (having a predefined thinking process) were two powerful tools that — when combined well — create new worlds of possibility. The transition for me started when I failed a grade in high school.

17-year-old me was very upset at being forced to redo a year because of a mediocre grade in Dutch (my native language). I had been clashing with close-minded teachers who didn't want to answer my questions. Specifically, one question: "but why?". All except my biology teacher who always answered (guess what I went on to study in university).

Ironically, the final straw was a grade I got due to having forgotten to bring a specific piece of administrative paper to a test. The teacher was, unfortunately, a closed-minded woman who didn't care that my Dutch was perfectly fine. Rules are rules you know.

That summer break I was angry. Angry and frustrated. In a conversation with my mother, I voiced how I basically felt a destructive urge to ignore school altogether. I felt betrayed and wanted nothing to do with teachers and their idiotic rules. My mother asked a very simple question: "but how is that going to make your life any better?"

Just like that, I went from hot to cold. Looking back it may have been a moment of mild sociopathy. I decided to use every tool at my disposal to show my teachers that they were wrong. Although the trigger might not have been exactly healthy it did cause me to take interest in productivity. Whereas before I saw structure as an imposed force from the outside, I learned to see it as a powerful tool.

My methods were crude compared to what I know now, but they laid the foundation for how I work now. Later that year, in a spiteful moment as only teenagers can produce, my physics teacher reacted to my (silent) contempt for his teaching by telling me I was welcome to not come to class and work in the hallway instead. I did, aced the test and he admitted defeat by asking me to come back to the class.

This was also the year where I learned the value of structure and self-motivation. Once I ignored the advice of my teachers on structure and made one that suited me, life suddenly became a lot easier. The last year of high school I had three jobs and still graduated with the Dutch equivalent of American A's.

After high school, I spent a few months in China doing kung fu at a school in the mountains. As far as discipline goes, it was next level. It gave me a valuable perspective on things people regularly consider hard. There is something sobering about getting up at 5 to do 2 hours of training before breakfast. I didn't learn much Chinese while I was there, except for the words 'water' and 'pain'. My teacher would always let us drink water, but when we were in pain from the so manyeth round of 50 push-ups he would laughingly respond "Ha! I game over you! Fifty more push-ahp!".

University served as a playground to develop my skills further. It is where I learned the value of collaboration. By year 2 I had set up a department-wide dropbox folder where we shared summaries for all available courses. I still keep those summaries and read through them once in a while.

I experimented with a great deal of productivity and health protocols those years. Ranging from the Everyman sleep cycle (5 hours of sleep a day) to intermittent fasting and more productivity software than I can count.

Everything came together in my second year on the job market, when I decided to keep freelancing and launching products but also do a full-time masters degree. For a year I got up at 6, spent the whole day working and learning and then got home between 6 and 10 at night. I still made time for exercise, meditation, reading books and learning new programming languages.

When I write it like this it sounds like hell, but it was actually a lot of fun (you can read about it in my post "How I Survive Multiple Full Time Engagements" (skillcollector.com)). As I'm writing this I'm not doing an insane amount of work. But knowing that I'm capable of it and remain happy is a feeling that is hard to describe.

Chapter
Learn faster

Principles for faster learning

- Start with a growth mindset
- Think in systems rather than facts
- Feynman: if you understand, you can explain it to a kid
- Choose the right content & structure
- Record your learnings in a reference format

In this chapter

- How parents have a habit of crippling their children
- Why calling someone talented is an insult
- How to approach learning new things
- The man who did the 4-year MIT computer science program in 1 year

Start with a growth mindset

Many societies have a tendency to glorify talent and genius. We say we value hard work, but as soon as someone excels we call them 'talented', which implicitly dismisses their efforts at developing their skill.

There are two ways you can look at your ability:

- A fixed mindset (I am talented)
- A growth mindset (I am skilled)

The first can be destructive, the second can empower you to grow [14]. Don't get me wrong, genetics is real. There are people who are born with an affinity for certain types of thinking or specific physical attributes.

> [14] The academic literature is still debating how to measure/prove this. Focusing on a growth mindset helped me personally to overcome self-limiting beliefs so I'm including it here. Your mileage may vary. ↵

But for every 'talented' sports player there are crowds of people with similar genetics who are overweight, and for every genius mathematician there is a taxi driver who never learned algebra.

Ask yourself, if you are going to cook, which equipment would win:

- A small pocket knife
- A set of sharpened chef's knives

But even with the chef's knives, do you think you could beat a well-trained Michelin star chef with a pocket knife? Would your "unfair advantage" beat the years of hard work this person put into their training?

From Even Geniuses Work Hard (ascd.org), Carol Dweck [15]:

> [15] She's at the time of writing a Stanford professor, though she taught at Harvard, Columbia and Illinois as well. See her Wikipedia page (en.wikipedia.org) ↵

A fixed mindset is limiting your potential:

> Students with a fixed mindset do not like effort. They believe that if you have ability, **everything should come naturally**. They tell us that when they have to **work hard, they feel dumb**. ... students

> with a fixed mindset tend not to handle setbacks well. Because
> they believe that **setbacks call their intelligence into question**

Contrasting to those with a growth mindset:

> Students with a growth mindset, on the other hand, view
> **challenging work as an opportunity** to learn and grow. ...
> Students with a growth mindset are more likely to respond to
> initial obstacles by **remaining involved**, trying **new strategies**,
> and using all the resources at their disposal for learning

Be vigilant to your self-talk and train yourself to change from fixed mind statements to growth mindset perspectives. "I'm not good at math" becomes "I've not had a lot of math training". "I'm a talented football player" becomes "I've trained to be a good football player" and so on.

Think in systems rather than facts

Imagine that I show you a large pile of bricks and tell you to memorise the position of all the bricks. You then close your eyes and I take one brick away. Are you confident you can tell me which brick is missing when you open your eyes?

Now imagine that we take those bricks and build a little house out of them. If I remove a brick now, it would be trivial to find out which. In fact, you could not only see which brick is missing, but you could make a very accurate guess at what kind of brick should fill up the empty spot.

Learning should work the same. Instead of jumbled facts brute forced into your mind, build trees and networks of knowledge. It is common to find this kind of reasoning in the sciences and engineering, but it can be applied everywhere.

Let's illustrate fact thinking it's extreme form. Say we are baking a cake, the ingredient list says:

- 200 grams of butter
- 200 grams of sugar
- 200 grams of flour
- 4 eggs

It turns out we only have 3 eggs in the house! A *fact thinker* might come to the conclusion we can't make the cake or have to choose a different recipe.

A *systems thinker*, on the other hand, will see that a recipe is fundamentally about ratios. Meaning we can create a smaller cake according to the recipe by subtracting 25% from the butter, sugar and flour. One less egg is 1/4 less, which is 25%.

Cooking is a very simple example, but this concept becomes incredibly powerful as you apply it more. It will also allow you to make connections across what are usually considered isolated areas of knowledge.

For example:

- **Ideas and religions compete for humans the same way viruses compete for hosts:** A *biological virus* is a piece of information stored in DNA. This virus enters the human and uses the human body to multiply and spread to other humans. Some humans are well-defended against some viruses, others are not. *Ideas* are pieces of information stored as thoughts. They are transferred from human to human through speech, text and other media. Depending on how powerful an idea is (how contagious) it easily infects people. Like with viruses some people are resistant to ideas and others are very receptive. Like a virus, an idea can spread through a community of people and benefit or harm it.
- **The internet works similar to the human nervous system:** Both transfer information through electrical charges. Both consist out of a number of nodes that through their connection to other nodes communicate. And indeed both systems lose their function if you cut important connections.
- **Blood vessels follow a pattern similar to tree branches:** Both optimise surface areas. Tree branches form in a way that tries to optimise the amount of sun its leaves get. You could say that a tree pushes branches away from each other to prevent leaves from growing in the other's shade. Likewise, blood vessels optimise surface area to spread oxygen and carbon dioxide. Like leaves, the vessels spread away from each other so they don't needlessly compete.

The more you connect things, the easier it becomes to understand new things.

Richard Feynman technique

Feynman was a physicist who was known for being able to explain nearly everything to nearly everyone. He exemplifies the concept that nothing is too difficult to understand. All it takes is the right understanding. The Feynman technique goes like this:

1. Explain a concept to a kid (real/imaginary)
2. Note down your gaps in knowledge
3. Research
4. Repeat

Many times people who think something is too hard to explain to a novice simply do not understand the concept well enough to break it down. Instead, they talk in circles and make things harder than they need to be. If you doubt this, look at Feynman explaining the chemistry and physics of fire [16] or Bawa explaining math [17]. Want something more recent? Take 2:41 minutes to learn how DNA is turned into proteins in your body [18].

> [16] *See the 4:42 video Richard Feynman Fire (youtube.com)* ↩
> [17] *See the 1:21 video Mathemagic - $(a+b)^2=a^2+2ab+b^2$ - But Why? (youtube.com) or the 6:38 Pythagoras Theorem Explained - Mathemagic with Bawa (youtube.com)* ↩
> [18] *See From DNA to protein - 3D (youtube.com)* ↩

I personally have had great learning success explaining materials to a rubber duck. The key to this technique is that explaining a concept to someone (or something) who doesn't understand the concept (yet) forces you to break it down to its core. If you explain the thing you are trying to learn to a fellow student, for example, you are likely to skip explaining steps that you both understand. This leads you to not breaking down the structure of the subject all the way to its core, which inhibits you fully understanding it.

Let's for example, say you are studying gravity. If you tell a kid that gravity is a force that pulls things together, you might get back all sorts of questions:

- Why do two apples not stick together?
- Why does a feather fall slower than a rock?
- Why does gravity exist?

You then turn to books, Google and notes. In a second attempt, you explain that:

- gravity is proportional to the mass of an object. Meaning apples are drawn to each other, but since they are small compared to, for example, the earth, you don't actually feel them stick to each other
- we don't actually fully understand where gravity comes from
- gravity pulls on all objects equally hard, meaning a feather and a rock have the same pull from the earth. The reason they fall differently is because of the air. In a vacuum, they actually fall equally fast.

Now you are doing better, but new questions arise:

- What is a vacuum? Do all things really fall equally fast in it?
- How large does something need to be to feel gravity from it?

And so on. Interestingly, the latter of these questions has an answer that will border on biology and chemistry.

My personal workflow when learning is:

1. Formulate what I want to learn
2. Do research
3. Explain to an imaginary person (out loud!)
4. Figure out the holes
5. Research more
6. Go deeper and deeper until I feel satisfied

The thing with this technique is that if you get good enough at systems thinking you will go down seemingly irrelevant rabbit holes. Physics will lead you to ethics, psychology to biology and chemistry to painting. Go down these rabbit holes as far as time permits. Be sure to keep your goal in mind.

Choose the right content & structure

You can spend your entire life trying to learn to cook if you only read books on painting. Choose your content wisely. A great approach is Tim Ferriss's DiSSS Approach which you can read about more in his free bonus chapters from the 4 Hour Chef (tim.blog). The steps in there are:

1. D - Deconstruct. What are the building blocks of this discipline? For example, words in a language.
2. S - Selection. What building blocks give the best output? For example, 20% of words with which you can have 80% of conversations.
3. S - Sequencing. What is the best order to learn elements? Don't assume the order of existing courses/books is the best one. Ask experts.
4. S - Stakes. See the motivation section. Set up a system that motivates you to keep going and punishes you for not continuing.

He suggests combining this with the CaFE approach:

1. C - Compression. Can the 20% most effective building blocks be represented in a one-pager? A cheat sheet or something you can hang on the fridge, for example.
2. F - Frequency. Schedule in an amount of learning that suits your needs and the discipline. Sometimes 10 minutes a day can do a lot, but for other things, it will not help you that much.
3. E - Encoding. Create mental anchors and tricks that work well for your mind. Things like mnemonics.

Record your learnings in a reference format

The human mind is usually not very good at being exposed to knowledge once and then perfectly retaining it. Recording it has two benefits:

1. You can refer to it later
2. It forces you to compress and structure

It is very valuable to be able to refer back to what you have learned. Either to solidify your learning by repetition, or by refreshing your learnings a while after you have completed a piece of learning.

Additionally, writing down your learnings in a structured format helps you better understand the things you are learning.

Personally, I enjoy writing down notes in a very terse format. Things that work very well for me are structured notes with bullet points as well as mind-maps. Specifically, using graphics in them is very helpful.

Note that the goal of your notes is to be terse. A big mistake is to write down superfluous information. Your goal is to condense information. I personally find it works well to:

1. Write an article for non-experts (usually on my blog)
2. Make a mind-map that only makes sense to people who have read the initial materials

Make sure to back-up your notes well. I take great pleasure in reading summaries I wrote years ago. I still regularly refer back to my own blog posts on the history of cholesterol (skillcollector.com), a summary of the 4-hour body (skillcollector.com) or basic post on the link between cancer, alcohol and longevity (skillcollector.com).

Getting started

Learning is a complex endeavour, but in my experience, there are two elements in this chapter that are fantastic starting points:

1. Embrace a growth mindset
2. Use the Feynman technique

If you do not start with a growth mindset, you are likely to cause yourself frustration and eventually you will quit. Remember the words of Carol Dweck earlier in the chapter:

> Students with a fixed mindset tend not to handle setbacks well. Because they believe that setbacks call their intelligence into question.

and

> Students with a growth mindset are more likely to respond to initial obstacles by remaining involved.

These attitudes are often deeply ingrained and partly subconscious. It is of the utmost importance that you monitor your self-talk and emotional response to learning experiences. Remind yourself in moments of struggle that this is what is making you grow. Like a weightlifter growing his muscles, your mental struggle is exactly what you need in order to grow.

From a very practical viewpoint, the Feynman approach of explaining what you are learning to a novice is incredibly powerful. In my experience the value comes from three aspects:

- It forces you to structure your thoughts
- It forces you to see the whole picture
- It identifies gaps in your understanding

Anyone who claims their field of study is too complex to explain to a novice either doesn't understand what they are studying or doesn't see the full picture. Remember Feynman talking about fire (youtube.com). I found this perspective very confronting since it often means that half of what you claim to understand or have learned is, in fact, incomplete understanding. Once you look past that confronting fact (growth mindset!) you can truly sharpen your learning.

When you are learning something, periodically take some time to explain what you have learned either to a novice or an inanimate object. As I write this there is a 3D printed baby Groot (thingiverse.com) sitting in front of me who fulfils the role of student. In the past, I have spent many hours explaining biochemistry to a plant on my desk, or programming principles to a rubber duck. It has been the single most powerful technique in my life to generate a deep understanding.

The general cycle of this technique is:

1. Learn (read, do, watch, etc.)
2. Explain to a novice (or inanimate object)
3. Identify points of incomplete understanding
4. Repeat from the top

Keep this going until you are reasonably certain you fully understand the concept you are trying to learn.

How I learned to learn

From an intellectual development standpoint, I am very lucky to have grown up in the household that I did. I'm not sure why, but my parents would argue over dinner, car rides and other idle time about the most random things.

I vividly remember my father asking "if glass would have a greater atomic weight, would this glass still stand or would the neck break?" over dinner. To be fair, my parents didn't find an answer and ended up in a very frustrated argument. But regardless of the outcomes of these arguments, I was, from a young age, conditioned into asking questions.

During high school, me and my friend observed that our class was filled with two kinds of students:

- Those who memorised materials and worked hard
- Those who grasped underlying principles and did not work

We called them memorisers and understanders. A side effect of being an understander was that you could often get away with studying very little and still passing. Memorisers, on the other hand, had to brute force knowledge into their minds and spent a lot of time on preparing for tests. Understanders tended to do well in disciplines like math, whereas memorisers scored well on languages.

Since then I've learned to separate memoriser/understander from worker/lazy. The current education system is not geared towards understanders in most regards. It rewards being able to reproduce knowledge rather than understanding principles. That means that understanders in my experience don't feel very engaged in school. At least this was the case for me.

A problem with being an understander is that the world is prone to call people who perform well with little effort 'talented'. Many cultures glorify the talented genius over the hard worker. This implicitly leads parents and teachers to tell children that their abilities are innate. Talent is not something you can develop, so as soon as you are branded as talented your agency as a learner is taken away.

On the one hand, it is nice to be called talented, but it puts constraints on your learning. I was lucky to be exposed to the idea of a growth mindset, through the internet, before leaving high school and it has served me greatly. Since then, I've always assumed everything can be trained unless explicitly proven otherwise.

It led me through great adventures in learning. Especially as a teenager in the Netherlands where downloading copyrighted content was not illegal at the time. I had access to courses on the most random subjects. By the time I was 16 I was following courses in hypnosis, massage, writing and a host of other things. I never intended to become an expert in any, but assuming I could learn something triggered me to seek out seemingly random knowledge.

Only during university did I realise that being an understander type learner was just a mental skill, a piece of software if you will. I started to consciously try to develop my systems thinking and learning techniques.

A great inspiration for me was Scott H Young who did something called the MIT challenge [19], where he did the entire 4-year MIT computer science curriculum in 1 year. Scott describes himself as not being exceptionally smart, but very skilled at learning. Seeing him complete something as seemingly impossible as doing an MIT degree 4 times faster than you are supposed to was very inspiring.

[19] *See his mit challenge progress logs (scotthyoung.com)* ↵

Since then I've tried to collect as many learning techniques as possible to find ones that suit my learning style, my favourite of which are discussed in this chapter. I intend to keep learning my entire life. Formal education has been interesting, but I'm strongly against the idea that after finishing your degree you are done and in some way "complete". Learning is a human need and I intend to do it as much as I can.

Chapter

Enhance your cognition

Principles for cognitive enhancement

- Draw a line between your software and hardware
- Hardware (body)
    - Treat sleep as work
    - Control blood sugar levels
    - Use caffeine together with l-theanine
    - Supplement Omega 3's
    - Supplement creatine
    - Consider Nootropics
- Software (mind)
    - Make targeted use of meditation
    - Practice professional mnemonic (memory) techniques

In this chapter

- Calibrating your sleep to your actual needs
- How to amplify the positive effects of coffee
- Supplementing DHA oil for structural brain changes
- Memory tricks used by competitive memorisers
- My journey for a magic potion that ended in Japan

Hardware versus software

What we experience as our mind can be viewed from two angles:

- The hardware (brain)
- The software (mental processes)

They are very much linked, but very much separate. Consider the following:

- How good can a person with good math software (a mathematician) perform math when the hardware is debilitated (he is massively drunk)?
- How well can an Olympic athlete (good hardware) solve linear algebra without any math education (no software)?

In order to perform at your best, it is important to tackle both elements of mental performance. That also means that you need to pick your battles:

- No amount of supplements will replace education & discipline
- No amount of genius can replace physical needs

Of course, there is a balance between these two. A genius who only eats doughnuts will still outperform a health-conscious gardener. But the genius in question is not using the full potential at his disposal, it's like driving with the handbrake on.

Take both the software and the hardware seriously. Optimise both, but do not exclusively focus on one or the other.

Treat sleep as work

Sleep is not wasted time, quite the contrary. It is what enables optimum performance in the waking hours. A mildly sleep-deprived person has similar cognitive impairments to an 80kg/18-lb adult who has drunk 2 shots of tequila [20]. Similarly to drinking, many sleep deprived people will deny feeling impaired when they are impaired.

> [20] *See Moderate sleep deprivation produces impairments in cognitive and motor performance equivalent to legally prescribed levels of alcohol intoxication (ncbi.nlm.nih.gov)* ↵

A traditionally sleep-deprived demographic is doctors-in-training, who tend to insist they are performing just fine. The intense work schedule of doctors, or in this case doctors-in-training, can cause a 36% increase in serious medical errors[21]. In other words, being treated by a tired person makes it significantly more likely mistakes will be made in your treatment.

[21] *See The Phantom Menace of Sleep-Deprived Doctors (nytimes.com)* ↵

Sleep is not a passive process. It is a very active collection of processes. We are not entirely sure how it works, but we know now that it has very concrete effects. Some of my favourite effects of sleep and their specific benefits:

Activity	Beneficial for
Clears metabolic byproducts like reactive oxygen species from the brain	Protecting brain health
Store energy in the brain as glycogen	Assuring mental energy & improved mood during the day
Explicit memory development (slow wave sleep)	Long-term storage of facts
Procedural memory development (REM sleep)	Improving automatic skills like driving or playing the piano
Growth hormone secretion	Support body growth and recovery

Sleep deprivation on the other hand causes[22]:

[22] *See the sleep deprivation Wikipedia page (en.wikipedia.org)* ↵

- Cognitive impairment (concentration, mood)
- Weakened immunity
- Obesity risk due to hormonal changes
- Cardiovascular disease risk increase
- Stunted growth hormone levels (growth, recovery)

There is no set sleep need that applies to all humans. Average sleep durations fluctuate between 7 and 8.5 hours per day[23]. For good sleep I personally have had good results with the following principles:

[23] *Those amounts are also optimal for longevity. Both more and less than 7-8 hours seem to cause harm. See Sleep Duration and All-Cause Mortality: A Systematic Review and Meta-Analysis of Prospective Studies (academic.oup.com)* ↵

- **Calibrate the amount of sleep you need:** take 2-6 weeks where you plan to be in bed for over 10 hours at the same time. Preferably set an alarm clock only after 10 hours of sleep and wake up naturally. In the beginning, you will spend a lot of time in bed, but as the weeks progress, you will stabilise around a time. Make sure to have light exposure in the morning, or your body will have trouble figuring out when the day begins.
- **Have a set time at which you get up:** respect your biological circadian rhythm. Neglecting your physiological sleep/wake cycle or shifting it during the week has been described as 'social jet lag', which has detrimental effects on health and prevents you from feeling rested [24].
- **Set your cycle using (sun)light:** the body clock is set based on light. Increase your light exposure in the morning, and decrease it at night. Preferably sit in a brightly lit location during the day (near a window for example) and decrease blue light exposure at night. I recommend turning down the brightness of your screens and installing an app like Flux (justgetflux.com") that filters blue light out of your screen later in the day. I also enjoy having an alarm clock that simulates sunrise (Philips wake-up light (usa.philips.com) or a smart light bulb set to a schedule [25]).
- **Went to bed late? Nap.:** if you went to bed late, don't sleep in but rather have a nap in the middle of the day. This prevents you from breaking your rhythm but allows you to compensate for the lost sleep. Try to nap earlier on in the day (before 17:00) but well after you have gotten up and have exposed yourself to bright (sun)light.
- **Have a bedtime routine:** in an ideal situation you set an alarm at night that reminds you to start winding down. No more screens, low light, no mentally stimulating input. I personally have a short stretch routine, meditate and read fiction.
- **Make your bedroom sleep-conducive:** especially at night have low light and low (but not freezing) temperatures. During sleep time assure a constant temperature and no light whatsoever. Ideally, condition your mind to view the bed as a place of sleep and nothing else. Do this by only using the bed for sex, sleep and pre-sleep routines like reading fiction. Personally, I use earplugs and a sleep mask, often even if I don't need them, purely as a conditioned response for my mind.

- **Take caffeine and alcohol early rather than late:** both interfere with sleep quality by suppressing specific sleep processes and/or cycles (even if you fall asleep fine). Caffeine has a half-life in the blood of 3-7 hours in healthy adults and a clearance time of 8-24 hours. Preferably use it only in the morning. Alcohol suppresses REM sleep so is preferably avoided.

> [24] See the book Internal Time: Chronotypes, Social Jet Lag, and Why You're So Tired (goodreads.com) by Roenneberg ↵
> [25] Personally I use a Chinese brand called Yeelight (aliexpress.com) but have heard good stories about Philips Hue and the Ikea smart bulb line. Just be sure what you choose has a timer function. ↵

Note that aside from the above you may want to consider strategic napping. Daytime naps have been shown to increase the retention of knowledge and boost energy levels throughout the day. Milage varies per person as some people (especially the sleep-deprived) will find it hard to wake up after a nap.

Control blood sugar levels

Where sleep is usually a once a day occurrence that influences your functioning, every time you eat can be a window to either support or destroy your capacity to function optimally.

Low blood sugar is known to make people grumpy and lethargic. But why do many people report low energy after meals? Shouldn't blood sugar be high?

Your cognition depends on your brain. Your brain depends on energy. No energy means no performance. Energy can reach the brain in two main ways [26] :

> [26] See the Wikipedia entry on brains (en.wikipedia.org), the nuance here is that there are some more molecules that can provide energy to the brain but the below are two biggest ones. ↵

1. Glucose
2. Ketones

If you have not heard of the ketogenic diet and generally eat more than once every 24 hours, you will basically rely on glucose in most situations. Glucose is the type of sugar your body uses for energy all over. In general, all carbohydrates are eventually converted to glucose during digestion. Glucose is kept within a certain bandwidth.

- Very high blood glucose (hyperglycaemia) can cause permanent damage to your body
- Very low blood glucose (hypoglycaemia) deprives your body of energy

Having optimal levels of glucose does not mean you should eat every 30 minutes to keep your body supplied with energy. Your body is very capable of regulating your blood sugar if you give it the food it was evolved to consume.

There are three components to blood sugar levels:

- Input/increase through food
- Storage/decrease through insulin
- Usage/decrease through usage

The key here is that insulin is released to store high blood sugar levels. If you cause a sharp rise in blood sugar your body will respond with a drastic insulin response potentially causing your glucose levels to drop below what they were before.

To keep your blood sugar within productive levels, the concept of glycemic index (GI) and load (GL) are very important. Both are a value assigned to a meal/food to predict the blood sugar spike they will cause. They are at length discussed in the weight loss chapter. For now, it is enough to know these generalisations:

- High GI causes a blood sugar spike. In general the sweeter and less fibre-rich a food, the worse it is.
- Low GI foods are fat, protein and fibre-rich.

You can look up GI lists online very easily. Consider the following scenarios as examples of the effect of GI on cognition:

Scenario	Effect	Cognitive performance
Large soda (high GI, high quantity) while working behind a computer (low energy)	Short lived higher blood glucose followed by an insulin-induced crash	Short-term increase, long-term reduction
Tablet of glucose (high GI, low quantity) while in the middle of a heavy workout	Small glucose boost, offset by high glucose usage by muscles [27]	Neutral/positive depending on initial levels
Low GI breakfast	Gradual and sustained blood glucose support	No decline the entire morning [28]
No breakfast	Waking up with low blood glucose, no external stimulation.	Lower performance, unless the body is adapted to it.

[27] *And high glucose absorption due to GLUT-4 migration in muscle membranes* ↵

[28] *See "A low glycemic index breakfast cereal preferentially prevents children's cognitive performance from declining throughout the morning" (sciencedirect.com)* ↵

Note that the last entry seems a bit vague. The fact of the matter is that different people are better or worse at self-regulating glucose levels. This is a combination of genetics and conditioning. I personally fast every day, usually until 14:00 or later. This intermittent fasting approach (see longevity chapter) has conditioned my body to more effectively regulate blood glucose and rely more on ketones.

As a general rule keep the following principles in mind:

Principle	Why
Eat low GI foods	Prevents a high insulin response.
Don't drink calories	Sodas, fruit juices etc usually have high sugar content and especially when consumed alone cause a blood sugar spike. If you are having one, keep the quantity in check and consume it slowly.
Eat protein, fat and fibre-rich foods	These generally have lower GI ratings.
Consume high GI in low quantities	Your body can handle even pure sugar if you don't consume too much. A little pick me up is not per se bad, but consume low quantities. Ideally, choose a low GI alternative.

Guidelines for meals:

- Reduce the glycemic load by eating low GI foods and combining higher GI foods with low GI foods and fibre.
- Reduce size to mitigate insulin response, the more you eat the more your body needs to work to handle the blood sugar response (of course mitigated by GI/GL).
- Reduce the speed at which you eat so your body doesn't have to handle everything at once.
- Do some mild exercise before and after eating. Ideally also 60-90 minutes after the meal. By doing this you mitigate the need for glucose since muscle movement decreases the need for insulin and increases insulin sensitivity.

Use caffeine in concert with l-theanine

Caffeine is one of the most used and abused substances in the world. The problem is that many people do not use it in a productive way to increase their performance but rather use it to cover up deficiencies in the management of sleep and blood sugar.

Caffeine:

- Does not provide energy, it blocks the effect of adenosine in the brain. In essence it prevents feeling tired, at least as a result of adenosine levels.

- In low dosages has healthy effects but in excess causes a host of issues [29] .
- In many people causes anxiety and nervousness to varying degrees.
- Has been shown to cause a peak of perceived energy, but after 2 hours also results in measurably lower levels of energy/focus than before using it [30] .

[29] *See Effects of Habitual Coffee Consumption on Cardiometabolic Disease, Cardiovascular Health, and All-Cause Mortality (onlinejacc.org), highlight: 4 cups of coffee max a day.* ↵
[30] *See Differential cognitive effects of energy drink ingredients: Caffeine, taurine, and glucose (sciencedirect.com)* ↵

To use caffeine effectively:

- Fix your sleep
- Fix your blood sugar
- Use it in the morning only
- Combine it with l-theanine

L-theanine is an amino acid found in green tea (and is also available as a supplement). The dosage of theanine depends very much on the tea type and quality. An average green tea bag will not contain much, whereas a high-grade Matcha tea [31] will contain far more.

[31] *You can spot good Matcha by color and flavour. Good Matcha is bright green and has no bitterness, even if you taste the powder straight.* ↵

Before going into the details, please note that:

- Caffeine, coffeine and theine are the same substance
- Theanine is not thymine or tiamine
- L-theanine can be metabolised by humans, d-theanine can't (as far as we know)
- When you read theanine without a prefix, l-theanine is implied

Theanine is an amino acid that can cross the blood-brain barrier and thus (like caffeine) affects the brain directly. Some effects of theanine can be described as the opposite of caffeine:

- A calming effect and stress reduction
- Increased alpha waves in the brain (focus)
- No crash after usage

Some effects are similar to what is experienced with caffeine:

- Better memory
- Improved attention
- Increased learning ability
- No increase in drowsiness

In short, one might say that where caffeine causes a restless and short-lived perceived energy spike, theanine offers a calm longer-term focus. In combination, caffeine lifts the calmer energy levels of theanine up, and theanine keeps caffeine from running out of control.

Combining the two has proven very effective for many people seeking to improve their cognitive performance with easily accessible materials. For effective usage:

- Experiment with 2:1 to 4:1 theanine:caffeine ratio
- Do not use this as frequently as coffee, I don't do this more than once a day (the effect is long-lasting)

If you have the habit of drinking coffee all day, consider switching to tea or decaf. You do not want to overload your system.

A note on safety: this combination is generally lauded as the safest cognitive enhancer on the market. The ingredients are easy to find and the side effects are considered to be due to the caffeine usage rather than the combination.

Supplement omega-3's

The human brain consists for nearly 60% out of fats (excluding water) [32]. Depending on what type of brain matter you look at 7-20% is cholesterol [33]. You can draw a simple conclusion from this: fats have a structural effect on the brain. There are fats that will have a structurally positive effect on your brain and those that will have a negative effect. An example of positive fats are omega-3 fatty acids. An example of negative fats are trans-fats.

[32] *See Essential fatty acids and human brain (ncbi.nlm.nih.gov)*
↵
[33] *See Lipid composition of the normal human brain: grey matter, white matter, and myelin (jlr.org)* ↵

There are three types of omega-3's relevant for human biology:

1. α-linolenic acid, ALA
2. Eicosapentaenoic acid, EPA
3. Docosahexaenoic acid, DHA

ALA is found mostly in plants. EPA and DHA are found abundantly in oil from sea organisms including fish and algae. Note that omega-3's are also found in meats and more so in grass-fed than grain-fed. The concentrations though often make it more practical and overall healthy to go with fish sources.

There are studies in which EPA and DHA show cognitive benefits, but also studies that show no benefit at all. The reason for that only became clear once those studies were compared. Studies supplementing under 500mg of DHA usually showed no benefit, whereas those in the 750-1500mg range did [34].

> [34] *See Omega-3s and Cognition: Dosage Matters (goedomega3.com), to my sadness many meta-analysis like Effects of omega-3 fatty acids on cognitive performance: a meta-analysis (sciencedirect.com) on the topic do not include studies with 1000mg DHA a day for a prolonged period of time. They find no relation between dosage and effect, but this is no surprise if there is indeed a threshold for effect. The ones that do, like Docosahexaenoic Acid and Adult Memory: A Systematic Review and Meta-Analysis (journals.plos.org), do find an effect.* ↵

In other words, if a researcher tests whether one push-up a day increases muscle mass and finds no results and another tests if 20 push-ups a day and finds positive muscle gain results, which one is right? The first, concluding push-ups have no effect on muscle mass or the second concluding that they do?

From here we can create a supplementation strategy:

1. We need DHA because it is the dominant omega-3 in the neurological system
2. We need a minimum of about 1000mg DHA a day for effect

One important thing to note is that omega-3 supplements are often made from fish. This is not a bad thing per se, but in case you didn't get the memo, you should know our oceans are polluted with plastics and heavy metals because of the bad life choices of the human race.

Supplement oil is filtered for toxins, but not all countries hold the same standards [35]. For this reason, when buying omega-3 supplements keep in mind the following guidelines:

[35] *Milk from the US is, for example, banned in the EU because of the entirely irrational health standards with regards to, for example, hormone usage.* ↵

1. Make sure it is according to EU standards which are currently the highest
2. Smaller fish lower on the food chain are preferential since they accumulate fewer toxins
3. Algae sources are of high quality, but often prohibitively expensive

Personally, I use a European brand that blends oils from anchovies, sardines and herring. Remember to check what the DHA dosage is in your supplement and to take s sufficient amount to reach 1000+ mg DHA per day. Often this exceeds the recommended amount since they are often based on old standards that differ widely by country.

Supplement Creatine

Creatine is a very common and well researched [36] fitness supplement used to increase strength & power output for athletes [37]. Creatine is a primary way in which cells, including muscle cells, store short-term energy. For athletes, this means an increase in power output, but for the brain it means a cognitive function increase.

[36] *See Safety of Creatine Supplementation (link.springer.com) and Effect of Short-term High-Dose Creatine Supplementation on Measured GFR in a Young Man With a Single Kidney (ajkd.org)* ↵
[37] *See Creatine Supplementation and Athletic Performance (jospt.org) & Effects of creatine supplementation on performance and training adaptations (link.springer.com)* ↵

In times of activity, the brain drains its stores of creatine to keep levels of ATP (energy) high [38]. By supplementing, creatine levels in the brain rise [39]. A 2009 study found effects on a number of cognitive performance tests, including IQ test performance, for subjects who supplemented creatine for 2 weeks [40]. A 2010 study found increased memory span in creatine users [41]. Contrarily, a 2008 study confirmed that for a number of other cognitive test measures did not improve [42] suggesting that creatine is most effective for tasks that involve complex reasoning. Interestingly, sleep-deprived and elderly individuals experience enhanced executive function with creatine supplementation [43].

[38] See *Effect of photic stimulation on human visual cortex lactate and phosphates using 1H and 31P magnetic resonance spectroscopy. (ncbi.nlm.nih.gov)* ↩

[39] See *Increase of total creatine in human brain after oral supplementation of creatine-monohydrate. (ncbi.nlm.nih.gov)* ↩

[40] See *Cognitive effects of creatine ethyl ester supplementation. (ncbi.nlm.nih.gov)* ↩

[41] See *Dietary supplementation of creatine monohydrate reduces the human fMRI BOLD signal. (ncbi.nlm.nih.gov)* ↩

[42] See *Creatine supplementation does not improve cognitive function in young adults (sciencedirect.com)* ↩

[43] See *Use of creatine in the elderly and evidence for effects on cognitive function in young and old (link.springer.com)* ↩

For optimal dosing take:

- first week: 0.3 grams for every kilogram of body weight
- after that: 0.03 grams per kilogram of body weight per day

For a person weighing 80kg that comes down to 24 grams per day in the first week and 2.4 grams after [44]. In the buildup phase, it is most effective to split the full dose into 4 smaller doses. Personally, I only supplement creatine in times where I for a number of weeks need to perform on an elevated physical and/or mental level.

[44] See *Pharmacokinetics of the Dietary Supplement Creatine (link.springer.com)* ↩

Consider Nootropics

Once you have optimised the basics (diet, sleep, blood sugar, supplements), you may consider nootropics. These are compounds used to improve brain function. I will not dive deep into them here as many are experimental and their long-term effect is often unclear. If you are interested in using nootropics I recommend having a look at the reddit Nootropic community that wrote a very helpful getting started manual of /r/nootropics (reddit.com).

Make targeted use of meditation

Meditation is like a stretching routine for the mind. Where in physical exercise muscles go tense and fatigued, the use of the mind too creates tensions and tiredness. We can stretch muscles to ease out tensions, prevent injury and increase range of motion. We can meditate to calm the mind, prevent breakdowns and increase stress resilience.

The premise of meditation is simple: focus on one thing and let distractions pass by like clouds in the sky. The focus element can be implemented in many ways, some common examples are focusing on:

- Your breathing
- A word or phrase
- A physical sensation

Meditation is about as religious as yoga, meaning it isn't. Both are linked to spiritual traditions, but historically almost everything has religious ties. If you like exploring spirituality please do, but also feel free to use meditation as a practical tool the same way you would choose to lift weights or stretch your muscles.

Learning meditation

If you have never meditated or would like to learn meditation in a structured way I recommend following an intro program. Great examples of these are:

- The 10-day intro course by the Headspace app (headspace.com")
- The free guided meditation Calm app (calm.com")
- Check out local meditation courses

If you just want to give it a shot without committing to a program or downloading an app, I recommend trying the following:

1. Find a calm environment where you can sit comfortably (any position)
2. Set a 5-minute timer and commit to meditating until the timer goes
3. Close your eyes
4. Breathe calmly and count your breaths
5. When thoughts arise don't interact with them, just bring your focus back to your breath

The above are a good place to start, but taking a multi-day intro course through an app or an offline course is very much worth your time.

My favourite meditations

I like meditating twice a day, once in the morning to prepare my mind for a good day and once at night to wind down and prepare for sleep. In the morning I take 10 minutes after my morning workout and at night I take 20 minutes before bed.

In the morning I meditate to put myself in a good mood and set my mind to a sharp and attentive state. It makes self-motivation much easier. Even if before meditating I don't feel like it, I never regret doing it afterwards. My morning meditation looks like this:

- Put in silicone earplugs to block out any sound
- Set a timer for 10 minutes (I use an app called Meditation Timer (play.google.com))
- Count 50 breaths without interacting with my thoughts, reset the count if I get caught up in a thought and lose track of my breathing
- Visualise the people that love me, telling me they love me
- Mentally tell people I care about that I love them and wish them well
- Go through things I am grateful for

It usually ends with a smile on my face.

My meditation at night is geared towards slowing down my mind and taking it from a convergent productivity mode into a divergent creativity and dreaming mode. It looks like this:

- Put in silicone earplugs
- Set a 20-minute timer
- Count 100 breaths without interacting with my thoughts, reset the count if I get caught up in a thought and lose track of my breathing
- Focus on the visual imagery that my mind spins up, don't interact with it and don't try to change it other than trying to make it more solid
- Towards the end, my mind is often calm and solid enough that I can 'walk around' in these visual daydreams

The above works very well for me probably because I have a visual mind. Note that in the beginning, it was a struggle to even focus on any visual aspect for longer than half a second. With practice, I find that this meditation puts me in a sleep-ready state.

Practice professional mnemonic techniques

Sometimes you just need to brute force some knowledge into your head. Shopping lists, credit card numbers and so on are not part of a system, meaning the aforementioned usual learning techniques don't apply. The solution to this problem comes from the competitive field of mnemonics. Memory championships basically.

As it turns out, with a few basic techniques you can learn to memorise seemingly random things. For an in-depth overview, I recommend having a look at the book Moonwalking with Einstein (en.wikipedia.org).

Memory palace

Let's say you need to remember a sequence of things, for example, the sections of a presentation you are going to give. The memory palace is one of the most well-known techniques for sequential memory. It relies on using a physical space you know very well in order to memorise a list of things. Take, for example, your house (palace) which has a number of distinct places:

1. front door
2. hallway
3. living room
4. kitchen
5. and so on

The memory palace technique works by linking unusual images to these locations so you can 'walk' through the list. Say, for example, you are going to do a work presentation and need to cover:

- the sales figures for the last quarter
- unexpected costs
- what customers brought in the most revenue
- plans for the next quarter

You can use the memory palace to remember these in a visual way:

1. You walk up to your front door and see a big sign above it proclaiming 'SALE!'
2. You enter the hallway which is covered in a stack of receipts to your knees
3. You walk to the living room where a group of people in fur coats are throwing money at you
4. You enter the kitchen where the walls are covered in calendars

While giving your presentation you can easily progress from topic to topic knowing you covered all topics in the right order.

The key to this technique is to have a 'palace' that is large enough and memorable. It doesn't have to be a house, it could just as well be your drive to work where you store ideas at landmarks and points of interest.

Sequential technique

This one is good for lists where you don't need to know at what place an item is. For example, a grocery list. It is similar to the memory palace but doesn't rely on your memory of a physical place. The principle is simple:

1. Make a list
2. Visualise each item in a crazy way
3. Connect the items in a weird way

For example, take the following list:

- Apples
- Cayenne pepper
- Cheese
- Coffee
- Mushrooms

The human mind usually doesn't like random things, it likes to see connections. It also doesn't remember most unremarkable things but likes remembering remarkable things. So in order to have our mind store the random unremarkable list, we need to make it a connected remarkable list.

We do this by creating a visual chain of remarkable images, where remarkable is anything unusual. Weirder is better, for example:

- We imagine a blood red **apple**, covered in a red liquid that may or not be blood
- This blood red apple starts growing spikes like a pufferfish which turn into pointy **cayenne peppers**. The apple explodes and the cayenne peppers shoot out like dangerous projectiles
- The peppers get stuck in a huge block of **cheese** turning it into a cheese-cayenne pincushion
- The cheese pincushion starts to mould into a mush of black fungus which dries up into **ground coffee**
- From the ground coffee **mushrooms** start growing

Visualise the above sequence and I guarantee that as you are walking the store running through it will be a trivially easy endeavour.

For the best results, make the visualisations explicit and as weird as possible. Your mind will spin up a whole bunch of weird stuff over time, just let it roam free.

Memorising numbers

What if you want to memorise numbers? Perhaps you are sick of having to look up your credit card number when ordering things online, or you want to be able to remember a telephone number as soon as someone mentions it to you. Numbers don't have shapes like physical objects so our previous technique is off the table. Or so it seems. We can fix this issue by giving numbers a physical manifestation:

1. Assign sounds to numbers
2. Use the sounds to assign objects
3. Chain the objects like we did before

For example:

- The number 1 is 't'
- We make the number one the object 'tie'
- We can memorise 1 as a tie

Step one is assigning sounds to numbers 1 through 0. The sounds are phonetic, meaning T and D are the same etc. It's about sounds as opposed to letters

1. **T/D**, it looks a bit like a 1
2. **N**, on its side, looks like an 2
3. **M**, on its side, looks like an 3
4. **R**, 4 mirrored it looks like an R without its leg
5. **L**, a sloppy 5 looks like an upside down l
6. **Sh/Ch**, a 6 is curled up like a cat (shhh, let it sleep)
7. **K/G**, a seven and upside down seven together look like a k, which in English sounds similar to a g (e.g. cable and grab)
8. **F/V**, an 8 is four v's stacked like < > < >
9. **P/B**, it looks like a mirrored 9
10. (zero) **S**, zero is nothing, like silence

Using the above we can turn any series of numbers into sounds, and thus into objects. Take, for example, this seemingly random string of numbers (which could be a telephone number for example):

98475234985 (I literally jammed my keyboard to generate random numbers here), they translate to PV RK LN MR PVL. Now we just think of a series of words using these consonants:

- **buff**
- **rack**
- **alone**
- **more**
- **buffalo**

Note that since the sound of a P and B are the same in English, we can remember PV and BF interchangeably since the sound of P (puh) and B (buh) sound the same. This is useful if you can't think of a word with the one sound but can with the other.

From here we can create a visual chain like we did before. So long as we memorised the sounds of the numbers we can now translate back and forth.

Memorising lists out of order

What if you want to be able to answer the question "which item is in the 19th place in the list of 30 we memorised?" The above techniques will become quite impractical. To make this work we are going to layer some levels of artificial structure on top of each other:

- Give numbers objects based on their sound
- Link the objects in our list to these objects

Let's give the numbers 1 through 10 some default objects, these are permanent associations you will make in your mind:

1. **T**ie
2. **N**ail
3. **M**an
4. **R**oad
5. **L**amp
6. **Ch**ange
7. **K**ettle
8. **V**eal
9. **P**otato
10. **T**oe**S**

You can choose your own if you'd like. I do recommend having some default ones for this particular technique. Now let's say we memorise the following list:

- Coconut
- House
- Grass
- Hat
- Tomato

We link them to their position visually:

1. Tie + coconut = a woman wearing a tie with coconuts growing from it
2. Nail + house = a house pierced by a nail twice its size
3. Man + grass = a construction worker eating grass
4. Road + hat = a long road lined with pink top hats
5. Lamp + tomato = a huge dripping tomato being used as a lamp

Now when someone asks you what was item 3 on the list, you can retrieve it from memory by tracing 3 > man > construction worker eating grass > grass.

In the competitive spheres, this technique is often implemented as a person-action-object (PAO) list. Meaning the numbers are people who are memorable to you and they perform an action on the objects you are memorising.

Getting started

It is very tempting to look for a magic bullet that will lift you to the next level. In practice, this will only hurt you and led to long-term failure. Get the basics right and take it from there. If you do nothing else, in order of importance:

1. Sleep 8+ hours a day
2. Eat food that keeps your blood sugar levels from fluctuating
3. Meditate

These are the most powerful techniques for nearly everyone. They are likely to lift your mood, improve your focus and make your reasoning clearer.

The first two especially are about designing your daily routines, refer back to the habit chapter for tips on doing this. Both of them have compounding effects in that they make everything you do in a day more effective. It's like upgrading from dial-up internet to 21st century wifi. No matter what you do after, everything will be faster, better and of higher quality.

To make them easier I have found the following techniques to be most helpful:

- Sleep
  - Set a bedtime alarm
  - No screens 1 hour before sleep and/or wear blue light blocking glasses
  - Calculate in 30 minutes of time to fall asleep
- Eat well
  - Have a predefined breakfast, make it low in sugar (eggs, salad, unflavoured yoghurt)
  - Ensure access to healthy food (bring lunch to work, buy groceries for the week on a full stomach)
  - Plan the meals of the week ahead of time to prevent bad 'in the moment' decisions
- Meditate
  - Do the free 10-day headspace course (headspace.com") through the app
  - Commit to meditating just for 5 minutes a day at a time you know yourself to have low energy/mood/focus

There is little glamour to these recommendations, no sparks or fire. It will take you a week or two to get them instituted properly and see results. They are however the most powerful things you can do to get started. From there optimise further.

The most common counterproductive responses I see from people on these recommendations are:

- **I can't sleep that much, I need more hours in a day not fewer:** which misses the mark by a mile. Which would you rather have, a pill that allowed you to stay awake for an hour longer every day with low energy levels or a pill that forced you to sleep 2 more hours but gave you perfect focus the entire day? You don't need more time, you need more focus and energy to get things done and enjoy life.
- **Eating healthy is hard:** the effort of eating right is far less than the pain of suffering through suboptimal mental states your whole life. What is hard is changing habits. But while it is not easy, it is far from impossible and entirely worth it.

- **I don't have time to meditate:** similar to the argument of not being able to sleep more. Every minute you spend meditating will effectively double the value of your time after (at least in my experience). Before sleep it will improve your rest, at work it will improve your focus and when you feel overwhelmed it will make you more able to deal with the pressure.

How I went from magic potions to Japanese tea

As a kid, it seems like the adults have everything figured out. They are infinitely wise creatures that understand things about how the world works. As the years go by you come to realise that adults are really just kids who managed not to die for a number of years. The disillusionment is quite confrontational.

I had always expected growing up meant I too would get the superpowers of an adult. To be able to understand nearly anything and to know the inner workings of the world. It was quite disappointing to find out there were no superpowers in store for me. It lead me to try and find ways to gain the superpowers that were so rudely stripped from my expectations.

When I was a toddler I would try to make magical potions with berries and plants from the garden, but luckily decided against actually drinking them. My teenage years were spent exploring meditation, hypnosis and supplements of all kinds. As teenagers do I was looking for the easy way out, a silver bullet that would take my mind to the next level.

As the experiments came and went I slowly came to the conclusion that there was no easy fix. At the same time, a hope developed that a slow fix was indeed possible. For example, a little meditation didn't give me the power of perfect memory, but over time it increased my ability to focus and see connections. Likewise, eliminating certain foods wasn't as glamorous as a magic potion, but it increased my capacity to work for longer periods of time.

As I grew out of my juvenile desire for a magic pill, I found out that there was a whole world of possibilities that would allow me to boost my mind's performance. Don't get me wrong, there is a part of me that is still looking for magical potions. From exotic Matcha tea to Scandinavian mushroom extracts, I'm game so long as there is some reasonable science I can read and evaluate.

Some experiments work out very well. Matcha tea, for example, is to this day my favourite way to ingest caffeine and theanine together. Other experiments worked out reasonably well but proved unsustainable, like following a polyphasic sleep schedule. And then there are those that end with the need to puke, like freshly juiced garlic and cayenne pepper on an empty stomach.

In the end, my most meaningful transformation was going from a desire for an instant fix to the knowledge that small changes implemented consistently outperform big temporary actions. The body and mind are a system and by expanding our understanding of it we can tweak it. The 21st century gave us a great many tools to improve what we can achieve with our minds and will only continue to give us more. The coming decades will be a golden age for those of us actively trying to improve our minds.

Chapter

Self management & productivity shopping list

For an up-to-date version of this list please use your always-up-to-date links to the pdf and eBook versions.

If you haven't claimed those yet, you can do so at smartworkbeatshardwork.com/claim or by scanning the QR code below.

Free digital copy claim

Software: Mobile & Desktop

- Text expander - If you type the same thing a lot, use a text expander like [45] to automatically type things with shortcuts. When I type $bank, for example, my keyboard automatically types my bank account number. $plan types a standard invitation to have a Skype meeting.
- Night mode - Flux (justgetflux.com") (Mac/Windows) reduces the blue light coming from your screen when the sun sets based on your GPS location. This prevents your screen from messing with your sleep cycle. Pair with automatic screen brightness for full effect. Android and iPhone systems also have a night mode.
- Pocket (getpocket.com) - If you read articles and/or blogs a lot use this to save articles into a reading stack. The articles save to your e-reader (Kindle/Kobo/tablet) as well. I use this to save articles I find and want to read at a later point.
- Todoist (todoist.com) - my favourite todo manager. Very structured, easy to customise and very powerful quick-add syntax.

> [45] *aText (trankynam.com) for Mac,PhraseExpress (phraseexpress.com") for Windows, Texpand (play.google.com) for Android, Textexpander (textexpander.com) for iOS and multiplatform* ↵

Software: Mobile

- Podcast Addict (play.google.com) App (Android) - a good podcasting app
  - Listen on 1.3x speed for most podcasts
  - Recommended podcasts: Darknet Diaries (hacking stories), 80,000 hours (how to have impact with your career), Tim Ferris Show (self-development), Kevin Rose show (self-development), Foundmyfitness (health, science), Rational Reminder (investing), The Drive (health, science), Joe Rogan (30% interesting, 30% comedians, 30% UFC, 10% whatthefuck), Nerdland Maandoverzicht (Flemish, science news).
- Greyscale mode - you can take the color out of your screen through the settings. This makes your phone far less interesting/addictive. Tech savvy rooted Android user? Try Tasker with CF.Lumen.

- Clipboard history manager - keeps a history of text/images/files you copy. Copy'em Paste (itunes.apple.com) (Mac) or ditto (ditto-cp.sourceforge.net") (Windows). Very useful if you copy-paste a lot and want to avoid accidentally losing what you copied.

Software: Desktop

- Window snapping - Having two windows on your screen side by side is very useful, for example, a note-taking app on the left of your screen and a document you are reading on the right. On Windows, press the Windows button plus an arrow key to align screens automatically. For Mac, download an app called Divvy (mizage.com).
- iA Writer (markdown editor) - If you like minimalist writing programs, try iA writer (ia.net). It was originally designed for architects but is loved by engineers and novelists alike for it's distraction-free interface.
- File backups - Make sure that all your useful documents and files are backed up using a service like Dropbox (dropbox.com"), Google Drive (drive.google.com) or Onedrive (onedrive.live.com"). This synchronises files across devices so you always have up to date versions everywhere and it makes sure that if your devices stop working your files are fine.

Automation

- Tasker (play.google.com) - an android app that allows you to link any trigger to an outcome. For example when "phone upside down" do "enable airplane mode"
- IFTTT (ifttt.com")/Zapier (zapier.com) - web services that let you link services to each other. For example if "email received with attachment" do "save attachment to Dropbox".
- Robot vacuum cleaner - Having a daily cursory clean of your floor saves quite a bit of time in cleaning the house. I like to run mine an hour before I wake up. You can get cheap €50 ones (aliexpress.com) from China or go for more premium models like the Roomba (irobot.com) series. The differences lie in how smart they are. The cheap ones randomly run around and will probably clean most of your floor whereas the newer ones generate a map of your house and clean it strategically.

Tools

- Liquid chalk markers - great for writing habit reminders on smooth surfaces like windows, mirrors and kitchen appliances.
- Elastic organizing board (aliexpress.com) - a laptop sized flat board with elastic bands across it. Wonderful to store your daily gear on.

Supplements

- Nordic oil fish oil (smile.amazon.co.uk) - a 'pharmaceutical grade' fish oil, meaning they are very strict about quality and purity. Remember to get the dose right for your intended effect.
- Creatine - this one has both strength and cognitive benefits. It's a simple supplement that you can get in any drug store (or online). I have no favored brand.
- L-theanine - to be used in conjunction with caffeine for a cognitive boost. I prefer the Dutch brand AOV (aov.nl), but buy international brands as well so long as it is suntheanine (a patented form with a specific production process).
- Twentyfive AM caffeine + theanine capsules (twentyfive.am) - dosing theanine with coffee is not an exact science. These capsules have a verified 2:1 ratio of theanine to caffeine for a good cognitive boost.

Self-tracking

- Smart scale - tracking your weight and bodyfat percentage can help measure your weight goals and show trends. I use a Withings Body+ (withings.com)
- Fitness tracker - mostly helpful if you are trying to optimise your sleep. It prevents you from lying to yourself. They are not perfect though. I wear an Oura Ring (ouraring.com) for sleep and HRV tracking.
- Rescuetime (rescuetime.com) - automatically tracks what you spend time on and lets you find time-sinks you may not be consciously aware of

Reading

- Pavlov's Dogs - understand the original experiment and how it relates to your behaviour. Wikipedia or a Youtube video are good starts.
- Skinner box - understand the original experiment and how it shapes your desires. Wikipedia or a Youtube video are good starts.

Chapter

Lose weight

Principles to lose/maintain weight

1. Eat fewer calories than your body uses
2. Eat food that makes you feel full
3. Minimise the number of choices you have to make
4. Institute habits that make it easy to make the right choices
5. Set up accountability measures that keep you motivated

In this chapter

- How to calculate how many calories your body burns
- How to estimate the calories in the food you eat
- What foods make you feel full (satiety index)
- What foods are absorbed quickly/slowly (glycemic index & load)
- Effective accountability and motivation tactics
- How a bet with my mother got me obsessed with weight loss for a few weeks

Eat fewer calories than your body uses

Weight-loss is simple.

The human body is a complex system, but it handles energy in accordance with the laws of thermodynamics.

> Weight change = energy intake - energy expenditure

Humans measure the energy they consume in calories [46]. The above means simply that:

[46] *Or more specifically kilocalories (kcal).* ↵

- If you eat more calories than you expend: you gain weight
- If you eat less calories than you expend: you lose weight

Energy In versus Energy Out Weight Gain/Loss

For anyone that thinks their body does not conform to this principle: If this were true, your body would be breaking the laws of physics. I assure you it is not.

The main principle for weight loss is thus simply:

> To lose weight, eat fewer calories than you expend. To gain weight eat more calories than you expend.

The exceptions

The above is a rule of thumb in the same way that 'if you jump from a first story window you will get hurt' is a rule of thumb. There are exceptions, but you shouldn't let them dictate your choices. For context, I do want to add some.

There are people whose genetics make it easier or harder to lose weight. This is often due to their genetic food preferences [47]. Genetics can however make it harder, but never ever impossible to lose weight.

> [47] *Fun fact. People who grew up hungry have a higher risk of diabetes because their body responded by increasing food cravings. See Famine Exposure in the Young and the Risk of Type 2 Diabetes in Adulthood (diabetes.diabetesjournals.org)* ↩

With regards to the fattening effects of specific foods, they do exist to a degree, but the most important ones are the satiety and glycemic index foods we cover below. The one that stands out most is fructose, which can be found in fruits (less in berries), table sugar (sucrose is 50% fructose) and high fructose corn syrup. Overdosing fructose triggers fat storage and a host of other health problems besides. For a deep dive see Peter Attia's interview with Rick Johnson (peterattiamd.com).

Losing weight happens in the kitchen

Your body needs energy to stay alive. The majority of the energy you use every day is used to pump blood, keep you warm and have your brain running.

The energy used to keep you alive is called Base Metabolic Rate (BMR). BMR energy expenditure is far greater than the energy you expend doing sports.

The average BMR can be estimated with this calculation [48] :

> [48] *See the wikipedia page on Basal metabolic rate (en.wikipedia.org)* ↩

- 370 + (21.6 x lean body mass in kg)
- Average for women: 370 + (14.4 x Body Weight in kg)
- Average for men: 370 + (17.3 x Body Weight in kg)

Note how the main formula requires you to know your lean body mass, which is your body weight minus body fat. If you don't know your body fat percentage, use the average formulas.

> For a male with average body fat (20%) weighing 78 kilos that
> means a BMR of 370 + (17.3 x 78) = **1719 kcal**

This same male would burn about **250 kcal** for a half hour of aerobic
sports (e.g., running). In other words, to use the number of calories he
burns by going about his day is equivalent to 9 half hour sports sessions.

If you want to do sports, good. But don't do it to lose weight. Change your
food intake to lose weight.

Eat food that makes you feel full

Your body does not feel full based on the calories you eat. The satiety
system responds to different factors, ranging from stomach fullness to
lipids in your digestive system and the corresponding hormonal response.

Some rules of thumb:

Filling	Not filling
Protein	Fat (caveat below)
Fiber	Sugars

Fat is an interesting one. It does help with satiety, but the effect is **delayed**.
Basically, it is digested slowed meaning you will feel full longer, but not
faster [49].

> [49] See *Effects of Fat on Gastric Emptying of and the Glycemic,
> Insulin, and Incretin Responses to a Carbohydrate Meal in Type 2
> Diabetes (academic.oup.com)* ↵

An interesting technique based on the satiety system is taking 30 grams of
protein within 30 minutes of waking. It suppresses appetite for a good
amount of time.

Glycemic index

A high glycemic index (high blood sugar spike) is bad for weight loss. Your
body is more likely to store the energy as fat, plus most high GI foods are
not that filling compared to their low GI counterparts. This is a rule of
thumb and not universal.

Your body transforms all carbohydrates into sugar. This is why all
carbohydrates increase your blood sugar levels, but fats and proteins do

not [50].

[50] *At least not directly. In practice, this rule of thumb is productive to use.* ↵

Depending on the carbohydrate type and what it's consumed in combination with, your blood sugar will spike to different degrees.

- Table sugar is absorbed as sugar, thus spikes your blood sugar a lot
- Pumpkin takes your body a while to break down, and then a while to break its starches down into sugar. It doesn't spike blood sugar all that much

One note: the glycemic index is a carbohydrate-specific measure. A more 'real world' measure is the glycemic load. Which takes into account the whole meal/food contents. It's harder to calculate on the go though.

Rules of thumb to identify high GI foods:

Level	Guesstimated GI
High (bad)	'White' carbohydrates like sugar, flour, bread, potato, rice, etc.
Medium (all right)	Sweet plants like fruits and starchy vegetables
Low (good)	Protein-rich foods. Non/less sweet/starchy plants like leaves.
None (no impact)	Pure fats. Water.

Minimise the number of choices you have to make

Whitelist instead of blacklist.

When losing weight you want to rely on your willpower as little as possible. Every time you have to make a decision on the spot there is a chance you will make a bad decision.

Therefore, don't choose the foods you will stay away from. Rather choose the only foods you will eat.

Instead of blacklisting:

> I will not eat candy, not drink soda, drink less sweet juice, put no sugar in my coffee, etc

Go with whitelisting:

> I will only eat meats, eggs and vegetables.

It is simpler and less error-prone. If you want to make your weight loss period even more foolproof, take a lesson from the Slow Carb diet and plan a set amount of meals and only eat those.

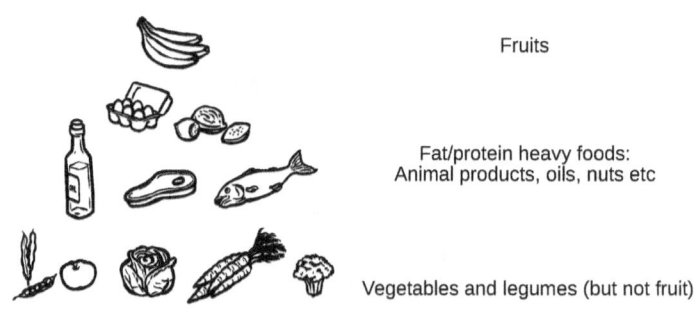

Fruits

Fat/protein heavy foods:
Animal products, oils, nuts etc

Vegetables and legumes (but not fruit)

Weight loss pyramid

Suggested food whitelist

What stuff	How much	Notes
Vegetables that grow above ground	As much as you want	E.g. cauliflower but not potato.
Meat & fish	Normal portions	Prefer lean, but fatty is fine.
Fermented dairy	Normal portions	E.g. Yoghurt, cheese. Only unsweetened.
Fruit	Very limited intake	Consider fruit candy. Its satiety effect is very short. Prefer berries over bigger fruits.
Nuts	Very limited intake	While low glycemic index, 100g macadamia nuts is 700 kcal. Equivalent to 4.5kg cucumber.
Can I eat...	Zero	If you need to ask, then you don't eat it. No 'superfood grains' or 'sugar-free' snacks. Simplicity.

Suggested meal types

Meal	Instructions
Soup	Boil vegetables, add salt, blend them (heatproof blender).
Salad	Chop things up, add olive oil and balsamic. Eat.
Stir-fried	Chop vegetables, put in a pan with hot oil, stir until they are soft-ish.
Yoghurt with fruits	Yoghurt + fruit in a bowl. Spoon it.

Never whitelist

Food	Severity	Example	Why
Sugar	Nuclear	Sugar in coffee	No satiety, lots of energy, fast absorption.
Drinks with energy content (kcal)	Nuclear	Fruit juice, soda	High calorie per second intake. Little satiety. Fast absorption.
Soft/white carbohydrates	High	Bagel, pasta	Low satiety, high energy, fast absorption.
Sweet fruits	Moderate	Dates, figs, grapes, cherry	Fruits have a short-lived effect on satiety and a high GI. Bad for weight loss, fine for long-term health.

Note: there are exceptions to all of these. There are very good kinds of pasta for example, that are decent in satiety and not too bad in GI. When trying to lose weight, don't complicate your life by adding 'maybe, it depends' foods. Simplicity.

Institute habits that make it easy to make the right choices

Habits are behaviours that stopped costing decision power. There is no question in your mind whether you will brush your teeth tonight. The universe would feel out of balance if you didn't. Imagine working out in the morning or eating healthy being as easy to do as brushing your teeth every day.

General advice

- Do not keep food in the house that is not whitelisted

- Prepare your meals in advance if you can
- Eat before shopping for food

Suggested routines

When	Action	Notes
Waking up	30 grams of protein within 30 minutes	5 eggs or 1 big protein shake.
Waking up	500ml (1 big cup, 2 regular ones) water	Cold water preferred.
Hungry at a non-meal time	Savoury broth	Any whitelist food is fine, but zero-sugar broth packages are easy to carry around.

Accountability & motivation

Humans are not very good at making a decision and sticking to it. It is therefore advisable to make a system that supports you in (read: forces you to) stick to your intention.

Humans are more risk-averse than goal-oriented. If you give a person €10 they will be happy. If you give them €20 and later steal €10 from them they will be sad. Even though in both scenarios they end up with €10. Use this to your advantage.

Popular options:

Strategy	Logistics
Betting pool	Set a goal with friends, put money into a pool (enough to hurt, not enough to be impractical) first to reach the goal gets the money, rest loses.
Punishment	Give a friend/service money. If you don't reach the goal, they donate it to a charity/cause you hate.

Suggested accountability

Either go with a betting pool or use a service like Stickk [51] to set up a donation to a charity you hate. Do not choose a charity you like, Stickk is a deterrent for you, it must hurt you to lose. At Stickk you will choose a good (but stern) friend who will decide whether you stuck to your goals.

> [51] stickk.com is a free service that will donate your money to a charity you hate if you don't commit to your goals. ↵

Formulate the cost of failure & gain of winning

Inspiration is fickle and temporary. You can keep it alive by continuously reminding yourself of the cost of failure and the profit from winning. It pays to formulate your cost/benefit reasons.

An example list, 'if I do not reach a healthy weight I will':

- Feel inferior to those around me
- Not have the energy to go for hikes
- Die younger than I need to

An example list, 'if I reach my desired weight I will':

- Feel proud of my body
- Feel good about my discipline
- Be able to enjoy physical activities better

Your reasons will always be your own. Formulate what matters to you, write them down and remind yourself of them at key moments:

- Recite your costs/gains to yourself in the mirror in the morning
- Go through your costs/gains before every meal

What gets measured gets managed

Measure your progress every day. Your first priority should be logging your weight and body fat. You can use an old-school scale and a notebook or a smart scale that makes pretty graphs. Notes on weight management:

- Measure at the same time of day each day for consistency
- Body fat % on scales are not accurate. Use them only for trends.

Note that if you do aim for muscle growth while losing fat as well, it is possible to progress with your weight remaining the same. This is the case if you lose fat at the same rate as you gain muscle. In this case, taking progress pictures might be more useful than measuring weight.

For those who like numbers, calorie counting is a great option. To be effective:

1. Set a calorie goal
2. Measure your intake

For the people who like accuracy, get an app that has accurate calorie counts for foods, I like using myfitnesspal (myfitnesspal.com") because of its huge database of products. When it comes to logging your food, a kitchen scale is your friend.

Rules of thumb:

Food	Guesstimated calories per 100g	Example
Vegetable	30 kcal	Asparagus, cauliflower, carrots
Fruit (N-European)	50 kcal	Apple, berries
Fruit (Warm places)	100 kcal	Pomegranate, banana, grapes
Starchy vegetable	100 kcal	Potato, peas
Cheese	300 kcal	All except explicitly low fat
Fish lean/fatty	50/150 kcal	Trout / eel
Lean/reg/fat meat	100/200/400 kcal	Chicken/Beef/Sausage
Egg small/large	50/75 kcal	

The above is extremely oversimplified. But *measuring something always beats measuring nothing.*

Getting started

As described in this chapter there are two main elements to losing weight: 1) the physics, meaning the thermodynamic truth that your body loses weight when you eat less energy than you burn and 2) the emotion, meaning how easy it is to stick to good behaviour.

For many people, starting with the second part will prove most effective. There are two elements to it:

- Your hunger
- Your environment

To keep your hunger in check I recommend starting with:

1. Eating 30 grams of protein within 30 minutes of waking up. This equals 5 scrambled eggs or a large protein shake.
2. Not drinking calories. That includes 'healthy' juices. Stick to plain coffee/tea/water.

From there start growing your food habits towards high satiety foods with a low glycemic index as described in this chapter.

For the sake of your environment, you want to minimise the occasions where you could make a bad decision. Most importantly:

1. Have no food in the house you are not supposed to eat. Only buy things that suit your weight goal. I recommend planning your food and grocery shopping on a full stomach.
2. Know what you will eat during the day. That can mean pre-determining the foods you will buy in the cafeteria at work/school or preparing your own lunches.

If you feel ready to do so, accountability is the next important step. Set up a betting pool or a Stickk (stickk.com") pledge.

How a single bet changed my life

It all started as a bet with my mother. At the time I was in high school and intensively practised trampolining. Think gymnastics, only on trampolines (it's an Olympic sport I kid you not).

While I was running on a teenager metabolism training 5 times a week, my body did not so much say 'jock' as it did 'meh'. My mom commented on this at some point, which led me to confidently proclaim "I bet you I can get ripped within 4 weeks". And so it began.

You see, at this point I did not know biology the way I do now. I mostly grabbed things for which my brain rewarded me with serotonin and dopamine:

- Energy drinks (4 cans in a row? Sure)
- Cookies (Google 'roze koek' for Dutch delicacy)
- Chocolate (multiple bars of course)

The epitome of my food habits at the time was a thing called boterkoek, which loosely translates to 'butter cake' because it's basically butter with some flower.

The bet changed everything. One thing I did have back then was my base personality traits. A big one of them is having an innate visceral resistance to the words "that is not possible". And so my obsession with all things food started. Experiments included:

- Eating only fruit

- Eating no food
- Smoothies
- No sweet things
- More sports

These were the days where Google hadn't learned to filter out spam web pages very well. I spent many days reading pages that were trying to sell me everything from magical weight loss bracelets to berry extracts. Through the noise, there was one approach that caught my eye: the Paleo movement.

Note that at this point the whole Paleo diet was not well known at all. This Paleo diet dictated a number of things that seemed to make sense, and some I would never agree to:

- No sugar (ok fine)
- No legumes (sure)
- No grains (ok, I think)
- Meat is good (oh god yes)
- No dairy (what, no, I'm Dutch)

Understand that the traditional Dutch diet looks very much like the opposite of the above. Breakfast is bread with chocolate sprinkles [52] with a glass of milk. Lunch is bread with cheese and a glass of milk. Dinner is potato with meat and some vegetables [53].

> [52] *Google hagelslag* ↵
> [53] *Google boerenkool or hutspot* ↵

It was incredibly hard for my teenager brain to summon the willpower to make the above work. My mom basically told me I can eat whatever I want, but if I want something other than she cooks it's my responsibility to buy and cook the food I want.

Over the coming weeks a number of things happened:

- I lost weight
- My acne ridden skin cleared up

Guess what teenage me really cared about. Screw the scale, my skin was a cause of great insecurity.

The months after that were spent reading research reports on everything to do with the relationship between skin and food. From eBooks to spam web pages and research papers I barely understood, I read everything I could find.

> My curse was my blessing, deviating from eating good food messed my skin up within 24 hours.

After a while, a pattern emerged. I learned that I could keep my skin in a good state by sticking to some simple principles:

- Low GI foods
- No searing hot showers (especially on my face)

As time went by I refined my approach. I tried supplements, fasting regimens and all sorts of hormetic exposure like hot (sauna) and cold (ice). A whole world opened up. I felt the world had lied to me, lesser-known but clever people told me that:

- Sugar (the refined kind) is bad for pretty much everything
- My acne was not just genetics but also linked to my food consumption
- Fasting is good for you
- Adult humans have brown fat [54]
- Weight loss is not about sports [55]
- Supplements are not just quackery [56]

[54] *A type of fat thought to be exclusive to babies. This type of adipose tissue burns energy. See the Wikipedia entry (en.wikipedia.org) on brown fat* ↵
[55] *This took me a long time to get over. Eventually, the base metabolic rate calculation convinced me.* ↵
[56] *Though I quickly found out a great deal of them are* ↵

As time went by I found more and more interesting information in the corners of the internet. I obtained audiobooks from questionable web pages, downloaded PDFs of books and discovered online forums. Half of the ways I obtained information back then are illegal now due to copyright legislation [57]. Teenage me without money was very grateful to communities like Demonoid [58], where people all over the world shared copies of books that I could not afford back then.

[57] *Stressing here that at the time everything I did was in compliance with Dutch law* ↵
[58] *Illegal now in most places, and the community seems dead* ↵

> This singular event, the bet with my mother, amplified by the power of the internet, kicked off everything I know about health and fitness.

In the years after I was strongly influenced by writers like Tim Ferriss who pioneered the slow carb diet. By the time he published this very effective weight loss approach, the principles came as no surprise to me anymore.

This is also the point in time where I had started university and was learning how to read actual research. This is the basis of much of the next chapters.

Chapter

Increase muscle mass

Principles to increase muscle mass

1. Verify that you actually want more muscle rather than less fat
2. Trigger muscle growth with resistance training
3. Modify your diet to support muscle growth

In this chapter

- What exercises are commonly recommended (both for men and women)
- How to choose your training weight
- Dietary guidelines for muscle development
- How to distinguish high quality from low-quality protein
- How a handful of writers made me ashamed I took 'broscience' fitness advice

Verify that you actually want more muscle

Keep in mind that most people don't want more muscle, but rather desire greater muscle definition (visible muscle lines). Many obese people have plenty of muscle mass. The goal there is to reduce fat so the muscles become visible. For this purpose see the weight loss section.

General advice

- Focus on good technique
- Use free weights where possible
- Rest is as important as training, do not overtrain
- Use the principles of the weight loss section to control fat levels

Gaining muscle: 2 variables

To increase your lean muscle mass there are many very effective techniques. They all rely on two basic variables:

1. Trigger muscle growth
2. Supply relevant nutrients

Any training program that supplies both of the above will yield results. There isn't one 'good' way of working out for muscle gain. There are however many bad ways.

Trigger muscle growth with resistance training

Triggering muscle growth is simple in principle. You want to send your muscles the signal that they are not sufficient. Exhausting your muscles by doing heavy things basically gives the signal: "I had to fight/run for my survival and these muscles were barely sufficient".

By stretching your limits in exercise you tell your body to activate the set of metabolic and genetic pathways that cause the growth of muscles. Some people have genes that make them respond very sensitively to certain stimuli, meaning a little exercise shows a great result. Others need a heavier stimulus.

Choosing your workout

What matters in choosing your workout is that you train your muscles in a way that exhausts them. Specifically, we're not looking for cardio exhaustion (like stationary bikes) but rather muscle exhaustion (resistance/weight training).

A good workout:

- Trains muscle groups (rather than single muscles)
- Exhausts muscles
- Is safe for long-term usage

In general, it pays off to do exercises that train multiple muscles at the same time. An example would be performing deadlifts rather than a lower-back only machine. Not only does it mean you target more muscles at once, but it also keeps the muscle growth in balance with the muscles in its functional vicinity.

For muscle growth, an important factor is exhaustion. The more you work your muscles to the 'I can not do this any longer' point the more you're triggering the signal to grow. There is some nuance in this as overtraining is counterproductive. This mostly pertains to workout frequency rather than workout intensity though.

Safety is of prime importance. If you do an exercise irresponsibly, you will in the best case prevent yourself from working out for a while and in the worst case cause permanent injury. Keep in mind that:

1. Technique comes first
2. Weight and muscle failure (exhaustion) come second

To compile your workout, the easiest is usually to ask a personal trainer at your gym to help you out. Often you will as you go along learn more and more about fitness and begin to tweak your workout as you go along. There are some recommendations to get you started in the 'getting started' section later in this chapter.

Suggested exercises

Note: there are many other great approaches, for example with kettlebells. The same principle applies: train till (near) exhaustion of muscles as long as you can maintain proper technique.

What matters here is exhausting your muscles with short and intense exercise. For most people talking to a personal trainer at a gym is the best idea (often a single consult is free). There are many good and bad trainers out there. If you think your trainer doesn't suit you, change to a different one.

Exercise	Target
Deadlift	Back, arms, legs
Barbell squat	Legs, butt, back
Bench press	Arms, chest

The below illustrations show you the basic movements of these exercises [59].

[59] The images were taken from Everkinetic (db.everkinetic.com) under the Creative Commons Attribution-ShareAlike 3.0 Unported (CC BY-SA 3.0) (creativecommons.org) ↵

Deadlift

Barbell Squat

Bench Press

Choosing your weight: 5x5

A repetition (rep) is one movement (e.g., lifting a weight and putting it down). A set is the number of times you do a rep.

A guideline often used is the 5x5, a detailed example of such an exercise plan can be found on the Stronglifts website (stronglifts.com). In essence:

- Find a weight where you can do 2 sets of 5 well
- Do 5 sets of 5 reps
- The last 2 sets or so you should just not be able to make 5 (remember, technique comes first!)

The moment you can do 5 sets of 5 reps, up your weight.

Note that this is just one of the many approaches you can take, many of which will get you results. The important thing to note is that hypertrophy (the technical term for muscle cell size increase) is mostly a volume game. More repetitions with more weight means more results. One example of a popular (and effective) philosophy is to not use 5x5 but sets with more repetitions (eight to twelve repetitions for example).

Modify your diet to support muscle growth

The second factor is feeding your body the building blocks it needs to grow muscle. In simple terms: proteins. There is a lot of nuance there that has to do with bioavailability and amino acid makeup, but in essence, it comes down to consuming sufficient high-quality protein.

Muscles are primarily composed of muscle fibres, which are protein structures. When your body is triggered to generate more muscle by exercise, it also needs to get nutrients to work with.

There are two classifications of protein intake that matter when building muscle:

1. Timed protein consumption (less important)
2. Total protein consumption (more important)

Bodybuilders tend to fixate on eating protein before, during and after a workout. The idea is that exercise causes the body to become catabolic (breaking down muscle) and it needs protein to turn anabolic (building muscle) again.

> From research on exercising while fasting we know that there is little to no loss of muscle when eating nothing for hours before, during and after a workout [60].
>
> > [60] *See for example Short-term modified alternate-day fasting: a novel dietary strategy for weight loss and cardioprotection in obese adults. (ncbi.nlm.nih.gov)* ↵

Additionally, many try to eat meals every 2-3 hours to 'supply a constant stream of nutrients'. This again stems from the faulty idea that not supplying protein will make the body break down muscle.

> Timing protein consumption has shown to be marginally effective at best, and without benefit at worst [61].
>
> > [61] *See The effect of protein timing on muscle strength and hypertrophy: a meta-analysis (jissn.biomedcentral.com)* ↵

If you want to be a full-time bodybuilder, go ahead and eat meals every few hours. If you are a regular human gaining muscle, don't worry too much about meal timing. Good rules of thumb are:

- Eating some protein after a workout is good, but not doing it is no issue
- Eating protein every few hours only is marginally better for muscle growth
- Having an adequate total protein intake is what really matters

Suggested dietary practices

Factor	Recommendation
Calories	Calculate your BMR, add calories you expend in exercise (unless you are aiming for weight loss).
Protein intake	Minimum 1.4 times lean body mass. This is the most important.
Protein type	High DIAAS score. This is important. See the protein quality section below
Protein timing	Regular if possible, max 40 grams per consumption. This is not a high priority.
Food types	Low GI, see weight loss section.

Choosing your protein intake

There are two factors in determining your dietary makeup for the sake of muscle development:

- Caloric intake
- Protein intake

From the weight loss section we know that the base metabolic rates for humans are about:

- $370 + (21.6 \times \text{Lean Body Mass in kg})$
- Average for women: $370 + (14.4 \times \text{Body Weight in kg})$
- Average for men: $370 + (17.3 \times \text{Body Weight in kg})$

> For a male with an average body fat percentage (20%) weighing 78 kilos that means a BMR of $370 + (17.3 \times 78) = \textbf{1719 kcal}$

Make sure you eat enough when trying to gain muscle. Keep in mind your exercise expenditure and set a daily target.

The rule of thumb for protein consumption is: 1.4x your lean muscle weight in grams. For example:

> A person weighing 80kg with 15% body fat should take about 80 minus 15% (which results in lean body mass) multiplied by 1.4 = 95 grams of protein in periods of muscle gain.

If you have no way of measuring your body fat percentage you can assume the average of 25% for men and 35% for women [62].

[62] *See Wikipedia page on typical body fat percentages (en.wikipedia.org)* ↵

Minimum protein consumption in grams for an average man/woman based on the above averages:

- 1.05x bodyweight for men (80kg weight = 80 grams)
- 0.91x bodyweight for women (70kg weight = 64 grams)

Please keep in mind that a gram of a food that contains protein doesn't count as a gram of protein. 1 gram of meat is not 1 gram of protein for example.

The above is a rule of thumb. Keep in mind that:

- This is a game of averages, don't go manic on exact numbers
- Protein counts as calories, protein shakes too
- Eating protein without exercise will not make your muscles grow

Note that these 2 factors (calorie and protein intake) do not describe a healthy diet. That would include choosing the right amount and type of carbohydrates and fats as well. If you would like to incorporate general health guidelines, read the guidelines in the weight loss section.

Protein quality

Not all proteins are created equal. Specifically, what matters is the ratio of amino acids and their bioavailability of the source. The currently used method to rate proteins is the *Digestible Indispensable Amino Acid Score* or DIAAS. It takes into account:

- The amino acid needs of a human
- The degree to which a protein is absorbed by humans

You can look up DIAAS tables online. In general animal source proteins (dairy, meat, eggs) are of the highest biological quality. This is why WHEY protein (dairy source) is very popular in bodybuilding.

This doesn't mean that plant proteins don't help muscle growth. However, it does mean that your body doesn't absorb them as well and might need a very diverse group of protein sources.

The (untrue) protein absorption limit

There is a lot of untrue common sense out there. In the fitness world, it is often referred to as 'broscience'. While it usually doesn't cause any explicit harm, it often tells people to do silly things.

For example, there is no limit to the amount of protein the body can consume in one meal [63].

> [63] *So no it's not 40 grams as many bodybuilders believe. This mantra stems from a misinterpretation of a study that found that 20-40 grams of protein was the most optimal per-meal consumption amount to stimulate muscle growth.* ↵

Later studies have found that the body is perfectly capable of absorbing far above 40 grams in one meal. An extreme example is that people who eat one meal a day absorb the protein from their huge meals just fine.

A side note to this issue is that there is a piece of 'common knowledge' that states that higher protein intake leads to kidney stones. A randomized controlled trial however show that this is not the case [64], that the major impact in generating kidney stones appears to be liquid and mineral intake as confirmed by later studies [65].

> [64] *See Randomized Controlled Trial of a Low Animal Protein, High Fiber Diet in the Prevention of Recurrent Calcium Oxalate Kidney Stones (academic.oup.com)* ↵
> [65] *See Dietary Factors and the Risk of Incident Kidney Stones in Men: New Insights after 14 Years of Follow-up (jasn.asnjournals.org), a nuance from that study is that men who are not overweight and eat a lot of animal protein do have an increased risk for an unknown reason.* ↵

Motivation and consistency

As with losing weight, things like accountability are very important. But while weight loss is an all-day endeavour, exercise is often more about routine and consistency.

For hypertrophy (muscle size) training it is advisable to have certain days or times of day where you exercise. Personally, I like going to the gym (and consecutively sauna) in the morning. Whatever works for you, schedule it. Put it on your calendar. Preferably have a friend or personal trainer to hold you accountable.

Getting started

Two of the most important principles to remember when it comes to the body are:

1. Temporary changes cause temporary results
2. Consistency beats intensity

Both of those principles point to a single conclusion:

> Choose a simple & sustainable routine and implement it in a way you will stick to it

Too many people decide they want to change their body composition, get started and then stop two weeks later. Someone who does 10 push-ups a day for the rest of their lives will have greater results than someone who has 2 weeks of intense workouts and quits.

Do not chase instant results or over-optimization, especially when getting started. Don't compete with other gym goers for who can lift the heaviest weights. Don't start using fitness supplements unless you are at a point you are willing to call yourself a weightlifter. Don't exercise isolated muscle groups with exercises like bicep curls.

Get yourself a personal trainer or experienced gym buddy. Focus on doing well-executed movements of the following exercises:

1. Squat
2. Deadlift
3. Bench press

Focus on establishing excellent technique and a reliable routine. Lifting heavier and heavier weights is fine, but consider it a side effect of your technical training.

Simplicity. Consistency.

Once you trust yourself to have good technique and a reliable routine, optimise for muscle gain with the principles in this chapter. It may take you a week, it may take you a month. This is not a competition, it is a personal journey to reach your goals.

If you are at a point where you feel like quitting, consider having a look at motivational videos like Even Ødegård's "Rise and shine" (youtube.com) or Jocko Willink's "Good" (youtube.com).

How I learned to ignore broscience

As my journey into health and fitness began (see weight loss chapter) I also started researching muscle. As any teenage boy insecure about their body will tell you, a little muscle definition never hurt anybody.

Before I knew it I was indoctrinated in the broscience world of fitness. Supplements, meal frequency, high protein diet and using my muscles to make repetitive motions. While I had some results, things were not moving as fast as I hoped.

My personal goals were to obtain:

1. Abs like Thor, please
2. Greek god chiselled muscles

While I was using my muscles very intensely (training 5-7 times a week depending on the season) I was not getting significantly closer to reaching my desired body. I was certainly in shape, but not where I wanted to be.

Enter Pavel Tsatsouline, Tim Ferriss, Martin Berkhan and Ori Hofmekler.

Pavel Tsatsouline is a strength guru who brands himself in line with his Russian background. He goes around calling people 'comrade' and generally just keeps a no-nonsense approach. He taught me through his writings that:

1. Muscle gain and muscle strength are not the same
2. You don't need a huge arsenal of equipment and exercises (squat, deadlift, bench press)
3. Kettlebells are a great one-stop shop

> Doing the perfect kettlebell swing alone is superior to 99 percent of the sophisticated strength and conditioning programs out there. *Pavel Tsatsouline*

Tim Ferriss collected a whole lot of valuable advice on all things health. For muscle gain, I was greatly inspired by the Occam's protocol. This exercise and food protocol uses 30 minutes of exercise a week to gain a lot of muscle in a very short span of time.

While I am not in favour of using this protocol in the long run, it drove home a very powerful point: time spent and results gained are **not proportional**.

> "It is possible to get huge with less than 30 minutes of gym time per week. *Timothy Ferris*

Martin Berkhan runs a blog called Leangains, and while it has been inactive for a while [66] it had a big impact on me. Him and Ori Hofmekler who wrote 'The Warrior Diet' showed me that broscience is wrong most of the time.

[66] *At the time of writing* ↵

Both of these men promote versions of intermittent fasting and time restricted eating. What they wrote went against common principles like:

- You need to eat every 3 hours for muscle gain
- Your body can only absorb x amount of protein per meal
- You should use machines for workouts
- You need to 'confuse' your muscle by rotating exercises
- Fat should be avoided
- And so on

The message from both was very encouraging: it's not all that complicated.

> Fuckarounditis is a behavioural disorder characterized by a mediocre physique and complete lack of progress, despite significant amounts of time spent in the gym. ... Fuckarounditis most commonly manifests itself as an intense preoccupation with crunches, curls, cable movements, belts, gloves, balance boards, Swiss Balls and Tyler Durden. Fear of squats and deadlifts is another distinguishing trait. Physical exertion is either completely lacking or misapplied (towards questionable or unproductive training practices). *Martin Berkhan (Read his total 'diagnosis' here (leangains.com))*

Many of the things written by them were the precursors for my current views on food and exercise. The principles that kept coming back were:

- Eat enough but not excessive amounts of protein
- Train your muscles until failure
- Use compound exercises that train many muscles at once

Based on these principles I began to experiment on my own body and thus developed my favourite blend of exercise. For me, that meant that my goals developed and changed. I wanted:

1. Low time investment
2. Portability
3. Strength & mobility

After a while, I came to the conclusion that I have no desire to be a muscle monster. I want to be strong and have well-defined muscles. I want to be able to move heavy things, make high jumps and move fluidly.

What this has ended up in is a combination of Pavel's teachings and that of Coach Sommer [67] (whose vision will be discussed further in the flexibility and mobility chapter).

[67] *Full name Christopher Sommer* ↵

I do only 10-20 minutes or so of exercise a day, consisting out of:

- One handed and one-legged push-ups
- Pistol squats
- Press handstands
- Pull-ups
- Kettlebell swings

All required a lot of training in strength and balance, but once I got there, doing an intense set of the above keeps me in good physical shape.

That said, I can't stress enough how important food is for muscle growth and general body composition. I have gone through periods of zero exercise (shame on me) where my body composition barely changed due to food choice and fasting practices.

Over time I learned the mechanisms behind the workings of hypertrophy (muscle cell increase), hyperplasia (increased muscle cell count) and strength systems. Personally, I only learned about the underlying mechanisms after I had experienced the effects firsthand.

Chapter

Increase muscle strength

Principles for strength development

1. Do high load exercises in low repetitions
2. Do not do exercises to muscle failure
3. Do many repetitions spaced out over the day (or in a gym, take breaks between sets)

In this chapter

- How strength training differs from muscle size training
- Effective full body strength exercises
- Progressions to help train towards technically difficult movements
- How a comic book guru's Discovery Channel show shaped my thoughts on strength

Do high load exercises in low repetitions

Strength is greatly neurological, the strength of a muscle depends not only on its size but also on how well you are able to activate it. Electrocution or tetanus, for example, can cause the muscles to spasm violent enough to break bones. Training for strength is decidedly different than training for muscle size gain.

While muscle size is one factor, it is not the only variable in muscle strength. The physical structure of the muscle determines theoretical output, just like how many seconds it takes for a car to accelerate to a certain speed if you give it full throttle. The neurological element is how well you are able to 'press the throttle' of your muscles.

What matters in practice is the neurological signal to exert force. There is a safety limit on the percentage of strength a muscle can theoretically and practically produce, which makes sense since we don't want to accidentally break our bones using our own muscle force like in the above tetanus example. When comparing bodybuilders (big muscles) to weightlifters (strong muscles) you will observe that weightlifters can lift far heavier weights than bodybuilders their size.

When training for strength you are in essence helping your body understand how much strength is safe to use.

Do not exercise to muscle failure

A popular approach to strength rather than muscle size is *Greasing the Groove* as described by Pavel Tsatsouline. This protocol consists of three tenets:

1. High load (lots of effort)
2. Low consecutive repetitions (no exhaustion)
3. Regular repetitions throughout the day

The **high load** refers to the need to use muscles close to their strength limit. It's not about exhausting them but rather about making one repetition of a difficult move.

The **low repetition** element is linked to the above. If you can do 10 repetitions of a movement, it is not hard enough for this protocol. Heavier exercises with lower repetitions are better under the condition you can execute them with good technique.

The **regular repetitions** refer to doing the high-load movements often throughout the day. Where muscle growth asks you to do a larger volume of heavy movements after each other, this protocol wants you to do single repetition sessions every hour or even half an hour.

The protocol as written by Pavel focuses on two body-weight exercises:

- One-handed (and/or simultaneously one-legged) push-up
- Pistol squat

One handed push-up with two legs

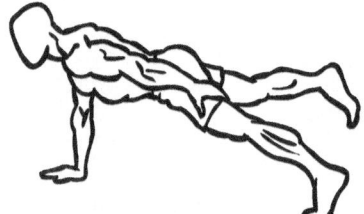
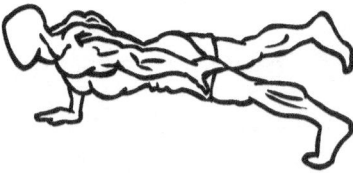

One handed push-up with one leg

Pistol squats

These are highly technical moves that stimulate a large number of muscle groups. The one-handed/legged push-up, for example, stimulates everything from triceps to pectorals to the core and even the upper leg.

The principles of this protocol, however, translate to many other exercises. Just keep in mind that this protocol is more dangerous with respect to injuries since you are training with high muscle-load. Technique is even more important than with regular resistance training.

Suggested exercises

The below two progressions are a suggestion on how to work your way up to one-handed and legged push-ups as well as the pistol squat. Start with the first one, and as you get stronger, build your way to the next exercise. Proper form is the bottleneck. If you can't do a movement with good form, don't go to the next one yet.

Progression one:

- Push-up
- One-handed push-up, downward motion only
- One-handed push-up
- One handed and one-legged push-up

Progression two:

- Squat
- Pistol squat, downward motion only
- Full pistol squat

If a pull-up bar is available, pull-ups are great.

You may modulate the difficulty of any exercise by doing it slower. A 5-second push-up is harder than a quick one for example. Some studies indicate that focussing on eccentric movement (downward in this case) is best for strength development.

Motivation and consistency

As with losing weight, things like accountability are very important. But while weight loss is an all-day endeavour, exercise is often more about routine and consistency.

For strength training, set triggers throughout the day. Try to make your home and place of work conducive to this. This might work better for some professions than others. Having a pull-up bar in the door to your office is, for example, a great way to do single-rep slow pull-ups throughout the day. Likewise, having space in your office to do a quick one-handed push-up will contribute to your consistency.

Getting started

Any structural changes to your body take structural behaviour changes. In the case of increasing your strength, that means consistently practising the 'skill' of strength. Before you emphasise what specific exercises you will use for your strength development, consider how you want to implement consistent habits.

Strength development depends on technically well-executed motions under high load and low repetitions. For most people that means either:

- Going to the gym and practising the big 3 (squat, deadlift, bench press) with high weight, low repetitions and long breaks between sets
- Practising intense callisthenics (one-handed push-up, pistol squat) spaced out throughout the day

What form this takes for you personally depends on how you live your life. If you spend your working days wearing a suit and tie, dropping for a push-up every hour might not be feasible whereas using the company gym at lunch could work great. If you work in a more casual workplace it may be totally feasible to do exercises at your workplace.

Start by instituting one habit and build from there. Even if that means you go to the gym and do 1 technically perfect repetition (after a warm-up of course), or you do a single push-up at lunch. Build the habit, and then increase the intensity and volume of your practice.

The most important element is consistency. You need to give your body the signal to get stronger (heavy exercises) and then give it time to adapt. Approaches I have personally found to work are:

- Going to the gym before work
- Do exercises next to my desk (some funny comments in week 1, week 2 nobody even notices, some even join)
- Lobby for a pull-up bar in the doorframe of the bathroom
- Do push-ups in the bathroom when you go. Do it right before washing your hands so your hands will be clean after

Find whatever helps you practice more regularly. I personally noticed I feel far less resistance to doing exercises if there is an easy to use space where not many people see me. Likewise, my morning exercises are easier to adhere to in the presence of a high-quality fitness mat.

Stan Lee's Superhumans

It took me a while to realise that muscle size and strength are not proportional per se. People like Pavel Tsatsouline said it many times. What really drove it home for me was a Discovery Channel episode of Stan Lee's Superhumans (excelsior Stan).

This particular episode covered a man called Dennis Rogers, a reasonably unassuming looking guy who proceeded to bend pans, wrenches and other miscellaneous items with his bare hands.

Of course, the TV show made a big show out of calling him the strongest man in the world, but I just couldn't deny that this man's strength to size ratio turned all the broscience spoken around the gym on its head.

From that moment on I took the whole strength versus size thesis more seriously. The common theme in recommendations on strength training I would include:

- Eccentric motion is more important
- Muscle exhaustion is undesirable

Eccentric refers to the negative part of an exercise, the part where the muscle stretches. For example, the downward part of a squat.

I started experimenting with all sorts of exercises, mostly in the gym. After listening to a podcast featuring Pavel Tsatsouline, I obtained some of his books. In particular, one called The Naked Warrior.

This book caught my eye because it focussed on bodyweight training only. The appeal of that approach to me is that I can keep practising when travelling or am otherwise unable to go to a gym.

The book focussed on only 2 exercises:

- Pistol squat
- Push up on one hand & one leg

The book also stressed the 'Greasing the Groove' approach, which sees strength as a skill. Under the motto of practice makes perfect, the book recommends:

- Doing intense exercises
- Never training to failure

The first translates to practising the skill of strength by tackling an exercise you find difficult. The second means you do not push your body to the point where you can't do any more exercises after.

In practice, the recommendations came down to doing pistol squats and one hand/leg push-ups throughout the day, getting your total count up as high as you can without ever exhausting your muscles.

The result of this is a signal to your nervous system that you are trying to use your muscles for more strength without triggering the muscle exhaustion response that is most effective for muscle gain. The result is more strength without all that much muscle gain.

The journey to reaching the point where I am now took a while. For the one-handed push-ups, it took me a while to build my way up. In the beginning, it took all my willpower to only do a downward motion one-handed push-up, but as I kept doing them throughout the day my strength levels increased reliably.

The nice and yet odd element of this approach is that you will be doing push-ups in the strangest places. I made it a routine to do some one-handed push-ups in the bathroom before I washed my hands, for example.

The pistol squat was even harder for me. Not just because it takes a lot of strength, but also because it requires balance and flexibility. For me specifically, the Achilles and calf were so tight that I would fall backwards whenever I attempted a pistol squat. I worked my way up by:

- Stretching the Achilles
- Holding some weight in my hands for balance

- Holding chairs/tables/etc for balance

By now, a pistol squat is no problem whatsoever, but it did take some time to get there.

I've also realised that a little warm-up is needed for these kinds of intense exercises. Nothing extreme, but if you are going to do a one-handed push-up at least warm up your hip and shoulder joints a bit.

My current exercise routine heavily depends on daily pistol squats and one-handed & legged push-ups. They are great portable exercises that activate a large set of muscles. Combined with a stretching routine (see stretching chapter) it takes care of daily physical fitness very effectively.

Chapter
Develop flexibility and mobility

Principles for flexibility

1. Choose stretching routines that target many and large muscle groups
2. Treat stretching as an active exercise
3. Treat stretching as normal length workouts
4. Stick with intense stretch workouts for at least 6-12 months
5. Consider Gymnastics Strength Training (GST)

In this chapter

- Why flexibility develops slower than muscle size/strength
- Recommended flexibility/mobility program
- My journey from not being able to touch my toes to 'that flexible guy'

Flexibility versus mobility

Flexibility refers to the ability to stretch into certain positions passively and is mostly a function of muscle and connective tissue flexibility

Mobility refers to being able to get into a position while maintaining strength and is greatly a function of how far the range of motion in your joints is

They are connected, but not the same. Flexibility tends to be static whereas the goal of mobility is to be able to use the body to move comfortably through physical motions.

An example of flexibility is a pancake motion forward without actively engaging any muscles:

Forward Pancake

Whereas being able to squat deeply with good form is an example of functional mobility:

No Weights Squat

In this chapter when the word flexibility is used, please interpret it as meaning mobility. The reason I use the word flexibility in the title of this chapter is that most people would have no idea what the chapter is about if I used the word mobility.

Optimally, the human body should be able to move in any number of ways that are, in our society, anything but standard. Many people are not even able to touch their toes while keeping their legs straight. Being able to make these motions makes the body more injury proof and prevents a host of common problems, like back pain.

Treat stretching as an active exercise

If you stretch passively, meaning without having your muscles under tension, you are not giving your body the right signals to promote active mobility. Instead you should be stretching while your muscles are actively under tension.

You body responds very differently to active and passive stretching:

- Stretching before exercise makes you weaker [68] and stretching before running makes you slower [69]
- Active dynamic stretches improve short-term performance and active static stretches do not have a negative impact like passive stretching does [70].

> [68] See Reduced strength after passive stretch of the human plantarflexors (physiology.org) and Factors Affecting Force Loss With Prolonged Stretching (nrcresearchpress.com) ↵
> [69] See The acute effects of combined static and dynamic stretch protocols on fifty-meter sprint performance in track-and-field athletes (search.proquest.com) ↵
> [70] See The effect of different warm-up stretch protocols on 20 meter sprint performance in trained rugby union players (ncbi.nlm.nih.gov) ↵

Over the long term, stretching actively conditions your body to facilitate active mobility and range of motion, rather than unidimensional passive stretch ability that will not carry over fully into your ability to move well. Passive stretching will still have some benefits, but substituting it for active stretches will result in better results.

One of the keys to the development of functional mobility is practising putting your body in a position while maintaining muscle tension. When doing these exercises we are training the body to do a number of things:

- To neurologically allow muscles to release tension
- To neurologically allow muscles to relax further
- To develop anatomical structures to handle greater ranges of motion

The neurological component of stretching

One element of mobility is the ability of your muscle to relax and lengthen. When you think of a tense muscle preventing you from stretching, this is partially not a result of an anatomically stiff muscle. Instead, there is a neurological pressure that is keeping the muscle tense. By stretching we are in essence sending neurological signals to let go of the tension.

Additionally, we are influencing the 'safety switch' on the muscles. You have probably noticed that your muscles reflexively contract when they stretch beyond a certain point. This is the body preventing you from doing permanent damage by moving into positions you can't (yet) handle. By stretching your muscles you are sending a signal that in essence says 'look here body, we can safely go this far, you should set the safety limits a little less strict'.

The role of slow-growing tendons

Lastly, there are a number of slow-developing structures like tendons that impact your ability to stretch and gain mobility, as well as potential muscular adhesions causing tension. These structures are slow to grow and change. While muscles take weeks to develop, these structures take months. Damaging them also means you will take a long time to recover.

Timeline warning

Note that the above tells you that you will most likely see some quick initial results, followed by a period of a plateau. The initial muscle relaxation is something you will notice even as you compare the beginning and the end of your workout. The further relaxation of the neurological range of motion will take a bit longer and the development of the tendons longer still.

When you reach a plateau, embrace it and keep going. Your body needs these signals over the long term. If you suspect that muscle tension and adhesions are holding you back, consider finding a (painfully) professional massage therapist.

Target many and large muscle groups

For most people tension is most severe and problematic in larger muscle groups. For example, hamstrings, quadriceps and the lower back. Of course, there are many other problematic areas like the calves and neck.

Often there are exercises that can target large and multiple muscle groups at once. For example, pancake motions when executed correctly can stretch the back, hamstrings and calves. Favour these kinds of exercises over very specific movements.

My favourite stretches

I do these stretches every day. They keep my main points of flexibility in shape but must be supplemented with more whole-body stretch workouts. Generally, I dynamically walk through these as a mini warm up and then hold each pose for 10 seconds. I spend extra time on the pancake and straddle stretches since those muscles tend to go tight fast for me.

1. Pancake (leaning forward)
2. Pancake (body flat on leg)
3. Straddle side stretch
4. Achilles stretch (leaning on one foot)
5. Glute stretch
6. Elevated bridge
7. Knees by ears (rolled on your back)

Forward Pancake

Side Pancake

Straddle Side Stretch

Achilles Stretch

Glute Stretch

Elevated Bridge

Knees by ears

General advice

- Stretching should be uncomfortable, but not painful
- Connective tissue grows and heals slowly, give it time
- Injuries of connective tissue take a long time to heal, don't overdo intensity
- Stretching isn't about relaxing, actively engage your muscles
- Any stretching beats no stretching, make it a daily routine

Treat stretching as normal length workouts

Exercise is something we use to give our bodies a signal for what development we desire. In the case of weight lifting, we are saying 'our muscles are not developed enough for this task, please develop them'. In the case of muscles, the body will activate synthesis pathways for muscle development.

With flexibility and mobility work, we need to give an equally strong signal that we want to develop connective tissue and muscle relaxation. To that effect, we need to take exercising for flexibility as seriously as muscle development.

Horizon: 6-12 months

Connective tissue develops much slower than muscle, meaning that you will notice that:

- Flexibility develops slowly as connective tissue changes over weeks and months
- Your range of motion often ends up being 'stuck' for a while, and then suddenly develops dramatically seemingly overnight

The upside to this is that once developed it takes a lot less effort to maintain flexibility and mobility.

Gymnastics Strength Training

Personally, I have had great experiences with the GST approach [71], specifically the fundamentals 1 series. It takes principles from gymnastics and translates them into gym-friendly workouts that increase your flexibility and mobility hand in hand.

[71] See the Gymnastic Bodies website (gymnasticbodies.com) ↵

The program is quite intense though and for a good few months had me doing daily workouts. The results are astonishing and I highly recommend this program to anyone who takes developing flexibility and mobility seriously.

If anything, this program is a good way to go from your current level to the level you desire to achieve. I found doing a workout every day unfeasible for me personally, but highly recommend following the program for as long as needed to get to your desired level. After that, you can institute maintenance routines.

Some observations:

- You will need some special equipment (that is available in most gyms or cheap to get)
- Some exercises require things like gymnastics rings. I ended up using whatever was reasonably close to the instruction video that was available in my gym

Getting started

For most people who read this, flexibility and mobility are most likely at the point where touching the ground without bending your legs is hard or impossible. The question I recommend you pose yourself is:

> How serious are you about your mobility?

In my mind, there are two approaches you can take. The first is intense, difficult and very rewarding within 6 months. It involves following an intense program like Gymnastics Strength Training. I personally took this approach and have made progress that I didn't think possible when I started. While effective, it is not for the faint of heart and requires at least 3 hours a week of exercises.

The second approach is more tempered and mild. It will certainly get you results, but they will be far slower. In this approach, you institute a less intense but consistent stretching practice. You may, for example, set up a daily stretch routine of 10-20 minutes that targets the most commonly tense large muscle groups.

If you take this approach, I have personally found the following stretches most helpful:

- Pancakes (sitting in a straddle and bringing your body down to the floor and your legs)
- Straddle side stretch (tension in these side muscles is the cause of a lot of back problems)
- Glute stretch (especially if you sit a lot)
- Elevated bridge (for the upper back and shoulders)

Set up a consistent routine, for example, a stretching session before bed. I personally enjoy stretching while consuming some entertaining but not too stimulating medium like a podcast (have a look at Dan Carlin's hardcore history (dancarlin.com)). Remember to do these stretches actively, meaning you don't relax into them but actively use your muscles to pull you into the desired position.

How I became 'the flexible guy'

Flexibility has never been my strong suit. My friends in high school all assumed I was flexible because I did trampolining, presumably because they thought it was like gymnastics. The reality was though that touching my toes with my legs straight has been hard or impossible for me at different times in my life.

As I started freelancing and developing a professional career I started being plagued by back and neck pain. I later found out back issues are prevalent in both my mother and father's families to different degrees.

I remember one incident where I was sitting against a wall cross-legged when suddenly - boom! - my back exploded in excruciating pain. For a good 3 days walking hurt, getting dressed hurt and pretty much everything other than lying flat hurt (and even that a little).

As any sane person would I visited a physiotherapist specialising in back pain within days of being able to walk again. He looked at me, had me do some postures and proclaimed we'd get things fixed in no time. Two times a week I visited the practice and was guided through a number of exercises.

Most of the exercises though focused on strength and joints:

- Deadlift motions without weight
- Lifting arms and legs on all fours
- Bending the back on all fours
- And so on

While I did start to feel better, I could feel that my back was not doing ok. From the way my muscles felt during the exercises I concluded that my hamstrings and core muscles were very tight.

Of course, I followed the advice of my physiotherapist, but could not resist reading some books on the topic of flexibility, mobility and injury proofing.

Through this search, I found a book called Becoming a Supple Leopard which pulled into question most things I knew about how a body should move. This book told me all the sensible and logical things that no gym coach or therapist had articulated to me. From body posture under stress to flexibility with relaxed muscles being an incomplete approach.

Meanwhile, I started trying all sorts of flexibility approaches, from the things I found in books to daily yoga classes at six in the morning.

I started to put these practices to use, but still nothing really clicked. That is until I found out about Coach Christopher Sommer. A former US national gymnastics coach with strong and unconventional views on what a normal healthy human body should be able to do.

He extrapolated his gymnastics philosophy into a set of workout routines designed to help both couch potatoes and inflexible muscle-heads to develop strong flexibility. Coach Sommer doesn't believe in strength and flexibility being isolated properties of the body. His workouts are designed for what he calls mobility, the application of strength in all relevant angles.

I started his gymnastics strength training series called Foundation and Stretch. These two had me in the gym multiple times a week for a good hour doing all sorts of stretches and strength exercises.

In the beginning, the whole thing was pure torture. Every 45-minute workout made me feel miserable. What kept me going is that after the actual workout, my body felt absolutely wonderful. For the first few weeks, I seemed not to progress at all. Then suddenly one day I was able to touch my toes.

Another few weeks passed without progress. Then seemingly out of the blue, I had no issue whatsoever bringing my face to my knee with a straight leg. Time progressed and before I knew it I had been training for a good 6 months and my body felt like it never had.

After the first few intense months I modified the workout into a short daily session I do to maintain my body's mobility. I have never since had any significant back pain and people compliment me on 'being such a flexible person' and complimenting me on my 'yoga workouts'.

Eat well to live longer

Principles of a longevity diet

1. Take care of the basics first
2. No brainer: do no harm
3. No brainer: eat vegetables
4. No brainer: eat complex carbs only
5. No brainer: eat healthy fats
6. Protein view 1: lower protein intake
7. Protein view 2: high-quality protein intake
8. Restrict your eating window
9. Eat a variety of foods

In this chapter

- Diet recommendations based on scientific research
- Using time-restricted eating as a powerful health tool
- The complexities of 'common wisdom' about things like saturated fats
- How university turned me into a lab rat

Take care of the basics first

Let's say your neighbour drives a car with a broken windshield. The same car has a squeaky door handle on the passenger side. Which do you think he should fix first?

In this example, it's obviously the windshield. But when it comes to health, people are for some reason predisposed to reaching for supplements or 'superfoods' before fixing their basic lifestyle. Your body is not going to thank you for taking an experimental supplement if you are obese, are out of shape or don't sleep enough.

Acting on the best information we have

The gold standard for medical studies is a double-blind placebo-controlled trial, but performing one on humans for longevity diets is near impossible. The study would likely be unethical and take at least one human lifetime. What the scientific community *can* do are:

1. Epidemiological studies (how long do people who smoke live? Can we draw conclusions?)
2. Animal studies (if it works on a worm, could it work on a human?)
3. Centenarian studies (how did the oldest humans live their lives?)
4. Clinical studies (what can we learn about healthy living from treating diabetics?)

There are some caveats I'd like to point out. Primarily, the recommendations in this chapter will likely be beneficial but are most likely incomplete.

The fact is that the studies leading to the conclusions are often not double-blind placebo-controlled studies. That leads to potentially infinite confounding factors. For example, looking at a country like the United States (where a lot of research is done) you will see many secondary relationships like:

- People who eat a lot of saturated fat often do so from low-quality food, they also tend to do less exercise and participate in a host of unhealthy behaviours
- Similarly, a high protein diet can easily be an indicator of a diet rich in fast food and thus likely high in glycemic index

These recommendations will change as research progresses and gives us a better understanding of human genetics and its relation to food and longevity.

What it comes down to is that the conclusions drawn from current science are **unlikely to do harm and potentially do a lot of good.**

No-brainer 1: do no harm

Remember that food is to humans what fuel is to cars. You wouldn't expect good things from throwing diesel into a regular petrol/gasoline car. It is important for us to figure out what our body thrives on and then makes sure it receives that.

There are a number of behaviour that we know to increase risks of cancer, cardiovascular and neurodegenerative disease. You probably already know them:

- Smoking (not strictly diet, we'll tag it 'consumption')
- Eating too much (and being overweight)
- Drinking over 1 glass of alcohol a day
- Eating processed foods & refined sugar
- Eating trans-fats and hydrogenated fats

If you have any of the above issues, fix them. It may be more than a trivial effort but you will be rewarded in a longer and healthier life.

No-brainer 2: eat vegetables

A study tracking 65,000 randomly selected adults from the UK basically found that more vegetable consumption decreases risk of cancer, cardiovascular disease and all-cause mortality.

Highlights from the study [72] [73] :

> [72] the study measured up to 7 portions a day. A portion is 80 grams meaning their study measured up to about 560 grams. ↵
> [73] See Fruit and vegetable consumption and all-cause, cancer and CVD mortality: analysis of Health Survey for England data (jech.bmj.com) ↵

- The first 400 grams/day are most important
- More than 560 grams/day has only incremental benefits
- The effect of vegetables seems more powerful than that of fruit

A variety of vegetables will supply a host of nutrients against a low glycemic load and calorie intake. When it comes to preferences I use glycemic load and index as an indicator. I exclude high-starch plants like potato from my consumption but consume high quantities of greens.

No-brainer 3: complex carbs only

I am not against carbohydrates as a rule but choose them based on the strain they put on my body. That means high glycemic load foods like fruit juices are a no-go, but vegetables, beans and legumes are fine. Based on those parameters I refrain from traditional staples like potatoes, rice and grain products (e.g., pasta, bread).

Glycemic index and load are your guides here, see the weight loss section for a detailed rundown of GI and GL. A low GI excludes refined sugars, starches and pretty much half of what you find in a typical western supermarket.

The effect a food has on your blood sugar is hard to guess without looking it up. For example:

- a portion of lentils (150g) has a glycemic load of 5 (reasonable)
- a portion of white rice (150g) has a glycemic load of 27 (no good)

See the Glycemic index list by Harvard University (health.harvard.edu).

No-brainer 4: eat healthy fats

I take the majority of my calories in the form of fats and most of my food volume as plants. A gigantic bowl of salad (half a kilo) with a shot glass of olive oil (50 grams) will supply about 150 kcal from the salad and 440 from the oil. Likewise, a kilo of tomato will supply 180 kcal and a large handful of nuts (100 grams) 600-700 kcal.

Choosing your fats

The saturated/unsaturated divide may not be helpful in separating the health effects on humans. So far, research is conflicting. A controversial study, for example, found that replacing saturated fats with a specific unsaturated one resulted in a *higher risk* of mortality [74]. Combined with the studies we'll discuss below I try to eat oils with a documented positive effect.

[74] *See Use of dietary linoleic acid for secondary prevention of coronary heart disease and death: evaluation of recovered data from the Sydney Diet Heart Study and updated meta-analysis (bmj.com)* ↵

Helpful heuristics:

1. Do not consume trans-fats and hydrogenated fats
2. Avoid vegetable/seed oils (e.g. sunflower, palm, rapeseed, soybean)
3. Fruit oils are fine (e.g. olive, avocado, coconut)
4. Fats from animal sources are fine in moderation and likely do low or no harm even at higher consumption (assuming they are of high quality)

This clears some well-known sources of good fats like nuts, fish, olive oil and filters out well-known culprits like palm oil [75].

[75] *Which is terrible for the environment too, try to avoid products with palm oil. See Social and environmental impact of palm oil on Wikipedia (en.wikipedia.org)* ↵

Olive oil has been reasonably well-documented to have positive health effects. Its major fatty acid content is oleic acid which seems to be beneficial. It is my oil of choice for non-cooking uses. I would like to stress that I recommend high-quality oil (you should be able to drink it straight and it should taste good) since low-quality oils are often fake and far less tasty.

Coconut oil is one my oils of choice for cooking due to its stability, reasonably high smoking point and shelf life. It is also high in medium chain triglycerides making it loved by those who aim for ketosis (see fasting section as well).

Animal fats such as meat and dairy are traditionally thought of as bad due to their saturated fat content. Since saturated fats in recent research have not proven to be reliable predictors of health risks (when not combined with other unhealthy foods), I don't worry about them too much. I have shifted my consumption of meat away from beef due to the environmental impact but am nutritionally not against high-quality unprocessed meat, that means yes to a good steak but no to fast food. Fats from fish are robustly documented to have a positive health impact so I have as much of those as I want.

Avoid vegetable oils

These I generally avoid, that includes margarine products.

There are a number of studies in humans showing that vegetable oils (specifically omega-6 polyunsaturated fatty acids) potentially correlate with cardiovascular disease and diabetes risk[76], cardiovascular disease and cancer risk[77] and inflammation[78].

> [76] See n-6 fatty acid-specific and mixed polyunsaturate dietary interventions have different effects on CHD risk: a meta-analysis of randomised controlled trials. (ncbi.nlm.nih.gov) and Diet and disease--the Israeli paradox: possible dangers of a high omega-6 polyunsaturated fatty acid diet. (europepmc.org) ↵
> [77] See New insights into the health effects of dietary saturated and omega-6 and omega-3 polyunsaturated fatty acids (bmcmedicine.biomedcentral.com) ↵
> [78] The data in humans is a bit scarce, but animal data is more abundant. For example in Rats (pubs.acs.org) and sea bass (sciencedirect.com) ↵

I specifically avoid oil high in the omega-6 fatty acid linoleic acid (not to be confused with alpha-linolenic acid which is an omega-3) as studies seem to indicate it has a particularly negative effect[79]. The animal data points to many other potential health risks like insulin resistance[80], cancer[81], reproductive issues[82] and mitochondrial issues[83].

> [79] See New insights into the health effects of dietary saturated and omega-6 and omega-3 polyunsaturated fatty acids (bmcmedicine.biomedcentral.com) ↵
> [80] See A high fat diet rich in corn oil reduces spontaneous locomotor activity and induces insulin resistance in mice (researchgate.net) ↵
> [81] See Dietary corn oil promotes colon cancer by inhibiting mitochondria-dependent apoptosis in azoxymethane-treated rats. (ncbi.nlm.nih.gov) ↵
> [82] See ffect of different dietary omega-3/omega-6 fatty acid ratios on reproduction in male rats (lipidworld.biomedcentral.com) ↵
> [83] See Induction of mitochondrial nitrative damage and cardiac dysfunction by chronic provision of dietary ω-6 polyunsaturated fatty acids (sciencedirect.com) ↵

Research so far seems to indicate that one of the main downsides to vegetable oils is that it upsets the ratio of omega-3 to omega 6 oils in the diet which is essential to health[84]. The fact is that there is no strong long-term study documenting health risks for vegetable oils compared to fruit or animal oils. The consideration for me is simple:

[84] *See Omega-6/Omega-3 Essential Fatty Acid Ratio: The Scientific Evidence (books.google.com)* ↵

> I have the choice between oils proven to be beneficial (e.g. olive) and oils that are potentially harmful (vegetable/seed), between those I choose the beneficial oil.

Note on Saturated fat

The recommendation to avoid saturated fats is one I expect to be altered in the coming years of research. The reason saturated fats are linked to poor health currently is likely that diets rich in saturated fats (think US diet) are often rich in other problematic ingredients like trans-fats, sugars and low vegetable ingestion. Additionally, not all saturated fats are the same with regards to health benefit or risk.

An early indication for this can be found in a paper that compared cardiovascular disease (CVD), all-cause mortality (ACM) for different sources of saturated fat (SFA) consumption [85] :

[85] *See Dietary fat intake and risk of cardiovascular disease and all-cause mortality in a population at high risk of cardiovascular disease (researchgate.net)* ↵

- Saturated fat intake showed an increased risk for cardiovascular disease and all-cause mortality
- Mono and polyunsaturated fats showed a decreased risk for cardiovascular disease and all-cause mortality

This seems to confirm commonly cited recommendations. However, saturated fat intake:

- From fish and nuts decreased cardiovascular disease and all-cause mortality
- From processed meats increased cardiovascular disease and all-cause mortality
- From dairy showed increases in cardiovascular disease, except for the study subjects who consumed the most dairy (highest consumption category the researchers used) where it was decreased
- From dairy showed decreased all-cause mortality for the second lowest consumption category, but high risk for high consumers

The above paints a confusing picture: Saturated fat is bad. Unless it comes from fish or nuts. And dairy is bad, unless you eat it in low quantities. But it's actually good for CVD if you eat it a lot.

What I mean to show with it is that things are more complicated than saturated versus unsaturated fats. The coming years of research will probably find that specific fats are beneficial or harmful as opposed to putting all saturated and unsaturated fats on the same pile.

Protein view 1: lower protein intake

According to the research compilation of doctor Valter Longo in his book The Longevity Diet (goodreads.com) it is recommended to have low protein intake for longevity with a split recommendation below and above 65 years of age.

Below the age of 65 keep protein intake low defined as 0.31-0.36 grams per pound of bodyweight, or the metric equivalent of 0.68-0.80 grams per kilogram of body weight. E.g. an 80kg/176lb person should consume around 60 grams of protein a day.

Above the age of 65 increase protein intake by 10-20%. Centenarian studies find that the lower levels of growth-related hormones need to be compensated for with slightly higher protein intake.

Protein view 2: high-quality protein intake

Similarly to saturated fat, there are studies finding seeming conflicts and definite complexities in protein intake. For example, a study on over half a million people showed [86] :

> [86] See Meat Intake and Mortality, A Prospective Study of Over Half a Million People (jamanetwork.com) ↩

- Red meat increased all-cause mortality, cardiovascular disease and cancer
- Processed meat increased all-cause mortality, cardiovascular disease and cancer
- White meat **decreased** all-cause mortality, cardiovascular disease and cancer (the effect was more pronounced in men)

Similarly, fish (a high protein food) consumption has been shown reliably to decrease cardiovascular disease and all-cause mortality. A study on a diabetic nurse population found a dose-dependent relationship [87] between fish and a reduction in risk for cardiovascular disease and all-cause mortality. The highest benefit was shown in those who consumed fish more than 5 times per week [88].

[87] *Meaning eating more means having proportionally stronger effects* ↵
[88] *See Fish and Long-Chain ω-3 Fatty Acid Intake and Risk of Coronary Heart Disease and Total Mortality in Diabetic Women (circ.ahajournals.org)* ↵

A meta-analysis including 222,364 people found a similar 'more is better' relation for fish, at least for cardiovascular disease [89]. These studies are not perfect, but do point to a more complex system than 'less protein is better'. Similar results were found based on WHO and FAO data [90].

[89] *See Accumulated Evidence on Fish Consumption and Coronary Heart Disease Mortality (circ.ahajournals.org)* ↵
[90] *See Fish Consumption and Mortality from All Causes, Ischemic Heart Disease, and Stroke: An Ecological Study* ↵

In general, most studies find higher mortality for populations that consume high amounts of protein [91]. Most studies point out though that these results seem to be primarily to animal protein consumption. Based on the aforementioned studies one might even hypothesise that if these studies would have split white meat, red meat, fish and vegetable protein sources the results would have been far more nuanced.

[91] *See Low carbohydrate-high protein diet and mortality in a cohort of Swedish women (onlinelibrary.wiley.com), Low carbohydrate-high protein diet and incidence of cardiovascular diseases in Swedish women: prospective cohort study (bmj.com), Low-carbohydrate–high-protein diet and long-term survival in a general population cohort (nature.com)* ↵

A note on dairy: the correlations so far indicate higher all-cause mortality and cardiovascular risks for milk consumption but decreased risks for fermented dairy like yoghurt [92]. This suggests that you should stay away from unfermented milk but are likely to benefit from fermented products.

[92] *See Milk intake and risk of mortality and fractures in women and men (bmj.com)* ↵

Restrict your eating window

I have been intermittent fasting for years and greatly enjoy it. Doctor Longo, the researcher that created the fast-mimicking diet, adds the extra dimension of having your eating window during the day due to keeping in sync with the circadian rhythm. I currently have an 8-hour eating window starting at noon, doctor Longo recommends a 12-hour eating window that falls such that you don't eat 2-3 hours before bed.

Eat a variety of foods

Remember to make a conscious effort to eat a variety of foods. By eating a varying selection of foods you make structural deficiencies far less likely. You may consider looking at the food patterns of your ancestors (within the confines of the above recommendations) to lightly optimise for your particular genes [93].

> [93] *Fun fact, evolution is slow but visible. Historically heavy dairy consumers like the Netherlands have a low incidence of lactose intolerance. Genetic pools like native Americans are quite reliably lactose intolerant or allergic.* ↵

Getting started

How you approach any sort of dietary intervention depends on your self-knowledge. Ask yourself whether you are a cold-turkey kind of person or whether gradual change suits you more. Take into account that this is an endeavour in structural change.

> A single behaviour permanently changed will have more impact than an intense temporary change

Personally, I have a propensity for radical change. If you are like me in that regard, I recommend you do the following:

- Document your rules, meaning what you will and will not consume and when
- Make a set of default meals and a shopping list
- Remove all non-desired foods from your vicinity

Writing down your rules as well as having them visually around (stick it on the fridge) will help you internalise them. Make very specific decision rules. When I started my rules were:

- I will read the label of everything I eat and refuse anything with sugar, glucose, sucrose, fructose, dextrose and maltodextrin on the label
- I will eat no (products of) grains, potato, rice or equivalents (e.g., quinoa, bulgur, etc.)

To increase the chance you adhere to your rules, make a list of easy to make meals that you will enjoy. Include snacks. I personally found that chomping on cucumber, tomatoes and chicory (Belgian endive, common in the Netherlands) make me a happy person. Likewise, there are a number of default salads and soups I turn to when in doubt about what to eat.

If you are not an "all or nothing" minded individual, first off congratulations on being more even-tempered than I. You will most likely benefit from a more gradual approach. What works great for many people is an elimination-based approach:

1. Eliminate one thing
2. Get used to it
3. Repeat

By cutting out single things you don't have to deal with intensely upending your usual habits. It is, in fact, likely that this paced approach will lead to structural changes that will benefit your health. I recommend doing the following things in the order presented:

1. Stop drinking sugars
2. Stop eating added sugars
3. Stop eating high GI/GL carbohydrates like white bread/rice/potato/pasta
4. Increase your intake of olive oil and fish
5. Start time-restricted eating

Those five things will radically change your health habits. If you want to optimise further from that point, look at the principles in this book and institute the things that suit your life and goals.

How university turned me into a lab rat

My bachelor's degree turned out to be a double blessing. Not only did I get to explore human biology through the curriculum, but many classes required me to write research papers on a topic of my choice.

It took some convincing in some cases, but in many cases I could use these papers to dive deeper into subjects that interested me. One pivotal moment was a metabolism paper I wrote called "Resveratrol bioavailability and Action". It was by no means a masterpiece but triggered the interesting notion that the human body has built-in mechanisms that increase lifespan.

You see, resveratrol was at the time considered a promising life extension compound. It's a powerful antioxidant that influences gene expression. It seemed to:

- Protect against cancer
- Activate the SIRT1 gene group whose equivalent extends life in other organisms
- Buffer the effects of high cholesterol

It turns out that resveratrol supplementation in humans is not all that effective since our liver metabolises it very quickly.

Nonetheless, my interest was piqued. The SIRT1 gene group spoke to my imagination. Specifically, the idea that the human body is capable of extending its lifespan if we take the right steps in our lifestyle.

This led me to an interest in epigenetics, the study of how the environment influences gene expression. One important thing to understand here is that genes are not a blueprint for the human body in the way that pop-culture sometimes presents it.

Human genes are an if-this-then-that system. If a certain stimulus is given human cells are programmed to respond in a certain way. For example, (simplified):

- Sunlight > activate melanin genes > darker skin
- Vitamin D > influences hundreds of genes > changes in bone, mood, immune system, etc.

I felt like I had discovered something magical. After hearing my entire life that genes are a static blueprint that make my body what it is, I now knew that my genes are just a large repository of potential outcomes.

While resveratrol seemed to be a bust, my interest in longevity was piqued. Specifically, many studies seemed to talk about insulin when talking about longevity. Even resveratrol had a close link to insulin and related measures. A later paper I wrote called "The role of insulin in fasting metabolism and gene expression" was my first touchpoint with what I would later learn to call intermittent fasting and the ketogenic diet.

Whilst researching this paper I found some things I at the time called counterintuitive, for example:

- Fasting increases growth hormone levels
- The body is perfectly capable of producing glucose without eating carbohydrates (or anything for that matter)
- Fasting periodically has similar benefits to limiting food consumption
- Fasting is good for the brain

In that particular paper, I learned the basics of FoxO and mTor functions and how they relate to fasting and longevity.

As much as I enjoyed the rabbit hole of academic research, I'm a practically inclined person. After handing in this paper I started a regime of 16 hours of fasting a day. I expected to find it very hard to do, but actually thrived on this approach. Since I had formulated some strict rules for myself as to what I do and do not eat, keeping myself fed throughout the day was a bit of a challenge. Not having to worry about food for the majority of the day was incredibly freeing! Not only that, but my mental and physical energy levels increased during the times I didn't eat.

Throughout my university years, I spent more and more time researching longevity and unconventional lifestyles to optimise the body. After the first two years of study I had converted myself to:

- Intermittent fasting
- Sauna sessions 5+ times a week
- Low carb leaning to a ketogenic diet

I also continued to experiment with:

- Cognitive enhancement supplements & practices
- Alternative sleep cycles

Through the years of experimentation, I learned to separate fact from fiction. Since then words like intermittent fasting and ketogenic diet have become more popular and mainstream. It's the first time I've been a hipster, I did it before it was cool. While my post-university years were when I refined a lot of my protocols and theories, the basis for all of it has been my years in the academic world.

My experiments do not turn into dogma. As new information becomes available I adapt. My goal is to make the best decisions based on the information I have at the time. My most recent change was to incorporate a larger portion of complex carbohydrates into my diet based on the longevity studies of dr Longo.

I continue to read, experiment and refine my lifestyle. Some people say it sounds exhausting, I say it sounds exciting.

Take blood tests and use supplements

Principles for blood testing & supplementation

1. Do not supplement blindly
2. Test for common deficiencies
3. Test for predictive markers
4. Consider health supporting supplements

In this chapter

- Recommended blood tests to get
- How supplements can be very harmful when used incorrectly
- The importance of recent research data
- Common and unusual supplements you can consider taking

Do not supplement blindly

Many people seem intent on using supplements blindly. It is in most developed countries however trivial to get a blood panel that tests for useful values.

Supplements should be exactly what the name implies, supplemental consumptions. They are not designed to replace a varied diet that supplies the nutrients your body needs. They can, however, offer ways to:

- Correct deficiencies
- Offer benefits that regular foods do not

Don't blindly take supplements:

1. Get your blood tested
2. Make a game plan (supplements/food)
3. Test again a few weeks/months later

Note however that blood tests are not like opening the door to a room to see what is inside. You can't just "test your blood" and expect a list of results to come back. You can only test for specific things.

When deciding whether you need to take a supplement, you can't just go by statistics, as they can be deceiving. If for example, 50% of a population is deficient in vitamin B12, that might persuade you to take a B12 supplement. If the underlying data, however, shows that the 50% that has this issue is over 65 years old, you may or may not change your standpoint.

For each of the things you test for there is probably a different test that needs to be run on your blood. It is therefore vital to know what you want to test for. Also, keep in mind that the unit of measurement sometimes differs per laboratory or country. If you are used to your levels of a marker being something like 2.5 and suddenly they are 200, ask your doctor what unit the test results are in. Probably they switched labs and went from one standard (e.g., mmol/L) to another (e.g., g/L). You can find conversion tools online or can ask your doctor to help you standardise the results.

The harm of supplements

Vitamin supplements are not without risk. Many people approach it with a "worst case it doesn't do anything" attitude. The thing is that excess vitamins too can upset the balance of your body.

The B vitamin group, for example, is well known to stimulate certain types of growth. This is why people take it to make nails and hair grow faster/stronger. However, these supplements could hypothetically stimulate the growth of undesirable cells like tumours as well. Some studies suggest excessive B6 and B12 supplementation could increase lung cancer risk for example [94]. This doesn't mean B vitamins are bad, but it indicates that taking them blindly can be problematic.

[94] *See Long-Term, Supplemental, One-Carbon Metabolism– Related Vitamin B Use in Relation to Lung Cancer Risk in the Vitamins and Lifestyle (VITAL) Cohort (ascopubs.org)* ↵

Likewise, for many male consumers taking extra iron is a terrible idea and has shown to increase risk for some diseases, whereas this is less so the case for women (who lose iron through menstruation).

> No supplement is inherently good or bad

Blindly taking highly concentrated supplements is a terrible idea though. Test yourself first.

Test for common deficiencies

On a statistical basis, there are a number of blood values that are out of whack for large portions of the population. Many of these could be compensated through diet and/or supplements. You should get yourself tested for the levels of these markers in your system.

I recommend asking your doctor for the original lab notes of your tests and keeping a spreadsheet of your tested values. Often a doctor will only tell you 'everything looks fine' without sharing the actual values. This is perfectly normal since most people have no desire to know about the specifics.

The following section discusses some commonly recommended tests.

Vitamin D

The effects of low vitamin D can be manifold (it affects DNA expression):

- Lower mood levels
- Suboptimal immune function
- Suboptimal cognitive function
- Weaker bone and teeth

Humans have two main sources of vitamin D:

- Food
- The sun

Some common reasons for low vitamin D levels include:

- Sitting inside all day
- Having darker skin in countries with less sun
- Wearing clothing that covers a lot of skin

When buying vitamin D supplements after having your blood tested, ask your doctor what is a good dose for you. It is important to know your target level. Consult with your doctor but do point out that:

- There is research indicating that the optimal level for a reduction of all-cause mortality is 100-150 nmol/L (equivalent 40-60 ng/ml) [95].
- From research, it appears to be the case that a vitamin D supplement [96]
    - Of 1000-2000 IU (the equivalent of 25-50 mcg) raises levels in the blood by 5-10 ng/L (equivalent 12.5-25 nmol/L) depending on the study
    - It seems to take about 6 weeks for the supplement to be reflected in blood levels
    - There are indications taking 2000IU/day or 50000IU/week have the same effect
    - Vitamin D3 (cholecalciferol) is the best form of vitamin D to take for humans as a supplement

        [95] *See Meta-analysis of all-cause mortality according to serum 25-hydroxyvitamin D (ncbi.nlm.nih.gov)* ↵
        [96] *See Vitamin D: Deficiency, Sufficiency and Toxicity, section 5 (ncbi.nlm.nih.gov)* ↵

Magnesium

This mineral is used in a large number of bodily functions ranging from the immune system to the brain. It's used by 300+ enzymes and without it, our primary ATP based cellular energy system would not function. There are no international population-wide statistics on magnesium levels in the blood, but depending on what study you look at as many as 60% to 80% of people are deficient in magnesium.

The problem is twofold:

> Many people don't consume enough magnesium and magnesium supplements are often low in quality

The issue with magnesium supplements is that different types are absorbed better or worse. Not only that, but it appears that different types are preferred by certain organs.

The important magnesium types to know [97] :

[97] *For more in-depth data see Bioavailability and pharmacokinetics of magnesium after administration of magnesium salts to humans (ncbi.nlm.nih.gov) and this European food safety authority (EFSA) Journal (2005) nr 167 pages 1-6 (docplayer.net)*
↵

Type	Bioavailability	Notes
Magnesium Oxide	Extremely low	Basically magnesium rust, can cause diarrhoea.
Magnesium Citrate	Good	Cost effective, mild laxative in higher dosages.
Magnesium Gluconate & Glycinate	Good	Harder to find, more expensive. Unpleasant taste in powder form.
Magnesium Lactate	Excellent	Harder to find, dissolves well into liquids. I like it in tea.

You can check for the type of magnesium in your supplement by checking the ingredient list.

Iron

Iron deficiency is often associated with low energy levels, but an elevated iron level can potentially cause a host of problems from cardiovascular disease to cancer [98].

[98] *See Moderate elevation of body iron level and increased risk of cancer occurrence and death (worldscientific.com)* ↵

There is a big difference in iron needs between the sexes as well since women periodically lose iron through menstruation and men don't. Iron should be tested for but never taken as a supplement unless a deficiency is found. Especially men should avoid multivitamins with iron in them.

When testing for iron you will likely be confronted with the following terms, which I'll explain in simplified terms:

- **Transferrin** is a protein used for iron transport in the blood. It transports iron from the intestines (food) to the cells. Serum iron is a measure for the amount of circulating iron that is bound to transferrin.
- **Total iron-binding capacity (TIBC)** is the amount of iron your body is capable of binding using transferrin.
- **Iron/transferrin saturation** is a measure of the amount of transferrin that is currently being used to hold iron.
- **Ferritin** is an iron storage (and to a lesser degree transport) protein that buffers against having harmful high or low levels or free iron. It is used as an indirect measure of the amount of iron in the body.
- **Hemoglobin (Hb)** is sometimes reported under iron tests and sometimes under haematology

Proteins like transferrin and ferritin have more functions than described here (e.g., immune function) but for the sake of your iron test, those are not essential to understand.

Test for predictive markers

Our understanding of predicting disease risks changes very rapidly. Based on that you should keep in mind that:

- The information in this book might be incomplete by the time you read it
- Your doctor may not be up-to-date on the latest research

In practice, that means that you should open a dialogue with your doctor about what tests could be useful for someone with your personal health profile and family history. If you doubt that your doctor knows about the latest research, ask them about their efforts to stay up-to-date. If they are not willing to work with you on a preventive approach, consider switching doctors.

Personally, I have experienced that doctors in bigger cities tend to be more up to date and flexible. This will be very dependent on the healthcare system in your country.

Homocysteine

Homocysteine is an amino acid that is not obtained through diet, it is an element in the cycle that handles methionine and cysteine which are both amino acids as well. Converting homocysteine to methionine and cysteine depends heavily on vitamins B 2,6,12 and folate [99].

[99] *See the Folate Wikipedia page (en.wikipedia.org) and homocysteine Wikipedia page (en.wikipedia.org)* ↵

The data on homocysteine and its effect on health seems contradictive:

- **Cardiovascular risk** is higher for people with higher homocysteine levels [100].
- **Cancer risk** is higher for people with elevated homocysteine levels [101].
- Lowering homocysteine directly by supplementing with folate **does not** seem to have a beneficial effect on cardiovascular or cancer risk [102]
- A randomised trial reports positive effects for a combination of folate, B6 and B12 for those who have undergone certain cardiovascular surgeries [103]
- Higher than RDA amounts of folate and B6 combined seem to reduce cardiovascular risk in women [104]

[100] *See Homocysteine and Familial Longevity: The Leiden Longevity Study (journals.plos.org) and Plasma Homocysteine Levels and Mortality in Patients with Coronary Artery Disease (nejm.org)* ↵
[101] *See Hyperhomocysteinemia is a risk factor for cancer and a new potential tumor marker (sciencedirect.com)* ↵
[102] *See Effects of Lowering Homocysteine Levels With B Vitamins on Cardiovascular Disease, Cancer, and Cause-Specific Mortality*

(jamanetwork.com) ↵

[103] *See Effect of Homocysteine-Lowering Therapy With Folic Acid, Vitamin B12, and Vitamin B6 on Clinical Outcome After Percutaneous Coronary Intervention (jamanetwork.com)* ↵

[104] *See Folate and Vitamin B6 From Diet and Supplements in Relation to Risk of Coronary Heart Disease Among Women (jamanetwork.com)* ↵

So, elevated homocysteine predicts issues. Lowering homocysteine seems to not do much. Based on that data there are a number of possible conclusions:

- Elevated homocysteine is the symptom of an (unknown) underlying problem
- The research done up to this point is not using the right typed/doses of vitamins

Either way, until better research is done getting your homocysteine tested is interesting as a health indicator even if we're not sure how to fix it if it's high.

The MTHFR gene

There is a particular gene that is important for the processing of homocysteine through the folate cycle. This gene is called "Methylenetetrahydrofolate reductase" or MTHFR for short. There are a number of versions of this gene in humans. If you have a variant called 677TT you will have severely reduced activity in the MTHFR enzyme which results in elevated homocysteine levels. Mutations in this gene potentially increase the risk of schizophrenia [105], dementia [106] and myocardial infarction [107].

[105] *See Meta-Analysis of All Published SZ Association Studies (Case-Control Only) rs1801133 (webcitation.org)* ↵

[106] *See Apolipoprotein E, Methylenetetrahydrofolate Reductase (MTHFR) Mutation and the Risk of Senile Dementia -An Epidemiological Study Using the Polymerase Chain Reaction (PCR) Method (jstage.jst.go.jp)* ↵

[107] *See C667T and A1298C polymorphisms of methylenetetrahydrofolate reductase gene and susceptibility to myocardial infarction: A systematic review and meta-analysis (ncbi.nlm.nih.gov)* ↵

If you have done a genetics test like 23andme you can check your MTHFR status by using a service like Promethease. This is a more advanced thing to do, so if you don't understand how it works either ask your doctor or don't focus on this aspect.

Hba1c (glycated hemoglobin)

Red blood cells interact with glucose in the blood, hence glycated (glucose modified) haemoglobin (red blood cell component). Hba1c is a form of glycated haemoglobin used on blood tests. Because red blood cells have a lifespan of on average 120 days we can use Hba1c to estimate the average blood glucose levels of the blood over the past 3 months.

By proxy, we can use this measure to estimate how well the body controls blood sugar levels. This test is usually done on diabetics to get a more long-term overview of blood sugar control compared to a fasting blood sugar test which could be influenced by many short-term variables.

While this test is commonly used for diabetics, studies suggest that it is also a health predictor in healthy non-diabetic populations. Elevated levels of Hba1c seem to correlate with increased mortality from all-causes and specifically cardiovascular and cancer risk [108].

> [108] *See Hyperglycaemia is associated with all-cause and cardiovascular mortality in the Hoorn population: the Hoorn Study (link.springer.com) and Relationship between HbA1c and mortality in a Japanese population (link.springer.com)* ↵

A study that followed 14099 individuals for 20 years found that even when the results were compensated for a large number of other variables (age, race-ethnicity, sex, lifestyle, cardiovascular factors, metabolic factors, red blood cell indices, iron storage indices, and liver function indices) they still indicated that elevated Hba1c levels correlated with higher mortality. A smaller study found similar results [109]. Additionally, a larger (24752 participants) study found that lowering Hba1c using a diabetics drug lowered cardiovascular and all-cause mortality risk [110].

> [109] *See The Impact of Diabetes Mellitus and Corresponding HbA1c Levels on the Future Risks of Cardiovascular Disease and Mortality: A Representative Cohort Study in Taiwan (journals.plos.org)* ↵
> [110] *See Early Glycemic Control and Magnitude of HbA1c Reduction Predict Cardiovascular Events and Mortality: Population-Based Cohort Study of 24,752 Metformin Initiators (care.diabetesjournals.org)* ↵

As always I must stress that these are observational studies, meaning we don't fully understand *why* Hba1c is correlated with higher mortality rates. What we do know is that it can be used to measure how well your body regulates blood sugar levels and that high blood sugar levels are predictive of a host of health issues.

If your Hba1c is elevated, consult your doctor and take a long hard look at your eating and exercise habits. Particularly the glycemic load you are putting on your body.

Lipid panel (cholesterol etc.)

A lipid panel tests cholesterol and triglyceride levels. The understanding of science has changed quite a bit in the past years. Particularly with regards to cholesterol.

The first important thing to understand is that the body relies greatly on fats and cholesterol for optimal function. The human brain is almost 60% fats (excluding water) [111] and contains a lot of cholesterol as well. Cholesterol makes up about 30% of our cell membranes to keep them fluid (read: flexible) [112].

> [111] *See Essential fatty acids and human brain. (ncbi.nlm.nih.gov)* ↵
>
> [112] *See the cholesterol Wikipedia entry (en.wikipedia.org)* ↵

The second important thing is that when a doctor talks about your cholesterol they are not talking about the cholesterol as you find it in food. In the blood, cholesterol exists mostly incorporated into larger complexes like LDL and HDL.

Your test will probably come back with the following categories [113]:

> [113] *Note that this breakdown is dramatically simplified.* ↵

- **Total cholesterol:** this value reflects your absolute cholesterol levels and does not make a distinction between types. Lower is not better! Indiscriminately demonising cholesterol is a grave mistake on our society's part, low serum cholesterol is, for example, associated with marked increase in mortality in advanced heart failure [114].

- **LDL:** or Low-Density Lipoprotein is a combination of fats, protein and cholesterol. It is a vehicle in the blood used to transport fats and cholesterol to cells that need them. The 'low' in LDL refers to it being less dense and more 'fluffy' if you will. There are many classes of LDL like ultra/very/intermediate/low-density lipoprotein (respectively ULDL, vLDL, IDL, LDL). While research on these types is being done, most countries still bunch them together on the same pile (LDL) when it comes to the medical system.

- **HDL:** or High-Density Lipoprotein is similar to LDL but are denser (less 'fluffy'). Where LDL transports fats and cholesterol *to* cells HDL transports it *away* from cells. Together they form the supply and drainage of lipids and cholesterol. HDL is often called 'good' cholesterol since people with excess LDL need HDL to balance it out, this is obviously inaccurate since balancing two things doesn't mean one is good or bad.

- **Triglycerides:** are what in colloquial speech we call fats. Olive oil is mostly triglycerides and your body stores fat as triglycerides. On a biochemical level, they are a head of glycerol with three tails of fatty acids.

- **Total:HDL ratio:** this is a measure of how much HDL there is in the blood relative to other cholesterol types. It is far more predictive of mortality risk than absolute cholesterol or LDL numbers. So far it appears to be the best simple lipid-based marker we have [115].

- **Particle counts:** there are indications that the most reliable tests that predict cardiovascular issues are the particle counts of specific LDL counts. Likely you would have to go out of your way to have a test like this done (this is at least the case in the Netherlands at the time of writing). I can highly recommend listening to this podcast (peterattiamd.com), a deep dive into heart disease. It covers some of the more recent efforts to understand cholesterol better.

> [114] *See Low serum total cholesterol is associated with marked increase in mortality in advanced heart failure (ncbi.nlm.nih.gov)* ↵
> [115] *See Importance of LDL/HDL cholesterol ratio as a predictor for coronary heart disease events in patients with heterozygous familial hypercholesterolaemia: a 15-year follow-up (tandfonline.com) and Association of Cholesterol, LDL, HDL, Cholesterol/ HDL and Triglyceride with All-Cause Mortality in Life Insurance Applicants (medscape.com)* ↵

What should you do if any of these markers are out of whack? First, listen to your doctor. But equally important is to follow recent science. These are some good rules of thumb to follow:

- Eating saturated fats is not per se a risk factor for cardiovascular disease
- Eating cholesterol is not per se a risk factor for cardiovascular disease
- Eating high glycemic index/load foods (especially sugars) is

If you want to know why many countries still believe a low fat and low cholesterol diet prevents cardiovascular disease please read my summary on the history of cholesterol research (skillcollector.com) or watch this excellent 80-minute presentation (peterattiamd.com) on it by doctor Peter Attia. If you like diving into the details, look at this in-depth blog series (peterattiamd.com) he wrote.

Testosterone

Humans are sensitive to testosterone levels for a number of physical and mental issues. Low testosterone in both men and women can manifest as fatigue, depression, trouble concentrating and sexual dysfunction.

In a study of older men (50+) testosterone levels were correlated with increased risk of death, even when other factors like age, body fat and lifestyle were taken into account [116]. A preliminary study confirms that testosterone therapy in older men reduces the mortality effects of low testosterone [117]. A German study on females aged 18-75 also found that low testosterone was associated with increased all-cause mortality [118].

[116] *See Low Serum Testosterone and Mortality in Older Men (academic.oup.com)* ↵
[117] *See Testosterone Treatment and Mortality in Men with Low Testosterone Levels (academic.oup.com)* ↵
[118] *See Low testosterone levels predict all-cause mortality and cardiovascular events in women: a prospective cohort study in German primary care patients (eje-online.org)* ↵

Low testosterone has been found to be associated with the well-being, mood and sexual function of both men [119] as well as women [120], though in women abnormally high levels have been shown to be associated with depression as well.

[119] *See Testosterone replacement therapy for hypogonadal men with SSRI-refractory depression (jad-journal.com), Bioavailable Testosterone and Depressed Mood in Older Men: The Rancho Bernardo Study (academic.oup.com) and Testosterone and Depression in Aging Men (ajgponline.org)* ↵
[120] *See Transdermal testosterone therapy improves well-being, mood, and sexual function in premenopausal women*

(journals.lww.com) and The impact of testosterone imbalance on depression and women's health (ncbi.nlm.nih.gov) ↵

Complete blood count

The complete blood count (CBC) checks the levels of a number of blood cells, proteins and other values. It is a generalised test often used as a general health check. By looking at the different types of cells (e.g., red, white, platelets) and markers (e.g. haemoglobin) in the blood, your doctor can estimate the overall functions of a large number of systems. Rather than being a specific diagnosis, if something in this panel is out of its normal range your doctor will probably suggest more targeted tests to find out what is wrong.

Consider health supporting supplements

There are a number of supplements that have the potential to support a good quality of life or to potentially extend lifespan. Many of these are quite experimental and have only been proven to work in theory or on animal test subjects. I list them here as interesting options to explore if you have taken care of the basics, I do not explicitly recommend taking them.

Lithium Orotate (mental health/mood)

Lithium is associated in high dosages with the treatment of psychiatric disorders. It is however in low dosages an essential mineral for optimal health. It occurs naturally in low dosages (up to 0.170 mg/L in tap water). The argument has been made in a New York Times article should we all take a bit of lithium? (nytimes.com) that we could all benefit from a daily low dosage of lithium. Suicide rates appear to be lower in areas where there is more lithium naturally in the drinking water, for example. From an older study (1994) using a dose of 400 µg/d:

> "... mental and physical activity, ability to think and work, mood, and emotionality. In the lithium group, the total mood test scores increased steadily and significantly during the period of supplementation" [121].

> [121] *See Effects of nutritional lithium supplementation on mood (link.springer.com)* ↵

From a more recent study (2001):

> ... low lithium intakes from water supplies were associated with increased rates of suicides, homicides and the arrest rates ... a provisional RDA for a 70 kg adult of 1000 µg/day is suggested [122]
>
> > [122] *See Lithium: Occurrence, Dietary Intakes, Nutritional Essentiality (tandfonline.com)* ↵

Epidemiological studies also find a tentative correlation between low dose lithium intakes and longevity in humans and other animal species [123]. Research continues on the role of lithium in preventing suicide, mania, ageing, dementia and cancer [124].

> [123] *See Low-dose lithium uptake promotes longevity in humans and metazoans (link.springer.com)* ↵
> [124] *See Is lithium potentially a trace element? (ncbi.nlm.nih.gov)* ↵

While large therapeutic dosages are classified as medicine (and rightfully so) the smaller dosed supplements are available for purchase from many supplement vendors. The dosages are greatly smaller than those in the medical form. Do not exceed low dosages in an attempt to self-medicate; enough tabs of a low dose supplement will land you in the medical zone. See this case study (link.springer.com) of an 18-year-old who thought more was better.

Collagen (skin/joints)

The human skin is kept in shape by a scaffold made of a protein structure called collagen. This part of the 'extracellular matrix' gives skin elasticity and keeps it from wrinkling. Likewise, it is an important structural component in cartilage that keeps our joints running smoothly.

Damage to the collagen structure in the skin is done by UV radiation, which causes wrinkles. This is why dermatologists hammer on using sunscreen all day every day. While preventing damage by means of sunscreen is good advice, it doesn't help your body to repair the damage that is bound to occur because of daily sun exposure. Note that sun exposure is positive for many health factors, one of the downsides to sun exposure is skin ageing.

Intuitively it makes sense that if a certain structure in the body breaks down (collagen) you can stimulate growth by consuming more building blocks (in the form of said collagen). Some argue that the body is perfectly capable of producing collagen if sufficient protein is consumed, but recent data seems to contradict this view. While the body is very capable of constructing collagen from other protein sources, consuming collagen seems to have positive effects on skin elasticity and joint health.

A study in rats has shown that radioactively labelled collagen derivatives can be traced to places in the body where collagen has a functional presence, like skin and cartilage [125]. Further placebo-controlled clinical trials showed that supplementation with collagen peptides improved skin hydration and increased collagen density in the skin [126].

> [125] *See Distribution of Prolylhydroxyproline and Its Metabolites after Oral Administration in Rats (jstage.jst.go.jp)* ↵
> [126] *See The effect of oral collagen peptide supplementation on skin moisture and the dermal collagen network: evidence from an ex vivo model and randomized, placebo-controlled clinical trials (onlinelibrary.wiley.com)* ↵

A double-blind placebo-controlled study also found that collagen supplementation (specifically undenatured type II collagen) decreased pain and stiffness in people suffering from knee osteoarthritis. It was found to be more effective than the often used regimen of glucosamine and chondroitin at very low dosages of 20-40 mg/day [127]. A randomised double-blind placebo-controlled study looking at athletes with joint pain found significant improvements in joint pain when walking, standing, at rest, carrying weight and lifting weight with 10 grams of hydrolysed collagen per day [128].

> [127] *See Efficacy and tolerability of an undenatured type II collagen supplement in modulating knee osteoarthritis symptoms: a multicenter randomized, double-blind, placebo-controlled study (nutritionj.biomedcentral.com) and Safety and efficacy of undenatured type II collagen in the treatment of osteoarthritis of the knee: a clinical trial (ncbi.nlm.nih.gov)* ↵
> [128] *See 24-Week study on the use of collagen hydrolysate as a dietary supplement in athletes with activity-related joint pain (tandfonline.com)* ↵

Note that those looking to supplement collagen don't have to put up with dissolving regular collagen (gelatine) into hot water and drink a foul-smelling mixture. There are great hydrolysed collagen supplements on the market that smell quite neutral and dissolve in cold water.

Fish oil (omega-3's)

Fish oil is known as a beneficial supplement in pop culture. The effects that are often touted include their beneficial effect on the cardiovascular system and cholesterol levels. More and more research, however, seems to indicate that omega-3 fatty acids also have many benefits for neurological attributes like cognitive function and mood levels.

For this supplement, it is important to realise that fatty acids are essential for the structure and functioning of cells. In essence, human cells are bags of water, filled with molecular machinery (DNA, mitochondria etc). The 'bag' that is the border of the cell basically uses lipids as an important building block. The right lipids keep the cell membrane flexible and functioning optimally. This is very important for many things, including nerve function.

On supplement bottles, you will often find references to EPA and DHA. These are two forms of omega-3 fatty acids that occur together in animal (e.g., fish) sources. Their structure differs and research indicates that their effect differs as well.

If you plan to take fish oil on a long-term basis make sure that you choose a reputable supplement that is adequately purified. The fish used to produce the oil may contain toxins like heavy metals (especially if the source fish is high up the food chain) that need to be filtered out.

With regards to toxins and oil quality, it pays off to look for products that:

- Are produced from animals low on the food chain (e.g., herring instead of salmon)
- Are filtered well (everybody claims this so it is harder to test)
- Has lab tests available on their website

Recommendations for supplements

Note: for all deficiencies ask your doctor if there is a reason you would have lower levels due to a reason other than low intake. B12 levels can also, for example, be low due to malabsorption.

Supplement Recommendation

Vitamin D	When far from 100-150 nmol/L (equivalent 40-60 ng/ml) [129] consider supplementing with at least 800IU/day [130] or supplementing 1000-2000 IU (equivalent of 25-50 mcg) for every 5-10 ng/L (equivalent 12.5-25 nmol/L) increase you want.
Vitamin B12	Supplement or increase dietary intake of animal products, specifically liver and meat [131]
Magnesium	Prefer citrate, chelate and glycinate over magnesium oxide [132]
Lithium	Do not confuse supplements with the drug. Go for low doses of 400-1000 microgram/day.
Collagen	For easy supplementation (cold water) choose hydrolysed collagen. For a cheaper option (hot water) consider gelatine.
Omega 3s	Consider using a dose that provides over 1000mg of DHA (see bottle) for additional cognitive benefits.

[129] *See Meta-analysis of all-cause mortality according to serum 25-hydroxyvitamin D (ncbi.nlm.nih.gov)* ↩

[130] *Equals 20 micrograms* ↩

[131] *It's also found in eggs, but humans only absorb about 9%. See Vitamin B12 sources and bioavailability (ncbi.nlm.nih.gov)* ↩

[132] *The magnesium type is on the bottle, just look at the ingredient section* ↩

You can find these supplements online at vendors like iHerb (iherb.com") (international) or your local Amazon if available.

Getting started

The most important thing is to simply get started and to plan in periodic measurements. Often this means going to your doctor, explaining what you want to test and getting blood drawn. In my experience it is of prime importance to 1) ask your doctor for a copy of the original lab notes and 2) not to let them dismiss you.

The fact of the matter is that doctors are in most cases not used to dealing with those of us who want to keep a detailed eye on your health markers. After every blood test session, I receive an email from my doctor's assistant saying "we found nothing out of the ordinary" to which I always reply "thank you for your email, would you be so kind as to send me a copy of the original lab notes?". I recommend making digital backups of your lab notes and if you like spreadsheets input the data into one.

The second hurdle when it comes to doctors not being used to people like us is that they will often dismiss us, at least initially. This is not bad will, but simply structured and somewhat rigid thinking. Expect to hear your doctor say "you don't need to test Hba1c, that is for diabetics" or "you are far too young to start testing cholesterol" and my personal favourite "you only need to start testing vitamin D once you exhibit symptoms, and you look fine". Stay calm, but don't take no for an answer. Be clear in that you are not doing this on a whim but based on the latest research, and offer to send them the research if they would like (send them a copy of this chapter, or some of the studies linked in it). If all else fails, switch to a different doctor since this one doesn't seem to value preventative healthcare principles.

Once you are comfortable asking your doctor for tests, most people have two important considerations when it comes to custom blood testing: availability and cost.

The first is usually a function of the healthcare system in your country. In the Netherlands, I am able to simply book an appointment with my doctor through their online booking system and get my blood drawn while I'm there. From friends, I know that the ease of access differs greatly per country and even within countries. I recommend booking a session with your doctor to explain that you are starting to gather preventative data about your health status. Ask them if this is something they are able to supply or if you need to contact private laboratories. In most developed countries your doctor should be able to help you. Make it clear that you have researched your options and in a very targeted fashion are looking to 1) spot and correct deficiencies and 2) monitor well established long-term health markers.

For the matter of cost, you will once again be dependent on the system in your country, and in addition how you are making use of it. In the Netherlands, every citizen is insured for health cost with a minimum 'pay it yourself' amount of about €300-400. In practice, this means that the first couple of hundred of test costs will fall on you personally, and after that, the insurance pays for everything. I recommend checking in detail what your insurance covers and does not cover. In some cases, it may pay off to go to a private lab (which you can find on Google) instead of your doctor since it can be cheaper. Then again, your insurance may cover the tests your doctor clears but not the ones you decide to get on your own.

In most cases, I recommend just going to your doctor and talking to them about options. If the cost in your country is prohibitively high (looking at you, US) consider doing some medical tourism. If you plan to go abroad to a cheaper country, you may consider finding a trustworthy lab that can do the tests at a fraction of the cost.

To summarise:

1. Get your doctor on board
2. Check cost and availability
3. Collect the lab notes (optionally record them in a spreadsheet)
4. Book periodic sessions

How I started taking responsibility for my health

In winter, I very reliably have a decline in overall mood. My mother used to refer to it as my 'winter dip'. I remember a year where things were particularly bad. It's not that I would be what is classically described as depressed, but every system in my body and mind would experience a loss of vividness. I was tired, lethargic and experienced the world as 'fuzzy'.

The year that had a particularly intense dip my mother sent me to our doctor. The man was a prototypical general practitioner. Male, middle-aged, not in shape, not out of shape, small round glasses and a calm but not intimidating authority. He also had no clue what to do. To him, I was just a moody teenager who was going through the natural cycle of hormonal changes and development.

Knowing what I know now, he could have helped me find my energetic self with a few reasonably simple actions. Starting with some diagnostic questions:

- How much and how well do you sleep?
- What do you eat?
- How physically active are you?
- When are you likely to feel good/bad?
- Do you have any other mental challenges?

The answers would have made health recommendations quite easy:

- I go to bed late and get up early, total sleep time 6-8 hours
- A lot. Mostly carbs. Candy and soda are a daily occurrence
- I am a competitive athlete and practice 5 to 7 days a week
- Every winter I have my winter dip
- I have intense panic attacks a few times a year and my parents fight often

Even based on those answers it is quite obvious what to recommend to a sleep-deprived teenager who is putting high strain on his body while in an episode of seasonal affective disorder.

The torturous months I lived through would have been easily improved with basic evidence-based recommendations:

- Sleep 8+ hours, teenagers have increased sleep needs compared to adults
- Reduce or eliminate low glycemic index carbohydrates from your diet
- Give your body time to recover from your sports performance, rotate intense/easy sports days
- Test for vitamin D levels and supplement to bring them up. Also, suggest increasing daylight exposure.
- Suggest stress resilience treatment (meditation, breathing exercises, psychologist, etc)

Instead of that happening, I suffered through this period and took a good year to get out of this particularly intense dip. On the plus side, this experience led me to do my own research. Since my doctor seemed not to grasp the intensity of my suffering, I turned to the internet.

If you think the internet is full of conflicting information now, imagine what it was like in the early 2000s. One of my primary information sources was the information section of a sports nutrition producer. This has the predictable effect that they talked me into buying and taking pretty much everything they had on offer. I spent all my pocket money on pills, powders and liquids.

Looking back at that time I was very fortunate since the company actually produced high-quality products. Many years later I met the owner and worked for them for a while. While their motivations were undoubtedly financial, this phase of experimentation taught me to think of the human body as a machine that operates based on set rules.

The cycle I went through with supplements at the time was 1) read about a supplement 2) get excited about the science 3) use the supplement and 4) decide whether or not it worked for me. The most valuable part of the whole process was learning that I found the biology of the human body and what food/supplementation do to it very exciting.

Keep in mind that at this time I was in high school and had nowhere near the sophistication to read scientific studies. The 'science' I did back then was mostly reading watered down science journalism and supplement labels. Only in the years after that did university teach me the more in-depth mechanisms of homeostasis and the art of reading the results of scientific studies.

An interesting turning point for me was when I heard the terms *evidence based medicine*, *preventive healthcare* and *personalised healthcare*. Imagine my confusion. I had always assumed my doctor's goal was to keep me healthy and to help me tackle the specific health challenges I faced. As it turns out, the global healthcare system is not geared towards that. Healthcare turned out to mean sick-care, the care of the sick. Additionally, many doctors operate not on the latest research, but on what they learned in school decades ago. When you get ill, most likely your doctor doesn't see you 'the patient' but rather a disease with too little regard for context of the person it is affecting.

The current system is certainly better than nothing, but advances in genetics and other recent developments are changing the game. We are learning that some drugs work well for some people, and that lifestyle is one of the most powerful facilitators of health. Most doctors are not ready for this. I remember the first time I brought my genetics report (done through 23andme (23andme.com")) to my doctor. They treated me like a child who made a drawing and wanted a sticker for their efforts.

Since then I have decided to take ownership of my health. I trust my doctors, but challenge them if I find reliable research that contradicts their views. I expect the world's healthcare systems to change a lot over the coming years, with the increased accessibility of genetic testing and a better understanding of preventive testing. Until my health is the job of a super-intelligent artificial intelligence, I will continue to spend time and energy on being responsible for my own health.

Use hormesis to stay healthy

Principles for using hormesis

1. Hormesis is the controlled triggering of the body's defences
2. Drink green and black tea in the right dose
3. Drink coffee in the right dose
4. Dose exercise for longevity
5. Extreme heat and cold exposure
6. Use different forms of fasting

In this chapter

- Ways to safely trigger metabolic self-defence reactions
- Different approaches to fasting for health
- Make sure you get the best time versus output for exercise
- Why I go without food for 5 days every 3 months
- The struggle of cooking bacon on an empty stomach

Hormesis is the activation of defences

The human body evolved in nature, which can be a very hostile environment. In order to survive as a species, we've had to develop ways to deal with things like:

- Temperature exposure
- Starvation
- Strenuous muscle use
- Toxic chemicals in plants
- Radiation exposure (UV from the sun)

In order to deal with this, the human body has a host of defence mechanisms. Because defence costs energy, these mechanisms are only activated when needed. For example, if we get bombarded with radiation (sun) we develop a shield of melanin pigment (tanning). We call this process of activating defences *hormesis*.

Hormesis has 2 interesting properties:

1. It overcompensates
2. Mechanisms are generalised

The overcompensation means that a little of a stressor can cause a disproportionately strong (and beneficial) defence. The generalised mechanisms mean that the body doesn't have highly specific defences but rather a handful of areas. For example, cold exposure and heat exposure both cause the body to make heat shock proteins.

Because of these two characteristics, we can activate the body's defences with harmless stimuli. These harmless stimuli are sometimes perceived as harmful, causing the body to strengthen itself. For example, saunas (heat exposure) have been shown to decrease a number of disease risks. Likewise, exercise (muscle stress) has many benefits. Drinking tea (a toxin) too can have benefits for health and longevity.

Hormetic responses in a controlled environment:

Trigger	Intensity/frequency
Sauna	More [133] & hotter [134] appears to be better [135]
Cold exposure	Colder is better, duration is less important [136]. The minimum temperature seems to be around the 14 Celsius mark [137]
Intermittent fasting	Common approaches are 16/8 [138] and 5/2 [139].
Multi-day fasting	While water fasts are most optimal, a 5 day fast mimicking diet approach has many of the same benefits

[133] *As measured by the number of days per week you enter the sauna* ↵
[134] *Commonly researched temperatures are 80 and 100 degrees celsius* ↵
[135] *See this excellent sauna breakdown (foundmyfitness.com) by Dr Rhonda Pattrick* ↵
[136] *20 seconds at 4.4 Celsius appeared equal to 2 minutes at -110 Celsius cryotherapy. See Effects of long-term whole-body cold exposures on plasma concentrations of ACTH, beta-endorphin, cortisol, catecholamines and cytokines in healthy females (tandfonline.com)* ↵
[137] *See Human physiological responses to immersion into water of different temperatures (link.springer.com)* ↵
[138] *16 hours of fasting per day, 8-hour eating window* ↵
[139] *5 days of regular eating followed by 2 days of fasting or low caloric intake* ↵

This chapter covers things you can expose your body to in a controlled fashion that can result in net positive effects.

Drink green and black tea in the right dose

Tea is often touted as a healthy drink. It turns out that tea has a likely hormetic response that is dose-dependent. In other words, in some quantities it boosts health and in others it doesn't. A meta-analysis study that analysed 18 green and black tea studies [140] found some interesting things:

[140] *See Tea consumption and mortality of all cancers, CVD and all causes: A meta-analysis of eighteen prospective cohort studies (researchgate.net)* ↵

1. Black tea had a reduced risk of **cancer** and **all-cause** mortality
2. Green tea had a reduced risk of **cardiovascular disease** and **all-cause** mortality

All-cause mortality basically refers to the odds of someone dying for any reason. If you remove some nuance:

- Green tea and black tea seem to increase lifespan
- Green tea seems to reduce cardiovascular disease risk
- Black tea seems to reduce cancer risk

Additionally, there is a dose-dependent response they found that indicates that:

1. Green tea has positive effects for 1-4 cups a day and the effect **decreases** but doesn't reverse if you drink more
2. Black tea has positive effects for 1-2 cups a day but the effect **reverses** if you drink more

The following graph shows the effect of tea dosage on all-cause mortality. Note that this graph is the result of the analysis of a larger number of studies [141], meaning the data is far from perfect. I suspect there will not be clinical studies of tea, so this is likely to be the best information we have for a while.

[141] *It is an adaptation of the results in the aforementioned Tea consumption and mortality of all cancers, CVD and all causes: A meta-analysis of eighteen prospective cohort studies (researchgate.net)* ↵

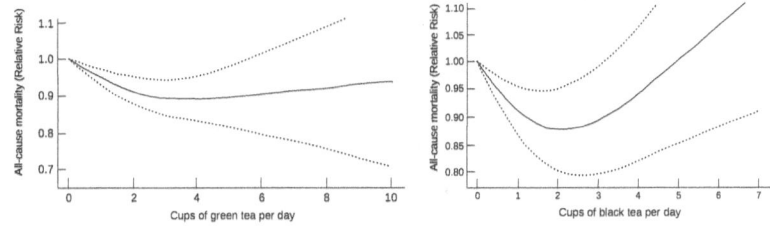

The effect of tea dosage on all-cause mortality

One can hypothesise that there are substances in tea that are mild toxins. In a low dose these trigger our defences, in higher doses they harm us. I personally translate the above into drinking green tea during the day, with a maximum of 2 cups of black tea.

Drink coffee in the right dose

Coffee has a reputation for being unhealthy, but the data is not that clear. From effects of Habitual Coffee Consumption on Cardiometabolic Disease, Cardiovascular Health, and All-Cause Mortality (onlinejacc.org):

> large epidemiological studies suggest that **regular coffee drinkers have reduced risks** of mortality, both CV and all-cause

> A daily intake of **~2 to 3 cups** of coffee appears to be safe and is associated with neutral to beneficial effects

and

> potential risks (which are mostly related to its high caffeine content) including **anxiety, insomnia, tremulousness, and palpitations**, as well as **bone loss** and possibly increased risk of fractures

Here is a chart of theirs showcasing how 3 cups of coffee seems to show benefits for heart failure risk:

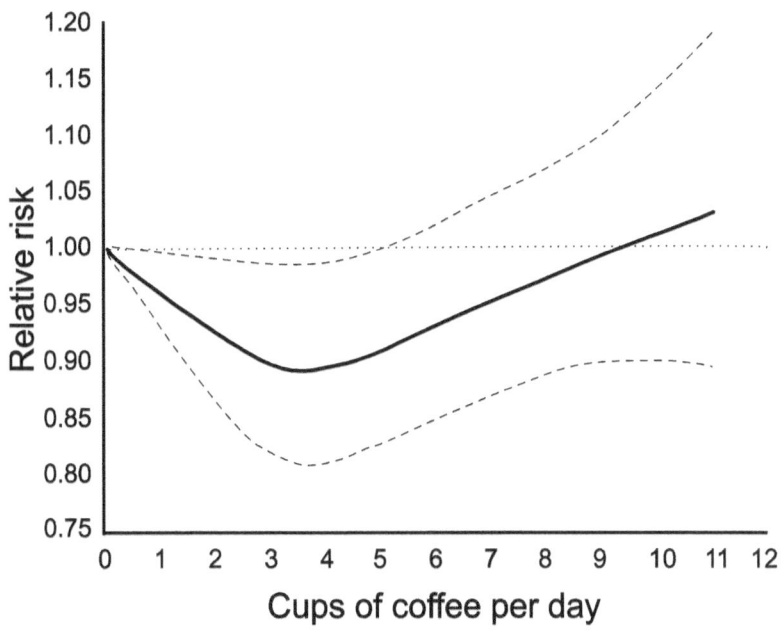

The effect of coffee on heart failure risk

Basically coffee is a tradeoff between cardiovascular and all-cause mortality benefits and mostly overstimulation side effects.

Dose exercise for longevity

Exercise is well-known to be healthy. There are however a number of cut-off points for the effectiveness of it, at least from the perspective of longevity. Look at these all-cause mortality improvements from an Australian study [142] :

[142] *See Effect of Moderate to Vigorous Physical Activity on All-Cause Mortality in Middle-aged and Older Australians (researchgate.net), the table in this book is based on table 2 in the paper.* ↵

MVPA	VPA	Improvement
0	0	0
10-150	0	40.4%
10-150	30+%	58.6%
150 - 299	0	47.5%
150 - 299	30+%	68%
300+	0	59%
300+	30+%	77.3%

MVPA: moderate to vigorous activity in minutes per week. VPA: vigorous physical activity as % of exercise. Improvement is relative to no exercise.

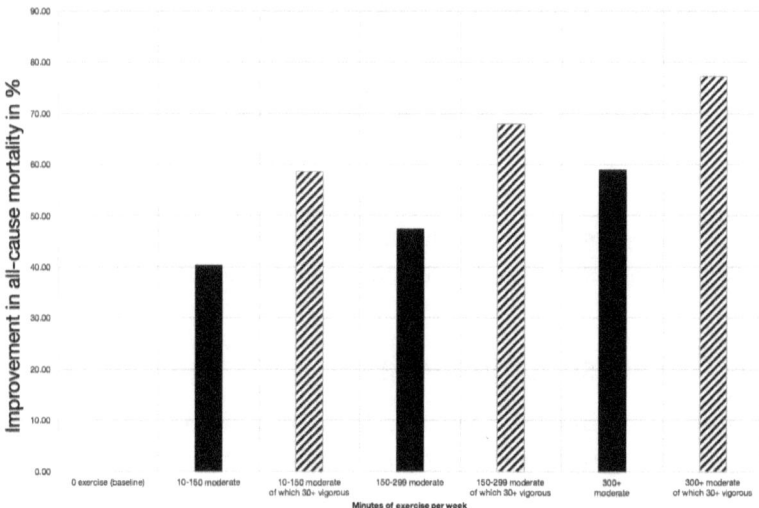

Effect of exercise (minutes) on all-cause mortality

In the above study 'vigorous' activity was defined as 6 or more metabolic equivalents (METs). One MET is equivalent to sitting still. Examples of activities that exceed 6 METs are jogging (7 METs), callisthenics (8 METs) and rope jumping (10 METs).

Another study that did a meta-analysis of 6 studies across the US and Europe [143] and found similar results:

[143] *See Leisure time physical activity and mortality: a detailed pooled analysis of the dose-response relationship. (ncbi.nlm.nih.gov)* ↵

Exercise	Benefit
0	0
under 60	20%
60-120	31%
180-300	39%

Exercise is defined as the number of minutes per week spent doing 7.5 MET exercise. The benefit is relative to doing no exercise.

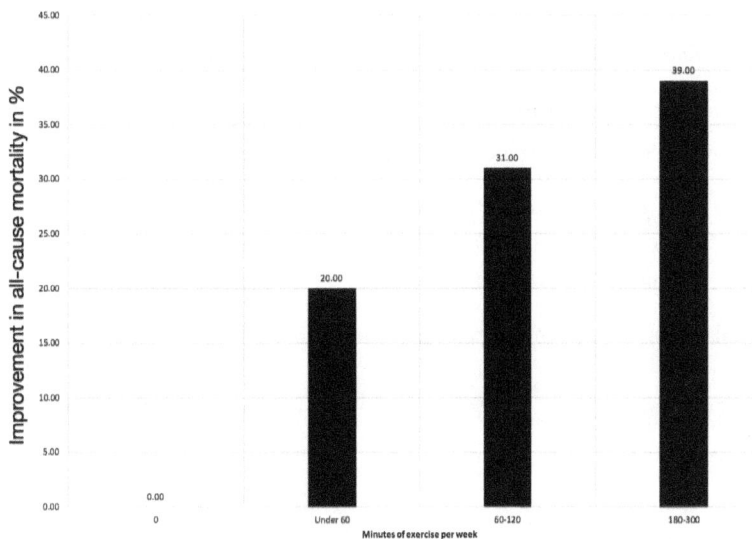

Effect of exercise on all-cause mortality

The above data suggests that:

- Any exercise is **greatly** better than no exercise
- Vigorous exercise has big proportional benefits (e.g., running versus walking)
- There is a decreasing amount of benefit the more exercise you do
- Around 150 minutes a week with 30% or more of that being vigorous exercise seems to be the optimal return on investment point

I'd like to stress that doing more than 150 minutes of exercise still showed benefits, but that the benefits are less dramatic than the effect of the first few hours.

Heat & cold exposure

The body gains a lot of benefit from controlled extreme heat exposure (sauna).

Saunas are in many countries relatively easy to implement as habits, through gyms that offer them. Benefits of saunas include both physical and mental effects. As for frequency, research so far seems to indicate that more is better. Going twice a week beats once, going 5 times beats 4 and so on [144].

> [144] *For a well-referenced overview of benefits of sauna use see dr Rhonda Pattrick's sauna report (foundmyfitness.com)* ↵

The opposite of controlled heat exposure, controlled extreme cold exposure (ice baths), also confers a number of benefits [145].

> [145] *For a well-referenced overview of cold exposure research check out dr Rhonda Pattrick's cold stress report (foundmyfitness.com)* ↵

Summarising the above two references in a table:

Effect on body	Stressor(s) causing effect
Athletic endurance	Heat & cold
Increased lifespan [146]	Heat & cold
Heat shock protein production	Heat & cold
Muscle growth	Heat [147]
Increased insulin sensitivity	Heat
Increased neurogenesis [148]	Heat
Improved cardiovascular function	Heat
Growth hormone release	Heat
Increases red blood cell count	Heat
Cold shock proteins	Cold
Reduced inflammation	Cold
White blood cell increase	Cold
Increased brown fat & thermogenesis	Cold

> [146] *In animal research and human models, it's all very experimental and not at all 100% proven* ↵

[147] *Cold when applied right after exercise actually reduces muscle growth gains* ↵

[148] *The creation of new neurons in the brain* ↵

Fasting & feasting

You can view the body as having two states, one of which can be dominant at a given time:

- Build new stuff
- Destroy/repair broken stuff

The building cycle is important since it is the time when we build new cells, proteins and so on. The destroy/repair state is important since broken cells and components can result in nasty things like cancer.

The caveat here is that these states can't optimally function at the same time. When the build state is dominant the repair state is less active and vice versa.

Interestingly, *eating stimulates building* and *fasting stimulates repair*. In other words, feeding your body will trigger it to use those nutrients. Not feeding your body will allow your body to repair itself on a cellular level.

- Feasting triggers growth
- Fasting triggers repair

One issue our society has is that we don't give the body enough time to enter the fasting restorative mode. We eat pretty much the whole time we're awake.

There are a number of fasting types to be aware of:

Fasting type	Effect
Juice fast/cleanse	This is *not* fasting. It will rest your intestines a bit but has little positive metabolic effect.
No calorie fast	Nothing with energy (caloric) content. Coffee/tea is fine, but only without sugar and milk. This is good for fasting but might reduce some of the benefits related to elevated oxidative stress.
Water fast	The most effective fast usually. Harder to use in regular life.
Full fast	No water, no food. While the purest fast the benefits compared to a water fast are not that much, plus is has far higher health risks.

Ketosis

When talking about fasting we must briefly discuss ketosis. The body usually relies on a glycolytic (sugar) pathway for energy. In other words, we usually run on carbohydrates. The body mostly supplies energy to the muscle and brain through blood sugar.

For many people, this is the reason they feel low when they have not eaten (low blood sugar) or when they have just eaten (blood sugar spike followed by an insulin spike). There is an alternative energy mechanism called ketosis. In this state, the body does not primarily break down carbohydrates but rather fats. Instead of using blood sugar for primary energy delivery, the body uses ketones.

Being in a state of ketosis has a host of health benefits. The list is very similar to fasting. Indeed a great deal of the benefits of fasting stem from the fact that fasting helps trigger ketosis. Entering a ketotic state is done by depriving the body of carbohydrates which can be done through a rigorous diet or through longer periods of fasting. A ketogenic diet is often over 80% fats as measured by the percentage of kcal consumed. Since longer fasts too result in ketosis they supply benefits similar to the ketogenic diet.

The benefits of fasting

The average human body can live for 3 days without water and 3 weeks without food [149]. Fasting can either be approached as an intermittent approach (eating only 8 hours a day) or as a multi-day endeavour. On a biological level not eating for a full day is really not that extreme. One might argue that in the human hunter/gather days it was quite common to eat a lot one day (caught an animal/found food) and nothing the next (caught no animal/found no food).

> [149] *This is an average based on the survival maxim of "3 minutes without oxygen, 3 days without water, 3 weeks without food".*
> *There are actually hilarious studies where obese people were fasted for 24 days just to see what the muscles in their forearms would do (jci.org). Gotta love 70s science.* ↵

Fasting and intermittent fasting have shown a number of interesting effects on both animals and humans. Note that this is very recent research so it's all still very experimental.

So far there are strong indications for:

- Reduced risk for certain cancers
- Reduced risk of mental disease
- Increased lifespan

There are a lot of cellular and metabolic effects that you can read about online [150]. While any extreme lifestyle change should be discussed with a medical professional, there are for most people no significant health risks involved in fasting.

[150] *See my blog post The science of fasting for longevity & health (skillcollector.com)* ↵

There is an additional caveat for women. If the fasting leads to a nutritional deficit they have a higher risk of side-effects, like hormonal and menstrual cycle dysregulation [151]. Potentially this is an evolutionary response where the body doesn't want to 'waste' a pregnancy in a nutrient-poor environment. If this troubles you 1) consider periodic over intermittent fasts and/or 2) if you experience side-effects, try a gentler protocol.

[151] *See Intermittent Fasting for Women: What We Know Now (marksdailyapple.com)* ↵

Time-restricted feeding

While not strictly speaking a fasting strategy, time-restricted eating is a time-dependent method of eating. The human body has an internal clock referred to as the circadian rhythm. There are two important factors that help your body calibrate its clock:

- The first moment you are exposed to bright light
- The first moment you use your liver

Bright light is a 'sunrise' mechanism. The liver is used to digest food but is also impacted by, for example, coffee. There are strong indications that eating within a window that falls in the waking 'daylight' time (e.g., 08:00 to 20:00) has health benefits. If you would like an overview of how and why this works watch Ruth Patterson, Ph.D. on Time-Restricted Eating in Humans & Breast Cancer Prevention (youtube.com) and this Dr. Satchin Panda on Time-Restricted Feeding and Its Effects on Obesity, Muscle Mass & Heart Health (youtube.com).

Intermittent fasting (daily)

It takes the body a while to enter recovery mode once you start fasting. When you eat something during a fasted state the countdown timer starts anew. In other words, if you have a juice after fasting for 5 hours, your fast is now broken and you have now fasted for 0 hours.

One approach to implementing fasting into your life is intermittent fasting. Popular approaches include:

- *The 16/8 approach* where you only eat for 8 consecutive hours a day and fast the rest of the day. For example, only eating between 16:00 and 24:00. At what times you set your window doesn't matter (caveats later on), what matters is that for 16 hours you do not eat or drink anything with caloric content. Most fasters do still consume coffee and tea without milk and sugar.
- *The 5/2 approach* in which you eat regularly for 5 days a week, but eat very little or nothing 2 days a week. While health benefits can be found with 2 days of very low on energy consumption, the body will only fully benefit if there is a period of actual fasting.
- *Alternate day fasting* is exactly what it sounds like. You eat for one day and do not eat the next.

Template: intermittent fasting

The most popular option (and most compatible with most people's lives) is the 16/8 approach. To get started, choose your eight-hour eating window. Keep in mind that the window needs to:

- Cover all your energy needs. E.g. 08:00 to 16:00 requires dinner before 16:00
- Be conducive to finding food. Evenings might work best if you work full time and cook at home.
- Compatible with your daily routine, think work(out), social activities etc.

Other important considerations:

- Most people I know report having the best mental focus when **fasting**.
- After adjusting many people report feeling sluggish when eating too early.
- Eat the right stuff, start with a protein-rich meal (for the sake of satiety). Focus on low GI foods, see the diet section.
- Have backup food on you, e.g. a box of nuts.

- Be strict but reasonable. Yearly family brunches are a fine reason not to fast.
- Biologically eating earlier in the day is advantageous due to the circadian rhythm

Fast mimicking diet (periodically)

This is fasting without truly fasting. Longer fasts result in more dramatic health benefits. They are however also harder to do and are not practical for certain target groups. There are, for example, indications that fasting reduces some side effects of chemotherapy[152]. Having a cancer patient fast is potentially not responsible or doable though.

> [152] *See fasting and cancer treatment in humans: A case series report (ncbi.nlm.nih.gov)* ↵

Dr Valter Longo pioneered a multi-day fasting approach[153] that still allows for some nutrition, but is very selective in what one is allowed to eat. The idea is to keep the effects of fasting, while not fasting entirely.

> [153] *See his book The Longevity Diet (goodreads.com)* ↵

The tenets of this approach are:

- 5 day fast
- Low caloric intake (under 1000 kcal)
- Low protein & carbohydrate (under 10% & 50%)
- High fat (over 40%)

Self-experimenters online also suggest using only high medium-chain-triglyceride oil like coconut oil as an energy source. Supplementation with salt is also advised since the body loses salt when glycogen stores are depleted during fasting.

Template 1: 5 day fast mimicking diet

In his book doctor Longo specifically recommends:

Day one

- 500 kcal from vegetables (complex carbohydrates)
- 500 kcal from healthy fat (olive oil, nuts)
- 25 grams of plant-based protein (nuts mostly)
- Multivitamin & omega-3 supplementation
- Sugarless tea (max 4 cups)
- Unlimited water

Day 2-5

- 400 kcal from vegetables (complex carbohydrates)
- 400 kcal from healthy fat (olive oil, nuts)
- Multivitamin & omega-3 supplementation
- Sugarless tea (max 4 cups)
- Unlimited water

Day 6

- Eat complex carbohydrates (e.g. vegetables)
- Minimise protein, saturated fat and sugar intake

Template 2: Multi-day ketogenic fast mimicking diet

This is an interpretation of the fast mimicking diet designed to support you reaching ketosis. It is a more die-hard version of a fast mimicking diet and has not been researched like the fast mimicking diet. I recommend using the above fast mimicking diet and only attempt this if you are a self-experimenter who knows what they are doing. *First off, a multi-day fast is quite extreme. Consult a medical professional if this is your first time.*

The rules are simple:

Hours/day	Rules
24h (day 1)	Coffee, tea, max 4 tablespoon coconut oil. Tsp salt.
48h (day 2)	Water. Max 2 tbsp coconut oil. Tsp salt.
72h (day 3)	Water. Max 1 tbsp coconut oil. Tsp salt.
98h (day 4)	Water. Max 1 tbsp coconut oil. Tsp salt.
122h (day 4)	Water. Max 1 tbsp coconut oil. Tsp salt.
day 6	Breakfast.

The coconut oil is rich in medium chain triglycerides (MCT) which are easy to convert into ketones. It is recommended to buy a device to measure your blood ketones [154]. Urine strips are not very accurate.

> [154] *For example, the Abbott Freestyle Optium Neo. You need to get both glucose and ketone strips. Ketone strips are markedly more expensive than glucose ones.* ↵

Tips to make the most out of your fast:

- Coconut oil is rich in MCTs, but you may elect to buy the more effective c8 MCT oil (in amazon for example).
- Have things to do.
- Don't be around food if you don't have to be.
- Go for a brisk 1+ hour walk on the first day (helps get into ketosis by depleting glycogen).
- If you must have coffee/tea the whole duration (suboptimal!) go for teas without antioxidants/caffeine (e.g. chamomile) and coffee without sugar/milk.

Getting started

I personally view my hormetic responses in three categories of frequency, those being 1) daily 2) weekly and 3) periodic. That division coincidentally also separates the hormetic responses discussed in this chapter by difficulty:

1. Daily - drink tea, of which a maximum of 2 cups black and the rest green & maintain limited eating window
2. Weekly - exercise and heat exposure
3. Periodic - intense fasting

The daily habit of drinking tea is a matter of finding the right teas and having the right equipment. I highly recommend switching to loose leaf tea and trying out a bunch of different flavours. You may even elect to go to a tea tasting (which is indeed a thing).

Maintaining a limited eating window can either take the limited form of intermittent fasting (8 hours) or a more relaxed but still beneficial window of 12 hours. I recommend starting with a 12-hour window, which for most people is enough of a challenge.

Exercise is a more structural habit that people find harder to implement, but has a large impact on quality of life and overall health. As discussed in this chapter there are indications that 1) any exercise is **greatly** better than no exercise and 2) around 150 minutes a week with 30% or more as vigorous exercise seems to be the optimal input/output point. That means that no matter how small you get started you will receive benefit. Try to aim for 150 minutes a week (20 minutes a day or three 50 minute sessions) for optimal results.

The way you implement heat exposure will depend on your access to sauna facilities. If your gym has a sauna you may use it as an after-exercise routine. If not, you might have to look for local bathhouses or spa facilities. If you are serious about increasing your heat exposure I recommend making sure you have some sort of subscription to a facility with saunas, or to buy your own unit. The latter might seem extreme, but over the course of 10 to 20 years it will likely turn out to be vastly cheaper than going to a spa facility if you want to get daily heat exposure. Remember, current research seems to indicate that more is better when it comes to heat exposure for health effects.

The practice of periodic fasting (or mimicked fasting) is very powerful but harder than the above habits since it is so different from most people's idea of 'normal'. The idea of drinking tea or doing more exercise sure is a change, but fasting is not something most people are confronted with regularly. While it is not something to take lightly, it is most certainly not impossible. I feel perfectly comfortable stating that, aside from a few medical conditions, anyone is able to complete a multi-day fast. It is simply how our bodies function. I recommend doing a multi-day fast every quarter (3 months).

The struggle of cooking bacon on an empty stomach

My latest addition to the list of hormetic triggers is a quarterly multi-day fast as described in this chapter. The biggest challenge I've experienced so far is cooking pancakes with bacon for guests while on an empty stomach for 4 days. The friends in question came over to the Netherlands and stayed over. Since I had previously promised them to bake Dutch pancakes with bacon I spent a good hour baking pancakes and bacon. Let's just say it was a great test of willpower.

Looking back at how I became such an experimenter, I can decidedly say my interest in longevity and health started early. My parents had instilled in me a great curiosity and desire to answer questions. My teachers at the time were unable to satisfy that curiosity with the cookie cutter curriculum of high school. Were I born a decade earlier that would have been that. Luckily, my last year of primary school things like computers at home and school became a thing.

At the beginning of high school, I bought a second-hand laptop (with a loan from my mother that would be paid off using my allowance). Suddenly I had unrestricted and mostly legal access to research papers I didn't understand, audiobooks I understood only 70% of (I was still learning English) and online communities discussing all sorts of things.

One of the first audio books I remember downloading and listening to was from a relatively unknown researcher who was explaining the effect of food on health and lifespan in a very in-depth way. Content like that opened up worlds my parents and teachers never could.

As time went on the internet gained more structure and my understanding of biology improved vastly. I continued to search for answers to questions that mattered to me at the time:

- How do I eat to perform best in sports?
- How do I live as long as possible?
- If medical science is so great, why are people obese?
- And so on

To my frustration, a lot of these questions had not been answered or answered in conflicting ways. After a while, a pattern did emerge, at least in some areas. Two of them were hormesis and homeostasis.

As I went through university, there was one particularly wonderful teacher (hello Andries) who taught courses on homeostasis. In essence, homeostasis is the body stabilising its internal systems. Examples include the management of heart rate to facilitate exercise, or the regulation of hormones to promote muscle growth.

What I learned in those courses was that in many cases illnesses are manifestations of a disbalance in the homeostatic systems of the body. Likewise, we encountered examples where turning a dial on the homeostatic system resulted in benefits ranging from lifespan to muscle growth or cognitive enhancement.

It was the first time the concept of hormesis clicked in my mind. The idea that you could tweak such homeostatic systems with external influences was very exciting. I started hunting for such mechanisms and discovered that many poisons and stressors in low dosages could produce a benefit. From alcohol to saunas there were a host of ways out there to tweak the balance of the body.

I feel incredibly grateful to live in a time where research and interpretation of such research has become very accessible. From podcasts like Dr Rhonda Pattrick's *foundmyfitness* to search engines like Google Scholar, I am learning more and more every year about hormetic triggers and how to use them.

Having already made myself a lab rat I went through a number of pleasant and less pleasant self-imposed experiments. My favourite addition to my daily routine was studying in a local sauna complex, which I discovered to be a hormetic trigger that supports both muscle and brain function. What I would call a lesser success is attempts to drink a glass of olive oil as a meal. I later learned you can totally pull this off with high quality imported olive oil, but that using supermarket level stuff will leave you retching over the kitchen sink.

Keep your skin and hair looking young

Principles for optimising cosmetic appearance

- Use Zinc Oxide sunscreen to prevent skin damage
- Slow the onset of wrinkles with retinol
- Moisturise for a smooth skin
- Exfoliate with a chemical peel
- Boost hair production with caffeine
- Replenish lost hair with transplants

In this chapter

- Learning to separate science from bullshit
- Why wearing sunscreen on cloudy days makes sense
- Why the best stuff is often cheap
- DIY solutions for more 'complex' products
- Why I used to smear toothpaste on my face

Use Zinc Oxide sunscreen to prevent skin damage

The reason skin looks smooth is the existence of a molecular scaffold made out of collagen. Your skin cells alone are just squishy blobs. The more rigid yet elastic grid of collagen fibers keeps it in a particular shape.

> Light is radiation, UV light is a type of 'color' we can't see but has a lot of energy.

Collagen is sensitive to UV light, in particular UV of type A (UVA). We can simplify and say:

- UVA radiation causes **wrinkles**: radiation damage to collagen in the skin
- UVB radiation causes **sunburns**: your body's reaction to short-term radiation overexposure
- Both of them increase a variety of cancer risks

In order to protect your skin from UV:

- Limit sun exposure so you don't get burned
- Wear sunscreen on wrinkle-prone areas like your face

When choosing a sunscreen, your priorities should be that it:

1. Blocks UVA and UVB
2. Uses a physical blocker, not a chemical blocker [155]
3. Isn't needlessly environmentally unfriendly [156]
4. Is a cream and not a spray [157]

[155] *Chemical blockers like oxybenzone, octinoxate, octisalate, octocrylene, homosalate and avobenzone work by interacting with UV light. They have limited safety data and some are absorbed by then skin and influence metanolism. See the Danish Survey and health assessment of UV filters (www2.mst.dk)* ↩
[156] *If you wear sunscreen and go for a swim to look at some coral reefs, it would be nice if you don't destroy them.* ↩
[157] *Sprays end up being inhaled, there is too little data in the damage of inhaled UV filters and blockers.* ↩

There is only one UV blocker that fits the bill: **zinc oxide** (zinc rust basically).

Since zinc oxide is a white powder, it makes you look pasty white. There are newer versions (micronised and nano) where the powder is so fine that is transparent. All data indicates they are safe for skin use [158].

[158] *See Support for the Safe Use of Zinc Oxide Nanoparticle Sunscreens: Lack of Skin Penetration or Cellular Toxicity after Repeated Application in Volunteers (sciencedirect.com)* ↵

You can check for this ingredient at the back of the bottle, it will be listed as zinc oxide or ZnO. Ideally zinc oxide is the *only* blocking ingredient. If others (like titanium dioxide) are mentioned this means there might only be very little zinc oxide in there.

Quality over SPF

SPF (sun protection factor) is mathematically defined as:

> How many more times can you stay in the sun, and have the same amount of radiation damage as you would without

An example of what that means:

1. If you would usually burn within 20 minutes of sun exposure where you are
2. Assuming you will be out in the sun for 5 hour straight
3. You could wear *SPF 15* and only be burned at the end of the day as if you tanned for 20 minutes without sunscreen (because 60*5/20=15)

That principle is *non linear*. Meaning SPF 30 is **not** twice as good as SPF 15.

SPF	% UVB Block	UVB let through
1	0%	100%
2	50%	50%
5	80%	20%
15	93.33%	6.67%
30	97.63%	2.37%
50	98%	2%

Of course you should wear a sunscreen that prevents you from burning, but rather that getting SPF 50 over 15 [159], I prefer making sure the sunscreen uses good blockers like Zinc Oxide rather than obsessing over SPF.

If you tan for vitamin D, do it at noon

Since UVB (high pitch, sunburn) is worse at penetrating atmosphere than UVA (deep bass, wrinkles), you'll get the most UVB relative to UVA at noon. We can then reason:

- Both UVA and UVB increase cancer risk
- UVB is the only one that helps produce vitamin D
- UVB is strongest relative to UVA at noon
- For most vitamin D for the least cancer risk, expose yourself to sun at noon

Wear sunscreen on cloudy days

On cloudy days UVB (high pitch, sunburn) is greatly reduced. UVA (deep bass, wrinkles) however penetrates much better. Wearing no sunscreen on a cloudy day means you get the worse deal ever:

- No vitamin A (no UVB)
- Yes wrinkles (UVA penetrates clouds)

Personally I mix an SPF 15 with moisturiser, with more sunscreen in summer than winter.

Wear sunscreen in winter (depending on location)

Countries near the equator don't have very cold winters since their distance to the sun doesn't change that much in winter. Places further from the equator have big temperature and UV differences in winter. Take Oslo, Norway[160] compared to the equator:

[160] See Daily, seasonal, and latitudinal variations in solar ultraviolet A and B radiation in relation to vitamin D production and risk for skin cancer (onlinelibrary.wiley.com) ↵

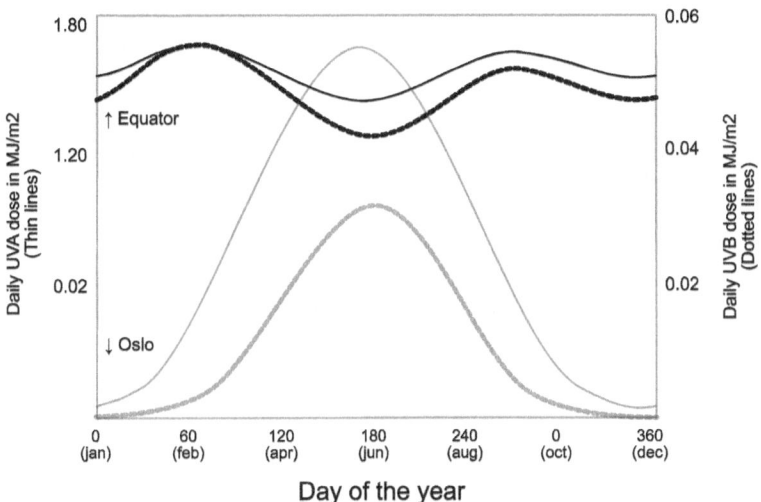

UVA & UVB levels in Oslo (0 °N) vs the Equator (60 °N)

- In Norway's summer
  - UVA reaches equatorial levels
  - UVB reaches far less than equatorial levels
- In Norway's winter
  - Both UVA and UVB approach very low level [161]

    [161] *Note that since UVB is needed for vitamin D production, people in Norway can't make significant amounts, even if they would walk around naked all day.* ↵

From an intra-day perspective, UVA and UVB are the highest at solar noon (near 'time noon') because the amount of atmosphere between us and the sun is the least then.

Slow the onset of wrinkles with retinol

Sunscreen prevents damage to the collagen scaffold that gives your skin firmness. Retinol is a compound that stimulates the production of collagen in the skin, this is why it works on fresh stretch marks too. It is applied to the skin.

Dosage is important [162]. The 'best dosage' is hard to define because it depends on whether you measure biochemical changes or visual changes in wrinkles and over what time frame [163].

[162] *See Unoccluded Retinol Penetrates Human Skin In Vivo More Effectively Than Unoccluded Retinyl Palmitate or Retinoic Acid (sciencedirect.com), Improvement of Naturally Aged Skin With Vitamin A (Retinol) (jamanetwork.com) and Application of Retinol to Human Skin In Vivo Induces Epidermal Hyperplasia and Cellular Retinoid Binding Proteins Characteristic of Retinoic Acid but Without Measurable Retinoic Acid Levels or Irritation (sciencedirect.com)* ↵

[163] *Plus, long term studies are expensive. And since cosmetics are not a medical necessity the research is not too well funded. The cosmetics industry might be big, but funding a 10 year study with a large number of people is out of their budget.* ↵

Averaging out the current data:

1. The minimum dose with biochemical effect: 0.025%
2. Best effect/side-effect ratio for wrinkles: between 0.25%-0.4%
3. Point of diminishing returns: above 1%

Based on that I personally use a 1% formulation. If you find your skin irritates with that dosage, try either putting it on every other day until your skin gets used to it, or get a lower dosage.

Practicalities:

1. Retinol is light sensitive, wear it at night[164]
2. Retinol is air-sensitive, close the bottle well
3. If a product doesn't specify what percentage of retinol it has, don't trust it
4. Retinol is the important ingredient, creams with more or better™ ingredients are usually not worth your time/money
5. Retinol is a cheap chemical, just use a trustworthy cheap source

[164] *It is commonly said that retinol makes you sensitive to sunburn, there is no substantial data to support this. See Retinoid associated phototoxicity and photosensitivity (sciencedirect.com)* ↵

On types and dosages

There are multiple retinoids you will find in anti-ageing creams, each with different availability (some are prescription) and dosages[165].

[165] *See Retinoids in the treatment of skin aging: an overview of clinical efficacy and safety (ncbi.nlm.nih.gov)* ↵

Clinical: Retinoic acid

Is one of the most studied classical retinoids. It is sold under brand name Tretinoin [166] and is considered a 'clinical formulation' (meaning it's prescription in many places). The upside of that is that the formulations tend to have science-based dosing.

> [166] *Note, the pill form is used to treat a specific leukemia type, for skin ageing only the cream is relevant.* ↩

It has been found effective in:

- making fine wrinkles less visible
- partially reverse skin photo-ageing (UVA damage)
- reverse some measures of intrinsic skin ageing

In lower dosages (0.01%-0.025%) it is effective, but shows the best effects after 6-12 months. There are experiments using 0.5%-1% formulations which show faster effects, but also far greater side effects.

Retinoic acid is known to cause a high degree of skin irritation in many people. The skin tends to adapt within a number of weeks.

OTC: Retinol

Retinol is an over-the-counter compound that has similar effects to retinoic acid. In fact it is a precursor (building block for) retinoic acid production in the human body [167].

> [167] *Though it doesn't appear that retinol's effect is due to the body turning it into retinoic acid. See Application of Retinol to Human Skin In Vivo Induces Epidermal Hyperplasia and Cellular Retinoid Binding Proteins Characteristic of Retinoic Acid but Without Measurable Retinoic Acid Levels or Irritation (sciencedirect.com)* ↩

It has similar wrinkle reduction/prevention effects as retinoic acid, but due to the fact that it is less potent [168] you will find that the strength of retinol creams as expressed in a percentage is higher than retinoic acid.

> [168] *It's an estimated 20 times less effective by some measures* ↩

On the upside, it is easy to obtain and has less skin irritation effects than retinoic acid.

Advanced 'next gen' formulations

There are other retinoids on the market, often marketed as 'better effects for less side effects'. One example is "Granactive Retinoid" products from the Ordinary. While I'm not against innovation, I would caution that:

1. These products don't yet have decades of scientific backing like retinol does
2. At the time of writing I found no significant studies for most of them
3. It appears most have proven less short-term side effects, but no long term effectiveness data

I recommend sticking with what we have the most data on: retinoic acid or retinol.

Moisturise for a smooth skin

Dry skin looks wrinkly, moisturised skin looks more smooth. Potentially, keeping the skin smooth will prevent wrinkle formation [169]. To increase skin-moisture [170], we can use a cream. It's not rocket science, in the words of Harvard medical school [171]:

[169] *There is some controversy over whether moisturisers prevent wrinkles. It seems plausible, but I've not found a meaningful scientific study confirming or denying.* ↵
[170] *Yes, it is literally about making sure there is as much water as possible in the top layers of the skin. That's why it is called a moisturiser.* ↵
[171] *See Moisturizers: Do they work? (health.harvard.edu)* ↵

> all moisturizers help with dry skin for a pretty simple reason: they supply a little bit of water to the skin and contain a greasy substance that holds it in

So why are there so many moisturisers? It's mostly about the short-term cosmetic properties:

> if greasiness weren't a problem, we might all go back to using ... 100% white petrolatum ... know as Vaseline

The diverse offer of creams is mostly about doing what grease does, without feeling greasy:

> One reason for the proliferation of moisturizers is the continuing search for a mix of ingredients that holds in water like petrolatum but feels nicer on the skin

The three most important components of moisturisers are:

- **Water**, the 'active ingredient'
- **Occlusives** as a protective layer to keep the water in (e.g. oils)
- **Humectants** are 'sponge' substances that draw water to the top layer of the skin
- **Emollients** to fill up little cracks in the skin (like putting wax on a car to make it look shiny and smooth)

Then there is a large list of ingredients that try to have some effect or another. Vitamins, minerals, amino acids, nonwords™ and so on. Ignore those, they have minor effects if any and increase the price of a cream mostly for marketing reasons.

Exfoliate with a chemical peel

Exfoliation is the act of removing some of the skin cells that make up the top layer of the skin [172]. This is known to even out and tighten the skin, as well as triggering internal repair mechanisms [173], including the production of new collagen.

> [172] *Contrary to old beliefs, the outer layer of the skin (stratum corneum) does not consist of dead skin cells. Rather they are at the end of their maturation cycle which ends in them being shed naturally form the skin. A process that takes about 14 days. See The Clinical Relevance of Maintaining the Functional Integrity of the Stratum Corneum in both Healthy and Disease-affected Skin (ncbi.nlm.nih.gov)* ↵
> [173] *See Skin anti-aging strategies (ncbi.nlm.nih.gov), section "Chemical Peels"* ↵

Think of peeling like taking sandpaper to a piece of rough wood. You are damaging the top layer to bring out the smoother looking layer below.

The superficial over the counter versions trigger skin repair by scraping off the top layer of the skin. The more extreme versions done by medical personnel cause heavier damage, with the most intense one killing and destroying the entire top layer (epidermis).

The easy to buy alpha and beta hydroxy acids (AHA and BHA) are superficial exfoliating peels. They have been shown to smoothen the top layer of the skin, increase epidermis (deeper skin layer) thickness, increase collagen production and even out pigment [174].

[174] *See Effects of alpha-hydroxy acids on the human skin of Japanese subjects: The rationale for chemical peeling (onlinelibrary.wiley.com)* ↵

The most important factors in choosing a peel is the acid type and the pH. The most effective AHA acids appear to be glycolic and lactic acid. The lower the pH, the more acidic and effective it is. The same goes for the concentration of the acid. Lower concentrations of 20% are considered safe for daily self-application, where higher concentrations of 70% with extremely low pH of 2 or less are considered safe only when applied by a professional [175].

[175] *See Cosmetic and dermatologic use of alpha hydroxy acids (onlinelibrary.wiley.com)* ↵

Some practicalities:

- Wash your face well before using a peel, you want to target your skin, not the oil on top of it
- Don't use a chemical peel if you shaved in the past 24h, it will hurt
- Don't use on wet skin, it will hurt

Boost hair production with caffeine

By age 50 about 50% of men are balding. To slow this process we can stimulate the hair follicles to produce hair. Caffeine has been shown to induce this [176].

[176] *See Effect of caffeine and testosterone on the proliferation of human hair follicles in vitro (onlinelibrary.wiley.com)* ↵

In both men and women applying caffeine to hair follicles [177]:

[177] *See Differential effects of caffeine on hair shaft elongation, matrix and outer root sheath keratinocyte proliferation, and transforming growth factor-β2/insulin-like growth factor-1-mediated regulation of the hair cycle in male and female human hair follicles in vitro (onlinelibrary.wiley.com)* ↵

- Increases hair length ("shaft elongation")

- Increases the anagen growth phase (hairs have a ~4 year grow/rest cycle)
- Stimulates the growth of hair-fiber production cells (keranocytes [178])

[178] *See Anatomy, Hair Follicle* ↵

When applied to your head for 2 minutes, a 1% caffeine shampoo measurably increases caffeine levels in the blood [179]. The blood levels of caffeine resulting from that are so low you don't need to worry about getting too much caffeine [180].

[179] *See Follicular Penetration of Topically Applied Caffeine via a Shampoo Formulation (karger.com)* ↵
[180] *The shampoo resulted in nanograms of caffeine in the blood, coffee results in milligrams. That is a factor million less. See Serum Caffeine Half-lives (academic.oup.com)* ↵

Instead of buying caffeine shampoo, I buy a bag of pure caffeine and dissolve it in water to create a caffeine spray I use on my head. It's odourless and cheap.

Replenish lost hair with transplants

The reason men get bald is that we have 2 types of hair follicles:

- Those sensitive to testosterone [181] (often top of head)
- Those not sensitive to testosterone (often side of head)

[181] *More specifically dihydrotestosterone, which is a specific form of testosterone.* ↵

This is why balding men retain some hair but not others. The hairs that are sensitive to testosterone die a slow death [182] at the hands of testosterone.

[182] *The actually enter a permanent sleep state* ↵

While (for now) those eternally sleeping hairs are a lost cause, the good news is that the non-sensitive hairs on the back/sides of our head will not disappear as quickly if at all.

To regain hair in lost areas, we can have someone take the non-sensitive hairs from for example the back of the head to the top of the head. The results are permanent.

If you are considering this, I suggest going with the HST variant. Instead of the older techniques of cutting away strips of skin this is a precision procedure. It's mostly painless (you get local anesthesia) and you don't need to shave your head.

- HST (hair stem cell) also known as stem cell FUE grabs only a part of the donor follicles at the back/side of the head
- FUE (follicular unit extraction/transfer) grabs hair follicles individually from one place and puts them back in another
- FUT (follicular unit transport) cuts small strips of skin form one place and inserts them in another

Note that since hair transplants are a cosmetic procedure and not a medical one, you need to pay careful attention to choosing your care provider.

So far only more advanced clinics offer HST. The way I chose mine was based on:

- It being in the Netherlands (I live here and I trust the medical system)
- The professional being trained medically [183]
- The professional having a long track record with good reviews from past patients

> [183] They don't need to be trained as a cosmetic surgeon per se, but I do want them to be educated as a nurse/doctor in the Netherlands for safety reasons ↩

Any good clinic will welcome you for a free consultation to talk about options. When in doubt, go have a chat.

After care post-transplant

First off: listen to your care provider. They should have the most up to date information on what recovery/care protocol is best for the treatment they gave you.

That said, after any surgical procedure I like to use a general wound healing protocol to support my body:

- Take collagen and vitamin c for 1-2 weeks (stimulate collagen production and use in the skin)
- Take a vitamin B supplement for 1-2 weeks (stimulate wound healing)

Let me repeat my position from the supplement chapter: I do not like taking supplements blindly, especially B vitamins.

Ideally you should know if any of your B vitamins are on the high end already. Taking a supplement for a week or two shouldn't cause side effects, but check with your doctor when in doubt.

Collagen and vitamin c have no downsides in high doses as far as I know.

Getting started

Skin appearance is all about setting up a routine. I recommend you consider how much effort you are willing to invest in it.

The easiest routine with the highest effect:

1. Wear sunscreen in the morning
2. Use retinol at night

You can upgrade this routine by introducing a moisturiser in both steps.

I recommend mixing the sunscreen with a moisturiser since you are unlikely to need full-strength sunscreen for an average day (depending on how and where you live). It also makes the sunscreen less heavy/greasy. I mix a 15 SPF sunscreen with my moisturiser in a ratio of about 1 part sunscreen 2-4 parts moisturiser depending on the season.

Adding moisturiser on top of the retinol will prevent your skin looking mildly more wrinkled as retinol can make the skin look a bit dry.

If you're willing to spend 15 minutes a week on using a peeling solution on your skin, I can recommend doing so. I set a weekly reminder and make sure not to shave the day before.

How it all started with smearing toothpaste on my face

In highschool I was a desperate acne-ridden teenager. While the final solution to that problem turned out to be modifying my food habits, the journey there consisted out of trying anything I could think of or read on the internet:

- toothpaste was supposed to dry out acne
- crushed aspirin apparently stopped skin inflammation
- I should wash my face multiple time a day
- I should not wash my face at all

While in the end none of that worked, it did focus my attention on the state of my skin. The only two things that stuck from that era were:

1. Acne comes from the inside out (for me at least)
2. Makeup cover sticks are super convenient

The latter was a gift from a female friend. I to this day carry a cover stick, which is basically a marker with skin-coloured goo/clay in it. It doesn't solve anything, but on days where there is a spot on your face it does wonders for your self-consciousness.

The deep dive into skin ageing only happened much later, when a new friend was trying to guess my age. She guessed my age at the time right on the mark:

> you are quite playful, but your fine wrinkles tells me you are not lower-twenties

Fine what now?

This was around the time I was starting to lose hair on the top of my head too, both of which prompted me to dive into the visual effects of ageing.

By biology background made the search much easier, and for the somanieth time I quickly got frustrated with the science to bullshit ratio in the commercial world.

Fast forward a few months and just like in diet, investing and productivity a handful of simple conclusions made all the noise obsolete.

While my main priority is still internal health, I do take pleasure in talking openly about the visual aspects of the body as well. Particularly as a man to other men. Aside from a few well groomed gay friends, most of my male friends look at me sideways the first time I mention skin creams, makeup or hair transplants. A few minutes later however they are usually asking for product recommendations.

Chapter
Health shopping list

For an up-to-date version of this list please use your always-up-to-date links to the pdf and eBook versions.

If you haven't claimed those yet, you can do so at smartworkbeatshardwork.com/claim or by scanning the QR code below.

Free digital copy claim

Supplements

- Magnesium - I favor a Dutch brand called Amiset for their lactate powder, but also use AOV's Magnesium AC + citrate, which combines bisglycinate and citrate forms.
- Vitamin d - in winter I have low levels (verified by blood check) so take 10,000UI capsules from Heathy Origins (smile.amazon.com) daily until I reach desired levels.

Gear

- Manduka Yoga mat (eu.manduka.com) - a non-slip mat I've been using this to stretch for years. The quality and feel of the mat makes the stretching experience much more pleasant.
- Gymstick pull-up bar (gymstick.com) - a very solid pull-up bar, I use it for pull-ups and to hang by my gravity boots.
- Gravity boots - You clip them around your ankles and you hang upside down. It elongates the spine and (in my experience) prevents and relieves back pain related to spine compression (sitting, workouts). Note that the original brand is called Teeter, but I got a knockoff from Gorilla sports (gorillasports.nl) because they were unavailable in the Netherlands at the time.
- Kettlebells - having one or two kettlebells at home and putting them in a place you see a bunch is a great way to get yourself to do a handful of kettlebell swings here and there. I have a nice cast iron 8kg and 24kg set from Gorilla sports (gorillasports.nl).
- Stretch band - I use this daily in my morning routine (to stretch the shoulders) and used it during my Gymnastics Strength Training phase to build my flexibility.

Food

Note on teas: the benefit of tea relative to exercise and diet is very minimal. I added these teas because I enjoy them.

- Matcha tea - a great caffeine/theanine kick. Note that matcha is like wine, bad one tastes bad, good one is more expensive but tastes good. Expect to pay over €30 for a 30 gram tin. For the purely cognitive benefits get theanine or caffeine:theanine capsules. Watch a youtube video on how to make it with a whisk.

- Shaded green teas - in the matcha creation process tea plants are put in the shade, triggering them to make all sorts of (delicious) compounds including theanine. You'll love them or hate them. You can find them under the names kabusecha and gyokuro. Very occasionally it's sold as sencha.
- Pu'er tea - a fermented black tea. It's very strong and when taken in large quantities has coffee-like overstimulation effects.
- Bulk buy nuts - nuts (not peanuts) are perfect on the go emergency foods. I buy a pecan/macadamia/almond/cashew/walnut blend in increments of 5kg. Buying in bulk makes nuts a very affordable backup foor (especially on a per-calorie basis).

Cosmetics

The majority of the products below are by The Ordinary. They are the only brand I found that sell active ingredients (like retinol) without any bullshit marketing, which gained my trust.

The only other brand is Moogoo, who I love for listing all their ingredients with an explanation of why they are in the product.

- 1% retinol in squalane (theordinary.com) - prevents and mildly undoes wrinkles. If you experience skin irritation, use it every other day or switch to a lower concentration.
- AHA 30% + BHA 2% peeling solution (theordinary.com) - reasonably strong exfoliating peel. I use it weekly and can recommend setting a reminder on a set day to take 15 minutes to go through the process.
- Squalane cleanser (theordinary.com) - used to remove makeup, sunscreen etc from your face. I tend not to use it if I didn't wear sunscreen but some people like using it as a daily wash.
- Natural Moisturizing Factors + HA (theordinary.com) - a non-greasy moisturiser with hyaluronic acid to pull moisture to the top layers of the skin.
- SPF 15 (theordinary.com) - a physical blocker based sunscreen. The zinc is not micronised so if you put on a thick layer you might look a whiter than usual. I mix it with a moisturiser for daily use.
- SPF 15 Cover up buttercup (moogoo.com.au) - my favourite body sunscreen. I sometimes use it instead of the Ordinary version.
- Soothing MSM Moisturiser (moogoo.com.au) - a moisturiser that makes you smell like cake. I'm not kidding, I think it's the vanilla extract. I love it as a body cream.

Further reading

- The Naked Warrior (amazon.co.uk): Master the Secrets of the super-Strong--Using Bodyweight Exercises Only by Pavel Tsatsouline
- The longevity diet (amazon.co.uk): Slow Aging, Fight Disease, Optimize Weight by Valter longo
- Foundmyfitness (foundmyfitness.com) blog and podcast by dr Rhonda Pattrick
- The Drive (peterattiamd.com) blog and podcast by dr Peter Attia

Chapter

Update your attitudes towards money

Principles for healthy attitudes towards money

- Money is neutral
- Money is not a goal
- Having money doesn't make you good or bad
- Money corrupts like any other power
- Having money doesn't mean you robbed others
- The rich don't have an unfair advantage (anymore)

In this chapter

- The rich don't have an unfair advantage, those with financial literacy do
- There are evil people and good people, money has little to do with it
- Why over a hundred billionaires committed to giving their money away
- My dad accusing his bank of being broke and being right

Money is neutral

Money is a resource. It has no brain, it has no emotions and it has no intentions. Like water, it simply flows where directed based on cause and effect. By extension, it can't be good or evil. Examine arguments that people use to call money evil or dirty and substitute money for water. Ask yourself:

- Is water evil because people drown?
- Is water evil because people are dying of thirst?
- Is water evil because it flows only in certain places?

Even though people die because of water for varying reasons, without it life as we know it could not exist. The same is true for money. Don't get me wrong, terrible things are done with and in the pursuit of money. But these are terrible acts done by humans. Terrible acts are done in equal measure for religion, respect, food and passion.

I could make a list of the benefits of money, but I think you know them. You are reading this paragraph on a medium that would not have been created without a monetary system. You have food tonight because the system of money allowed your supermarket to offer a remarkable array of products. Fantastic things like healthcare and the internet would never have arisen without a monetary value system.

There are plenty of issues in the world related to money and the global financial system. But those are not due to money, those are due to bad incentives that make people act against the interest of others. A powerful force, be it money or water, needs to be constrained for the safety of those around it. We build and maintain structures like riverbanks and dykes to prevent water from causing catastrophes. Likewise, a properly set up financial system needs checks and balances that keep those who manage money in check. How that needs to be done is a different discussion altogether. But it is a discussion about managing human actions, not about managing money.

Money is not a goal

Seeing money as a goal is thoughtless. I have yet to meet a person who expressed a desire for money itself. Humans don't care about money but rather what they think they can get with it:

- Physical objects (car, phone, house)
- Social status (respect, admiration)
- Self-image (confidence, belonging)
- Experiences (travels, events)
- And so on

You wouldn't say your goal in life is having lots of water. Your goal is *never dying of thirst*. Likewise, your goal is never money, but rather a sufficient quantity to facilitate the things you want in your life.

One of the keys to a healthy relationship with money is examining why you are striving to earn it. It all comes down to the previous paragraph: money is just a resource. In the end, many people have similar goals:

- Not to have to work unless they want to
- To travel and see the world
- To feel secure about their survival (food, shelter, etc.)
- To have a purpose in life

In all of these things, money is not the only factor. In fact, you often need far less money than you would expect to achieve the goals above, which is what we'll cover in the coming chapters.

Having money doesn't make you good or bad

There are people with money who do good things and there are people with money who do bad things. The money, however, is not the reason for either of their behaviour. In the majority of cases people who are generous stay generous when they have money, and people who were frugal remain frugal.

For some reason, there is a common belief that people with money are nefarious. Perhaps the source of that belief is the assumption that the only way to make money is to disadvantage others. While those cases certainly exist, as a rule, money is gained in return for something people want. In many cases, people trade their money for something they desire out of their free will.

Don't get me wrong, there are terrible situations where people are bled dry of their money and have no other viable choice than to pay. Examples of situations like those are healthcare systems that overcharge customers, or predatory loan practices.

But in the majority of cases, people spend money on things that make their life a lot better. Things that used to be incredibly challenging for a human to get. Like food, housing, education, healthcare and technology. In order for people to be able to buy those things, there need to be people offering them. By extension, for people to spend money on things, there need to be people receiving them.

That means that so long as we like having things to spend money on, the people offering them to us will receive money for them and grow wealthy. So long as those people do not abuse their position, there is nothing wrong with that (or them).

Having money doesn't mean you robbed others

I had initially not included this perspective in this chapter since it seems so obvious to me, but in the past weeks I noticed it's a recurring theme in people with what I consider unhealthy relationships with money.

The example that comes to mind is an exchange on Twitter where a user accused Elon Musk of being an unethical hoarder of resources (money) from 'the rest of us'. Musk took the time to respond with:

> No, it means I created jobs for 50,000 people directly and, through parts suppliers & supporting professions, ~250,000 people indirectly, thus supporting half a million families. What have you done? [184]
>
> [184] See the original tweet (twitter.com) ↵

I'm not saying that on a philosophical level any human should or should not be a billionaire, we can have very lengthy debates about that. But the fact of the matter is that money represents the value others put on your activity and service.

Every time you spend money you in essence say 'I appreciate the effort you took to provide me with this product/service'. The reason Apple (the company) makes so much money is not because they are evil, but because people willingly buy the products they create.

Note that there are most certainly cases where people are unfairly robbed of their money, but that is not fundamentally how economic systems work in most developed countries.

People who make money don't rob others, they do things that others value enough to give them money for it. This goes for small-scale entrepreneurs like your local carpenter as well as large-scale companies like Apple.

Money corrupts like any other power

It is well-known that power can have very corrupting effects on humans. Money is a form of power and with that can have a corrupting influence on people. As a species, we have tremendous respect for people in positions of power who resist corruption and are down to earth and humble.

We too appreciate people with financial fortune who handle it gracefully. Did you know that Warren Buffett (one of the most successful investors in the world) whose net worth tops $85 billion still lives in the house he bought for $31,500 in 1958? That is an example of a down-to-earth and humble person, and the world respects him for it.

I can never deny that there are people who are corrupted by money and take despicable actions, but that is true of any form of power and/or authority. From doctors who abuse patients [185] to fund managers hiking drug prices by a factor 56 for profit [186], the abuse of power is quite obvious.

> [185] Like the former US gymnastics team doctor Larry Nassar who abused those in his care ↵
> [186] See Martin Shkreli who jacked up the prices for a life saving drug by a factor 56 just because he could. ↵

Some fall to corruption and some do everything in their power to improve the world. Take The Giving Pledge, an initiative that asks the ultra-rich to commit to giving away the majority of their wealth to philanthropic causes. As of 2017, a total of $733.96 billion was committed by 158 individuals (en.wikipedia.org) like the aforementioned Warren Buffett. These are prime examples of people who want to give back to society even though their fortunes were built by being useful to humankind.

The most important thing here is that there is nothing special about money. Shunning money because it can corrupt means you should be shunning all sorts of power and authority from doctors to teachers and politicians.

The rich don't have an unfair advantage (anymore)

The nature of compounding returns math means that the more you have, the more you will receive. On the face of it, that translates unceremoniously to "the rich get richer". The thing is that in the past the methods of gaining money the rich had access to were inaccessible to the poor. The recent decades have seen a tremendous development in financial products. While some are ticking time bombs, others open up low-risk sustainable investment vehicles of the ultra-rich to anyone with €50 or more.

- **Real estate investment** used to only be for those who have a big pile of cash ready to invest. By now we have investment vehicles called Real Estate Investment Trusts (REITs) that allow you to own a fraction of a whole bunch of buildings at a fraction of the cost.
- **The stock market** used to be a place for people with money, expertise and a high risk tolerance. Thanks to John Bogle we now have low-cost index funds. This means that entering the stock market with complex diversification and risk management is now incredibly easy and cheap.

The problem in our current system is that knowledge is not equally distributed. With the right knowledge, a couple with cubicle jobs can retire in their thirties, which is exactly the story of the internet legend Mr Money Mustache (mrmoneymustache.com) who writes about his personal tactics online. So why do the majority of people work until they have lost the most vital years of their life? Because they do not have the knowledge and systems they need.

This is not a conspiracy by "the 1%". All of the information is out there on the internet. This book is but one example where you will find the information you need. The problem is that the majority of cultures on our planet do not teach their members financial literacy. It feels a bit like the middle ages when the majority of people in western society could not read. The difference this time around is that we have the technology to rapidly teach people, this book is one such attempt.

Finally, there is the undeniable math of compound interest. The longer you let money grow, the faster it grows (we will discuss the finer details in the coming chapters). Instead of seeing this as unfair, try instead to see it as the benefit it is. It means that your own personal financial development will only get easier with time. The longer you let your money grow, the faster you will gain wealth. All you need is the right knowledge.

Getting started

I have a number of friends who, because of the way they grew up, have what I would call unhealthy views of money. They say things like "money feels dirty" and "rich people must have disadvantaged others to get their wealth". The interesting thing is that when you examine those feelings, they are usually not based in reality. Sure, there are bad people with money. But I would venture to say that there is an equal amount of bad people without money.

When looking at your own attitudes towards money, try to finish the following statements for yourself:

- I think having money is ...
- Rich people are ...
- The idea of winning the lottery makes me feel ...
- The idea of asking for a twenty percent raise makes me feel ...

With these things in mind, ask yourself:

- What in my upbringing may have caused these attitudes?
- Are my assumptions based on actual reality/statistics?

With your background in mind, ask yourself whether your current attitudes will:

- make your life easier or harder?
- put you in a position to help others?

The best way to improve your relationship with money is to learn more about it and start taking control of it. Start maintaining a budget that makes you feel free of money worries, start investing small amounts of money just to see how it works and read more about how other people are dealing with the issue of money. As you learn more about navigating your financial life you will likely find that the reality of money differs greatly from what most people assume.

The financial bipolarity of my parents

The attitudes of any adult are strongly linked to how they were raised and I am no different. My father is an entrepreneur down to the bone whose last job working for anyone was probably a job he had in a restaurant when he was a teenager. He grew up in the time after the largely communist Yugoslavia broke into pieces. My mother is an entrepreneurial woman but works in the Dutch education system and has been planning for retirement since I was born. Growing up, my father taught me money is just a resource and not too interesting. My mother taught me how to manage money and to plan ahead.

One of the pivotal events that compounded my fathers perspective of money came in the form of his adventures setting up a large starch processing factory in Croatia. He had secured funding through a number of parties and had built a project he was very proud of. I remember going to the opening and walking through this huge complex that was going to deliver employment for people in the region. It was a grand affair with local and international politicians who were using this project in a lesser industrially developed region as a PR opportunity.

In the time after that, the financial crisis of 2007-2008 started to destabilise a number of banks that had committed to supplying funding to my dad's project. It's quite hilarious to hear him tell the story of accusing his bank representative of not having the money to support the project. According to him they puffed their chests and assured him such an assertion was ridiculous. A short while after, the bank in question was in danger of collapse and had to be bailed out by the government of the host country.

Quite understandably, the topic of banks will trigger a monologue from my dad describing banks as corrupt institutions that should have been allowed to collapse for their greed and stupidity.

Listening only to my father could easily result in disdain for the entire financial system and a desire to see it crash and burn. But my mother has always been a balancing force to my father. She doesn't really preach, but asks questions that make me examine the assumptions I had made:

- Do you think it is good if the retirement money of the entire population goes up in smoke?
- Remember those pictures from history class where people had cartloads of an unstable currency worth one loaf of bread?
- What do you think happens in a country where all the youth is unemployed?

She never told me what to think, but helped me build a more holistic view of money and finance. Her perspective was shaped by being on the inside of a government-funded operation like the Dutch educational system, where from day one you start building a pension for retirement. She has great faith in the ability of the government to provide for the population.

And to be fair, historically the Dutch government has been very reliable in taking care of the disadvantaged, ill and elderly.

Being in the middle though I am shaped as much by my father's blatant distrust of the financial system and my mother's near blind trust in the system. I do not believe the government is making the right decisions with regards to pensions in the light of demographic change (the Netherlands has a similar issue with baby boomers as the US), but think this is a problem that improved financial structures can solve and do not require a wholesale implosion of the system.

I am grateful to my parents for exposing me to their views but have learned to go beyond their understandings by learning about the fundamental forces of the world economy. While I'm no economist or stock market wizard, I understand the majority of large forces that govern the system. By listening to the calm and generous voices of people like Ray Dalio (en.wikipedia.org), Howard Marks (en.wikipedia.org) and Warren Buffett (en.wikipedia.org) I have learned about the structure of the financial world and let it shape my personal strategies.

As time passed, I had to admit that the systems that govern our money do a lot of harm but also a lot of good. Like so many things, it's complicated.

Chapter
Reach financial independence / retirement (fi/re)

Principles of financial independence

1. Calculate your desired yearly income
2. Invest 25 times your desired yearly income in low-cost index funds
3. Consider different types of fi/re
4. Track your progress

In this chapter

- How to calculate the yearly income you need to survive
- Why it is safe to assume a 4% withdrawal rate on your investments
- Why it doesn't matter how long you will live if you use the 4% rule
- How a billionaire and his special ops friend talked me into investing

Calculate your desired yearly income

Our goal is to create a perpetual money growing tree so that we can become financially independent / retired, abbreviated as fi/re. This is irrespective of age.

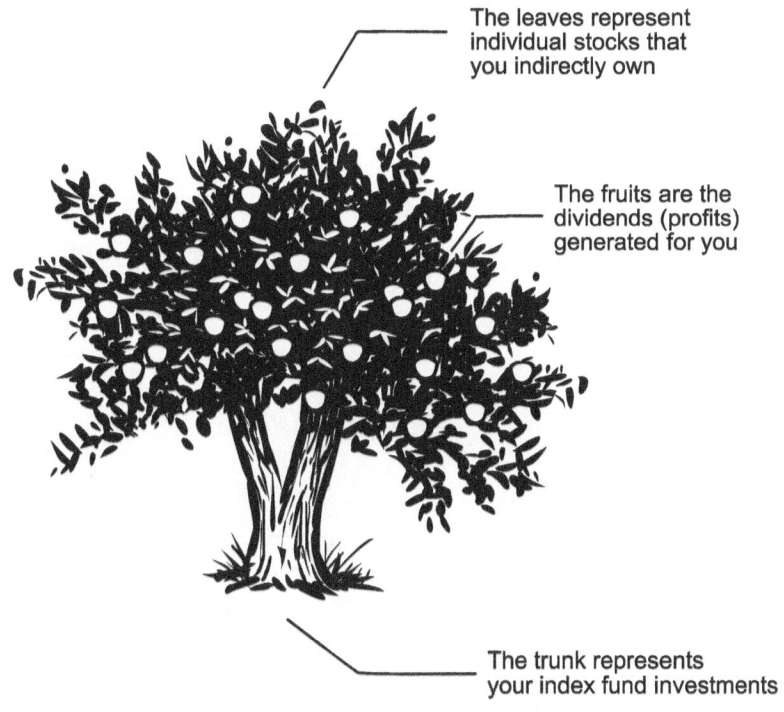

The leaves represent individual stocks that you indirectly own

The fruits are the dividends (profits) generated for you

The trunk represents your index fund investments

Money Tree

The goal of your money tree is to generate money for you. There are 3 steps to building your tree:

1. Calculating the size
2. Growing the tree
3. Eating the fruits forever

For most people, retiring on a money tree is feasible, especially if you start early.

There are three money amounts we will calculate that you need in order to reach:

1. Survive - meet your basic needs
2. Thrive - allow you to spend on fun
3. Freedom - let you live your perfect lifestyle

For each of these three, we need to come to a specific number.

Note: The below examples are a simplified illustration of the process, they are not meant to be 100% accurate.

Survival: not having to work to survive

Your basic needs come down to food, shelter and obligations. Calculate your monthly cost and multiply by 12 to calculate what yearly income you need.

Things to keep in mind here:

- Rent
- Food
- Insurance
- Non-optional costs

Do not include fun in here. The idea of your survival number is that you will not go into debt if you stop working. The survival level is not about retirement as such, having this amount will grant you certain perks like:

- No stress about not making rent
- Freedom to quit your job be able to take months finding your next one
- All your additional income is now available for fun

Make this category as bare bones as possible.

An example from when I lived in Amsterdam:

Expense	Monthly size in €
Rent (incl. gas/water/electricity)	780
Food	200 [187]
Cellphone plan	15 [188]
Healthcare insurance	100 [189]
Total	€1095

€1095 times 12 months equals €13,140. This is the after-tax income I need to survive.

Thriving: include fun

The second amount we calculate will include the spending desires you have. In this level, we include regular stuff you currently do, but not yet your crazy dreams like holiday homes, private islands and space travel.

An example:

Expense	Average expenditure per month in €
Massages	200
Foodie foods	200
Gym membership	35
Better healthcare	50 [190]
Optional insurances [191]	50
Travel	200 [192]
Total	**735**

[190] *If you are from the US this sounds strange, but maximum healthcare is about 150-200 in the Netherlands including dental etc.* ↵

[191] *Property, travel, etc* ↵

[192] *€2400 a year is worth 5-10 trips within Europe.* ↵

Survival (1095) plus fun (735) equals €1830. This equals a yearly (12 months) amount of €21,960.

Note that this number will vary greatly per person and location. Many big-city Americans will marvel at the low rent/healthcare/food costs while rural Italians will scoff at these exorbitant numbers.

There are no wrong answers. This is about how you personally want to live your life.

Freedom: the dreams

This category is not about spending as much money as possible but rather about fulfilling your dreams. Note that this might take some research.

Many people think they want to buy a yacht to sail the Mediterranean seas. But in the words of secondhand yacht salespeople: *the only days you will be happy about your yacht is the day you buy it and the day you sell it*. For the vast majority of people, the cost of maintenance, storage etc is a nightmare.

Think instead about how you can have the *experience* you want. For example:

- Buying a yacht is expensive, renting it for a week is cheaper. Are you really going to spend 6 months a year using it?
- Same for private jets. Chartering a jet often beats owning one.
- House on the beach? If you use it only a month a year perhaps budgeting for a high-end Airbnb suits you better.
- And so on.

An example calculation:

Dream	Yearly cost
Spending winter in Spain	6000 [193]
More massages	5200 [194]
City trip every month	4500 [195]
Fun shopping	12000 [196]
Total	**€27,700**

[193] *3 months of €2000 gets you a sweet time in Spain. Lower cost places like Thailand will be even more extreme.* ↵
[194] *100 times 52 weeks* ↵
[195] *500 per trip times 9 months (since we are in Spain in winter)* ↵
[196] *1000 a month seems good to me, maybe you like it higher or lower* ↵

This (€27,700) adds to the previous survival & fun (€21,960) to: €49,660

Invest 25 times your desired yearly income

There is a well-established rule in investing that a balanced portfolio can over time safely support a 4% withdrawal rate [197]. Note that this section and chapter cover how much to invest but not yet how to invest. The practical details on how to invest are the subject of the 'have your money generate money' chapter.

> [197] *See the 1994 paper Determining Withdrawal Rates Using Historical Data (retailinvestor.org)* ↵

There are many news outlets that will gladly proclaim that the 4% number is wrong because the study is from 1994 where interest rates were higher. These sensationalist non-experts lack long-term historical perspective. In fact, the original researcher recently crunched the numbers based on recent market data and in his own words:

> The "4% rule" is actually the "4.5% rule"- I modified it some years ago on the basis of new research. The 4.5% is the percentage you could "safely" withdraw from a tax-advantaged portfolio (like an IRA, Roth IRA, or 401(k)) the first year of retirement, with the expectation you would live for 30 years in retirement. After the first year, you "throw away" the 4.5% rule and just increase the dollar amount of your withdrawals each year by the prior year's inflation rate. [198]
>
> > [198] *See this wonderful 'Ask me Anything' (reddit.com) on reddit* ↵

Note for non-US citizens: the IRA/401(k) mentioned above is how the US allows its citizens to invest money for their own pensions. Most other countries do not work like this. In the Netherlands, for example, I can only open a regular investment account and get no tax benefits for saving for retirement.

Note about the 4% versus 4.5%: the 4.5% referenced people who retire at a later age and only need to support themselves from retirement onward. As we'll cover below, the 4% rule should cover infinity based on currently available data.

Of course, there are possibilities that a black swan event occurs and everything we thought we knew about money goes out the window. This chance is however quite low and leaves us with no strategy to plan.

We will act based on the best information currently available to us.
Which is to assume a 4% withdrawal rate.

Based on the calculations of the previous paragraphs:

Yearly income	Assumed withdrawal	Needed money tree
€13,140	4%	€328,500
€21,960	4%	€549,000
€49,660	4%	€1,241,500

A little math trick: to get your money tree size based on 4% take your yearly income and multiply it by 25 (the calculation behind that is 1/.04 = 25).

Money forever?

But won't your money run out at some point? Not if the 4% rule remains reliable. Take the (simplified) example of wanting a yearly income from investments of €13,140. According to the above technique of multiplying your desired yearly income by 25, we would need to have €328,500 invested. If your money has an average return of 4%, then every year the 'money tree' grows by €328,500 * 4% = €13,140. Which means that when you take €13,140 a year, you are always left with the original €328,500.

But can this really work? Well, **the best information we have says yes.**

As Bill Bengen notes [199] :

[199] *His specific comment can be found here (reddit.com)* ↵

> I find that the state of the "economy" had little bearing on safe withdrawal rates. Two things count: if you encounter a major bear market early in retirement, and/or if you experience high inflation during retirement.

In the above comment a 'bear market' means that the stock markets are trending down and thus not performing very well. Inflation basically means that money becomes less valuable in the sense that you can buy fewer things with the same amount of money.

But what about the major financial crashes we've had the past years?

> So far, I have not seen any indication that the 4.5% rule will be violated. Both the 2000 and 2007 retirees, who experienced big bear markets early in retirement, appear to be doing OK with 4.5%.

His exact words on withdrawals forever:

> If you plan to live forever, 4% should do it.

How do we make sure we get a 4% return while current (2018) interest rates on the average bank account are near or under 1%? We'll get to that in the investing chapter.

If you still have a nagging feeling in your stomach about the feasibility of a 4% yearly return, look at the data we have of the averaged yearly return (inflation adjusted) of the best and worst performing countries from the year 1900 to 2016 [200] :

[200] *See Credit Suisse Global Investment Returns Yearbook 2017 (plus.credit-suisse.com) who copied the data from "Triumph of the Optimists" by Dimson, Marsh, Staunton* ↵

Country	Average return [201]
Finland	9.3%
South Africa	9.3%
Japan	8.7%
Portugal	8.4%
US	8.4%
Australia	8.3%
Germany	8.1%
...	...
Italy	5.9%
Spain	5.8%
France	5.8%
Belgium	5.3%
Austria	4.8 %

[201] *As defined by the arithmetic mean* ↵

If you'd like to do some more reading on the topic of investing, you may want to have a look at the following titles:

Goal	Book
Passive investing without effort	Unshakeable (Tony Robbins)
Active investing & stock picking	The Intelligent Investor (Benjamin Graham)
Historical perspective	Conserving Client Portfolios During Retirement (William Bengen)

Consider different types of fi/re

There are many ways to become financially independent/retired (fi/re). Lean fi/re defined itself as going fi/re with household expenses < $40,000. Fat fi/re want to retire with more than that. It all comes down to what lifestyle you want to live. If you derive joy from living in the woods and fishing, you may choose lean fi/re. If you find happiness in sailing a private yacht and eating in 5-star restaurants, you may be more of a fat fi/re type. The lean fi/re community argues that being able to retire sooner and spending time on things that actually increase happiness is more valuable than taking more time to work towards fat fi/re.

There is a class of people that calculate their financial goals not on where they live now, but on where they could live. For example, living in Thailand is significantly cheaper than living in New York City. I suggest calculating this amount based on where you *currently* live. You can always move.

Finding a low cost of living (CoL) area to fi/re to can shorten your time horizon greatly. If you live in New York City and pay thousands in rent, moving to a smaller town or even a cheap country could mean you can retire in years instead of decades.

Think well and hard about how and where you want to fi/re. It can have a large effect on how you will live a great part of your life.

Some things to keep in mind:

- Most people who fi/re keep working anyway, usually on more fun things
- Moving to a different country is nice, but keep in mind travel costs

If you'd like to engage with online fi/re communities, I suggest looking at the following:

- Lean fi/re subreddit: r/leanfire/ (reddit.com)
- Fat fi/re subreddit: r/fatFIRE/ (reddit.com)
- Financial independence subreddit: r/financialindependence/ (reddit.com)

Track your progress

Long-term goals are notoriously hard to work towards. One element that makes long-term goals so tricky is that you often only see their result far in the future. In the case of working towards financial independence, there are some helpful ways to track your progress.

The first is that once you have calculated the amount of money you need, you can track your progress towards your goal. Depending on how you like to keep track of things this can be done in a spreadsheet or just on a whiteboard. One creative approach I found online was an individual who every month drew their progress on a fridge whiteboard. Personally, I like keeping track through my budgeting software which draws pretty graphs.

Another good motivational calculation is figuring out how much income you can currently generate. If you look at your investment portfolio, the current total divided by 300 is the current monthly income it can support. In other words:

- Every €300 you invest can support €1 of monthly income
- For example, €150,000 invested can support €500/month of income

The math behind this is that based on the 4% rule, your yearly income is equal to 0.04 (which is 4%) times your invested money. Multiplying something by 0.04 is the same as dividing it by 25 (because math). By extension, your monthly income is your nest egg divided by 25 and then divided by 12 to make it monthly instead of yearly. Dividing something by 25 and then by 12 is the same as dividing it by 300 in one go.

Getting started

The questions you are going to be asking yourself are going to be big and life-changing. The process is not complicated as such, but it will require you to take a detailed look at your financial life. The steps you will go through are those mentioned in this chapter.

Begin by calculating your monthly income needs. Give a good amount of thought to the kind of life you are currently living and how you ideally want to live. Ask yourself if you would be living where you are right now if it were not for work. Likewise, you may come to the conclusion that you will spend less money on food since you might eat out less if you had time to cook. Dive into the different fi/re approaches and based on that make a conscious decision on your goals. Once you have done that, start calculating:

1. Calculate how much you need to survive (food, shelter, mandatory costs)
2. Calculate how much you need to thrive (all the above + fun)
3. Calculate how much you need for full financial freedom (all of the above + dreams)

Convert the monthly needs to yearly (multiply by 12) for easier calculations in the next step. This will leave you with three numbers. For example, €13,140 (survival), €21,960 (thrive) and €49,660 (freedom). These are made up numbers based on my calculations in this chapter, your numbers will most likely be different.

After this, we can calculate how much money we need to have responsibly invested to have this income indefinitely. To do this, we multiply the three numbers by 25. This transforms our income goals into the amount of money we need in our investment portfolio based on a 4% safe withdrawal rate:

- €13,140 x 25 = €328,500
- €21,960 x 25 = €549,000
- €49,660 x 25 = €1,241,500

Knowing these numbers gives you clear targets. Once you reach the first, you may decide to quit your job and pursue another passion. The nice thing is that if your survival needs are taken care off, you can live quite a lavish lifestyle even if you make minimum wage.

How to actually invest the money is something we will cover in the following chapters. Before going through these give some thought to how you want to track your progress. Some people don't really track their progress and just keep in mind their number. This is fine in theory, but if you like the motivation of a concrete graph type progress bar, I suggest thinking of a visual way to go about it. A close friend of mind would undoubtedly recommend getting something called a bullet journal (bulletjournal.com") where you can go nuts on pretty looking graphs.

How I discovered never working again is an option

When I was a little boy, I once asked my mother how much money a person needs to never have to work again. We were driving in my hometown at the time so she was focussed on the road. She casually said that she thought she could live a comfortable life on a million guilders (the currency we had before the euro).

At the time I had no conception of how the monetary system works. I had heard banking commercials proclaim "geld moet rollen" (money must roll) and "in het verleden behaalde resultaten bieden geen garantie voor de toekomst" (past results do not guarantee future prospects). As for what they meant, that would take me another decade or two.

The first time I was really confronted with a big savings goal was when I decided I wanted to go to China after high school, to do kung fu in the mountains for a couple of months. My parents supported the idea and promised to finance a part of the trip. It left me to save about two thousand euros in a year. It seemed like an infinite amount of money at the time. I worked as a gymnastics teacher after school and often cleaned houses after those training sessions.

Working hard for the money I needed for my trip gave me the feeling of ownership and pride. It also made me forsake a lot of things I would have bought with the money I made if I would have had no goal. The insurmountable goal of an infinite amount of money (two thousand) started to actually feel within my grasp.

The lessons learned in high school carried over to my university years. I always kept a budget and most of the time knew exactly how much money I would have left at the end of the month. Then in rapid succession, I learned about growing money from some unlikely sources:

- A bitcoin loving billionaire with a penchant of wearing superhero ties (hello Tim)
- A special ops/heart surgeon speech
- A man drawing graphs on a wall

All of them happened when I was attending a programme called Draper University in 2013. I had met the program founder, Tim Draper, in New York earlier that year. I had no idea who he was at the time. We were having a conversation sitting around a table about the future of 3D printing and what you could do with it. Tim (tall man, superhero tie, big grin) went on to suggest that personalised sex toys would be a terrific idea. He later proceeded to tell some of us at the table to apply for his summer program.

Only later did I learn that this particular Tim was one of the founders of the venture capital firm DFJ. As the son of the first venture capitalist, he was a bit of a legend in Silicon Valley. I just knew him as the sex toy guy in my head. When I entered the DU summer program, I learned Tim was acquainted with the founder of Jimmyjane, a high-end sex toy producer. Suddenly his suggestion made a lot more sense.

While Tim didn't give us investment advice per se, he was a big fan of bitcoin. At the time it was worth about $80 per BTC. At the time of writing this, it is more like $8000, though it may spike up or downward anytime. His enthusiasm triggered my curiosity and the following months were a bitcoin rollercoaster for me. In the bitcoin world, I learned the meaning of:

- Initial Public Offerings or IPOs (a platform called Havelock investments was hosting a bitcoin company only stock market)
- Buy low, sell high as a principle (and failing at implementing it)
- The pain of losing 60% of your wealth within 24 hours
- The value of hodling (not a misspelling)

The months after my DU experience I poured all the money I could into bitcoin. I was riding the wave of crypto hype. I started buying bitcoin at a price of $100 and kept on accumulating until the peak that year of over $1000. Meanwhile, those bitcoins were invested in companies that promised ever more bitcoins. Mining companies, bitcoin banks, hardware manufacturers, you name it. I learned to read IPO prospectus papers, valuation graphs, candlesticks and so on. My experience went like this:

- Month 1: buying stocks
- Month 2: OMG I have doubled my money!
- Month 3: I am a professional now, I do IPOs and stuff
- Month 4: I can never lose
- Month 5: Where is all my money?!

You see, I went through a full market cycle and education within the span of a year. The beginning months were a total party. It is what wall street traders in a bull market must feel like. Every stock you pick wins (yay look at how smart you are) and your money grows every single day. Sushi ordered using bitcoin became very commonplace. My study debt was as good as paid off in my mind.

Then the bubble burst. The mining company I invested in bought old hardware causing the stock to crash, the value of bitcoin dropped, controversy ensued worldwide due to money laundering allegations, etc.

The year after was spent coming to terms with the emotional aspect of investments. I came out on the other side with some solid principles:

- Only invest if you can handle 50%+ fluctuations in price
- If you feel FOMO (fear of missing out), tread extra carefully
- If you make a decision, only act on it when you've slept on it

A number of 'basic' principles I later learned were common advice in the regular stock market:

- Buy low, sell high. When the market is exuberant sell, buy in times of crisis
- Buy things you believe in and hold them (related to the value investing approach of Warren Buffet)

When all these lessons settled in, the final thing I did before deciding to not track the bitcoin world daily was to invest in a group of people who promised a thing called Ethereum. A few years of patience was rewarded with a triple-digit return on investment factor.

Throughout my bitcoin days, I failed to reflect on two other pieces of advice I got while in the US. They were very similar suggestions from a guy who everyone called 'doc' and the financial planner of Tim Draper. In short, they said to:

- Start investing early
- Invest in index funds

They both did it in their own way, but the message was clear. Don't get burned by waiting to invest, or by trading individual stocks. When looking at large markets they seem to go up and down all the time, but when you zoom out they are trending upward. So don't worry about weekly fluctuations. Invest now and ride the years-long wave of developing markets.

A few years later I read a book called "Money: Master the Game" by Tony Robbins. The book drove home the lessons I had been presented. Within a few days I had:

- Calculated the money I needed to retire
- Opened an investment account
- Set up automated monthly payments to said account

I have since read more and more about investing on a long time horizon, and can only conclude that consistent periodic investment in world index funds is the way to go for the vast majority of people.

I know my own nature though, and protect my long-term financial health by having a smaller amount of money set aside for risky investments I do for fun.

Chapter

Manage a budget

Principles of budgeting

1. Chart your expenses
2. Set up multiple accounts for different purposes
3. Give money a job as soon as it comes in
4. Age your money (spend money you earned last month or longer ago)
5. Automate your finances as much as possible
6. Learn from others

In this chapter

- How to calculate your expenses ahead of making them
- How to channel human nature to help you with your budget
- Recommendations for automating your financial life
- How ice cream played a central role in my financial education

Chart your expenses

Let's get one thing straight: budgeting is about freedom.

I love budgeting. It gives a feeling of control and freedom. After my monthly budget session (30 minutes) I have zero anxiety over money.

The goal of a budget is not to make you feel like you are limiting yourself. It is about being in a situation where you can spend money without the anxiety of wondering whether you can afford something.

A good budget:

- Plans for expenses (rent, food)
- Incorporates fun (a 'guilt free' budget)
- Makes you feel in control

Certain expenses

Begin by making a list of expenses you know you reliably make on a monthly basis. For many people, this includes things like rent, food and transport.

It is of paramount importance to know exactly which financial responsibilities you have. Below is an example of my budget when I lived in Amsterdam.

Expense	Average expenditure per month in €
Rent (incl. gas, water, electricity)	780
Food	400
Cell phone plan	30
Healthcare insurance	110
Gym membership	35
Property insurances [202]	25
Total	1380

[202] *Dutch people insure pretty much everything* ↵

The above expenses are things I was 100% sure would be charged to my account.

Variable expenses

The above are expenses that are out of my control to the point that I can't just decide to not pay for them for a month. Besides these, there were a number of things that were optional, but quite reliably expenses. Go through your bank statements and find patterns.

Expense	Average expenditure per month in €
Massages	200
Espressos	20
'Splurge foods'	100
Total	**320**

The above expenses are reliable enough to calculate into your budget in a flexible manner. For me personally the above translated into a monthly budget category 'wellness' of €200 and a 'guilt free spending' of €200 to account for other variable expenses.

Create spending categories

How you categorise your expenses is up to you, what is important however is that only a very small amount of unforeseen expenses are allowed to be without a category.

For me personally, the budget looked as follows:

Budget category	Average expenditure per month in €
Rent (incl. gas, water, electricity)	780
Food	400
Cell phone plan	30
Healthcare insurance	110
Gym membership	35
Property insurances [203]	25
Wellness	200
Guilt free	120
Total	**€1700**

[203] Dutch people insure pretty much everything ↵

Based on this table I know that I need €1380 every month to survive and another €320 to do the things I love (massages, irrationally expensive tea).

The above table means that:

- Every month I knew I had (or didn't have) enough money
- I knew how much money to save to have 6 months of living expenses saved (which is a permanent savings goal I save)

Set up multiple accounts

It is a good idea to have 3 accounts for different purposes. One called 'centre' for automated expenses (your paycheck goes here) of which the card is not in your wallet. One account called 'guilt free' which is in your wallet and contains limited money for food and fun (maximum of €200 on there per week, or whatever is relevant in your situation). And one account called 'savings' for stashing money.

The centre account is very important. It is where you set up all automated expense payments. By making sure all your bills are paid automatically, rent and other expenses will never take extra effort or decision power.

The key purpose of the guilt-free card is that your wallet never contains a lot of money. Since cards entered our society your wallet has access to your full wealth and lines of credit. Before paying by card became the norm we were limited by the physical cash we had on us, we can now spend more money at once than we could ever carry in a wallet.

The savings account exists to separate your wealth from your money. Money is the stuff you spend to survive, wealth is the money you use to create freedom of choice in your life. I recommend this to contain 6-12 months of living expenses and the money you have not invested (yet).

Give money a job as it comes in

Decisions about money and spending should be made ahead of time. This is similar to the advice not to go food shopping when you are hungry. Give your money a job as soon as it comes in and make that decision based on your financial goals.

The key here is to work with rather than against human nature. For example, *have a guilt-free category*. This category is money you can spend without justification. Don't make it too much, but enough for smaller fun expenses.

Sharing the love is one of my favourite categories. It is a small budget category that you can only spend on other people. From charities to taking a friend out for dinner. It's a very fulfilling (optional) budget category.

I highly suggest getting a free trial of You Need a Budget (YNAB) and giving it a shot. It has been a significantly positive effect on my financial life.

Age your money

It is surprising how many people live paycheck to paycheck when it has little to do with their amount of income. It seems to be a human habit to want to spend the money that comes in. This is why one of your major goals should be to age your money, meaning you save money up to the point where you pay your expenses from saved money.

In other words, you should spend the money you made in the previous months, or preferably last year. Especially if you have not budgeted before this might sound impossible or undesirable. Funnily enough, once you start charting your expenses and assigning money a job as it comes it, it becomes almost natural to only spend aged money.

Spending aged money will allow you to build up larger financial buffers and as a general rule, reduced financial stress greatly. It means that you have a comfortable buffer, and if you don't have income for a month or two you are not in financial trouble.

Automate your finances

I mentioned it before in the accounts section, there should be one account dedicated to automatic payments. It is perfectly doable to set up a structure in which the human factor (you) plays no role. By automating as many payments you will:

- Never miss a payment (and thus never fear the consequences)
- Not spend money you shouldn't
- Spend less time and energy on administration

The more you automate and refine your finances the more freedom from money you will feel. All money automation tools you need are free. Banks offer automated transfers, credit cards offer automated payments and most subscriptions can be automated as well.

Learn from others

There are many great online and offline communities that share their fails and victories. I personally enjoy:

- The Personal Finance subreddit r/personalfinance/ (reddit.com)
- The YNAB Method (youneedabudget.com)
- The Frugal subreddit: r/frugal/ (reddit.com)

Getting started

Budgeting has an intimidating ring to it for many people. Luckily the reality is not at all scary, complex or painful. When setting up your budgeting structure make sure it is one you feel comfortable with. Don't cut yourself unnecessary slack, but a budget too strict to stick to makes no sense whatsoever.

Begin by charting your expenses. If this seems intimidating, start by only doing the big things:

- Food
- Shelter
- Insurance

You are of course welcome to chart everything in one go, but if you feel like it's too much effort or too confronting be sure to start small.

Once you have an overview of your expenses, set up three bank accounts:

1. **The central account:** where you receive your income, from which you will also pay big and predictable expenses like rent and insurance. The key for this account is that the card for this account is never used to pay for anything. It is only to be used for automated expenses. Set up a weekly automated transfer that sends money to your 'wallet card' described below, if you opt for monthly payment instead there is a bigger risk you will overspend and run out of food money before you planned.

2. **Hot wallet or 'guilt free' account:** of which the card is in your wallet. This card only receives money from the central account. The power of this account is that you do not need to track every expense to it. The money transferred to if from the centre account should be in balance with your budget. From there on you should feel free to use the card as you want. Don't top it up though. Especially in the beginning there will be moments where you realise the card does not have enough money to make an expense (like a coffee or dinner out), this is your budget reminding you that you previously made the rational decision not to spend money on this. It's self-protection.

3. **Savings or investing account:** your centre account should not be holding more money than it needs to. For one, you will be tempted to spend it, plus you will be missing out on interest. This third account is also where you will start building your financial independence from.

If you do nothing else, the above will probably already vastly improve your spending habits. It is however only a basic structure that does not incorporate a proper budget just yet. The next step is to choose a budgeting tool to keep track of expenses. I use YNAB (youneedabudget.com") but there are plenty of good tools out there. The key to any successful budget implementation, in my personal opinion, is to make sure money gets a job as soon as it comes in. In practice, this means that the moment your paycheck hits your bank account you should open up your budgeting tool and categorise the money.

For example, using made up numbers: if you received €2000 in wages your first step should be to give €800 the job of rent for next month, €400 to food, and €200 to insurances. The remaining €600 is for you to divide amongst other categories. If you are saving aggressively so you can retire as soon as possible you may put €550 towards investing and €50 towards fun. Or maybe you feel more comfortable spending €200 on fun and €400 on early retirement.

The key priority is to make sure that the moment money comes in, you give it a job. When you are considering making an expense, don't open your bank account to see if you can afford it. Open your budget application instead and check if your budget allows you to buy something. If it does not, you may come to the conclusion the purchase can wait. If not, you will have to take money from one category (investments, savings, etc) and allocate it to another category. Personally, I noticed that I hate removing money from my investment budget category because I know I am sabotaging my own personal financial freedom. In the end, it leads to better decisions.

Once you get used to assigning money a job, you will notice that it feels good to build up bigger and bigger buffers for your expenses. There is an incredible amount of relief that comes from seeing that your 'rent' and 'food' categories have enough in them to survive for a number of months. It takes a while to get there for most people, but you will notice that taking money away from impulsive spending to financial freedom feels very gratifying.

Most likely you will spend half an hour or so every month updating your budget. When you do that, see if you can spot recurring purchases that you can automate into your budget. The more automated a budget is, the more fun it is to maintain.

How ice cream shaped my financial life

My father has done a lot of entrepreneurial projects in Croatia. For the family that meant we went to visit this sunny Mediterranean country pretty much every summer. One thing that got me and my brothers in a frenzy was the difference in currency. One euro was usually the equivalent of 7 Croatian kunas. The weeks before the holiday we turned the house upside down for kunas, either those left from last holiday or pocket change my dad left lying around.

Money played an important role for us children in the holidays. We each got 10 kunas a day to spend as we saw fit. In practice, this meant it was ice cream money. It's not that my parents didn't buy us ice cream, but we didn't get to decide when they would buy us frozen deliciousness.

After having breakfast we would spend the morning arguing what was the best ice cream to get:

- The water-based ice cream sticks were cheap so we would get 5 of them
- The creamy ice creams were more expensive, often allowing only 1 a day

- The Magnums were often over 10 kunas, meaning getting one meant abstaining from ice cream for a day

Obsessing over ice cream taught me many things about managing money. Especially about balancing the desires you have right this second and how they relate to the possibility of a novel experience (or ice cream) at a later date.

Aside from teaching us the rudimentary principles of a budget, many times we ended up finding ways to make more money. Either we would bet against each other, or we would dive up pretty shells and sell them as necklaces in town.

Once we got older and had our own bank accounts, we no longer had the constraint of 10 kunas a day, but the lessons remained.

While the foundation for my current budgeting skills was laid in my childhood, it took me until university to crystallise it into a solid and specific budget system. University was an exercise similar to my childhood holidays. The Dutch government would give me a specific amount of money each month and I had to survive on it.

The first months I played by ear and mostly managed. I like being self-sufficient, so the idea of asking my parents for food money because I failed to plan properly was horrifying. I knew they would help me, but I viscerally didn't want to need help. Truth be told I had to ask for help anyway in the first year, which fuelled my desire to figure out my finances.

A world opened for me once I started really measuring my expenditures. Using apps to track my spending meant I could at the end of the month diagnose where exactly my money went and why. Not only that, but the act of recording my spending made me think twice about whether the expense was justified.

I reached my budgeting heaven when I discovered You Need A Budget (YNAB). At the time, it was still a standalone piece of software which I bought through the gaming platform steam. It's ironic that my favourite budgeting program was purchased during a game discount sale.

Using YNAB and their structure made me feel excited to do my monthly budget. Honestly, I didn't have enough money to even use the functionality to its fullest extent. I was supposed to save up enough money to cover the expenses for next month, what YNAB calls 'ageing your money'. I started saving towards it and expected to take 6 months to a year to get there.

YNAB really had an impact once I started working. By this time I had a good handle on my money, I knew my expenses and how to manage them in a predictable manner. Now that money actually started flowing in I started accumulating a buffer and even investment money. I was not making all that much, but because I had a good budgeting structure I grew my net worth quicker than any of my friends.

I learned from these developments that what worked for me was to:

- Start budgeting before you have a proper income
- Consider saving a present for your future self (I even labelled saving transactions as such)
- Set aside reasonable money for guilt-free spending

I've now solidified a budget structure I find a joy to work with. I've set aside 6+ months of living expenses so I can take my time switching jobs if I want, have money set aside to invest in different things and get to buy toys & tech without feeling guilty over it. I even have a budget category for money I can only spend on other people (thank you, Tony Robbins for that suggestion).

It was a revelation for me that budgeting doesn't have to be painful but can be fun instead.

Chapter
Have your money generate money

Principles for investing

1. Remove emotion from the equation
2. Find a low-cost provider of index funds & bond index funds
3. Set your profile to your age in a bond index fund and the rest in a stock index fund
4. Set up automated investing on a monthly basis
5. Get advice and coaching if you need it

In this chapter

- Why the rich get richer and how you can use that to your advantage
- How investing doesn't have to be very risky
- The power of compound interest (and danger of compound fees)
- How to actually get started
- How I almost gave up on investing until I called Vanguard

Remove emotion from the equation

Before we go into the particulars, it is important to stress the importance of logic in this process. Long-term financial planning has no place for emotionally driven decisions, it is based on making a solid plan and sticking to it.

The reality is that markets/investments go up and down. The biggest danger to any investor is making bad emotional decisions at key moments. Recessions, for example, happen every few years pretty reliably (every 1 to 10 years). They are hard and nearly impossible to predict, but it is inevitable that you will encounter them. Have a look at the Wikipedia page for US recessions (en.wikipedia.org) for a little taste of how common they are.

The fact of the matter is that on the long term, these recessions don't matter all that much for disciplined investors. In fact, a recession is a great opportunity, the stock market is 'on sale' so to speak.

Remember that in the financial independence chapter we discussed that the long-term performance of a portfolio makes it safe to assume you can withdraw 4% every year. **This includes recessions**. Based on the available data, we know the best decision to make is to use proven strategies and stick to them.

There is a maxim amongst stock traders: "Sell high, buy low". Warren Buffet's "be fearful when others are greedy and greedy when others are fearful" sends a similar message. What they mean by that is that when stock prices fall in a recession, many people panic and sell their investments while disciplined and intelligent investors buy instead. Anyone with a long-term perspective knows that recessions are temporary. If you look at history you can rationally conclude that selling your investments when the stock markets go down is a terrible decision. In fact, great fortunes are made by those who invest heavily in times of crisis.

The highs and lows that occur periodically in stock markets are like seasons, only a bit less predictable. Selling your investments when things are bad is like selling your sunglasses because the weather has been dark and gloomy for a few weeks.

The short of it is that you should make the best plan you can based on logic and data and stick to it. When emotions try to pushing you to deviate from that plan, ignore them.

Buy index funds & bond index funds

Investing is basically people who have money right now giving it to people who have no money but do have the expertise/opportunity to turn money they are given now into more money at a later point. A real-world example is a real estate developer borrowing money because he believes building an apartment complex will net him more profit than the money he is borrowing. Another example is a high tech startup (think Google, Tesla, Airbnb) asking investors to give them money now in exchange for the profits they will generate later (which is done through giving then shares in the company).

Example: a chicken business

Let's say I have a small chicken business with 10 chickens that each produce an egg a day, which I can sell for €10 to my neighbours. That means I have a €10 daily income (€1 for every egg). This would equal 10 times 365 equals €3650 yearly revenue.

Let's say you have €1000 available to invest and believe investing in my egg business is a good idea. You offer to give me this €1000,- in return for 25% of my egg profit (which would give you 25% of €10, so €2.50 every day). In essence, you are saying that:

1. you have money but not the expertise/time/will to build a business using that money but
2. believe that I will be able to build a business using your money.

> When you buy shares in a company, you are buying the rights to their profits from that moment onward.

This would give you 2.50*365 = €912.50 every year. So after 2 years, you would have €1825 which is a lot more than the €1000 you gave me. So why would I agree to trade your money for 25% of the profits? Well, perhaps I:

1. Want to buy more chickens so I make even more money (which is also good for you since you own a percentage)
2. I am short on cash and need money now rather than later
3. I took out a loan to buy the chickens, and want to pay it back

It's a silly example, but this is the basic mechanic of how the stock market operates.

The sections below will cover the essential concepts for you to start your investment journey and why:

- Low-cost index funds beat high fee mutual funds
- Stock index funds beat individual stocks
- Bond index funds beat individual bonds
- Low-cost asset providers beat investment fees of most banks

Individual assets are risky

Let's say we buy 5 of the 100 stocks of a fictional company called Acme Incorporated. This means we own 5% of the company and have a right to 5% of their profits every year.

So long as Acme does well we will gain 5/100 = 5% of their substantial profits. But what if Acme goes bankrupt? Then we lose it all...

Index funds for stocks

To decrease the risk of our investments, we can buy shares of an index fund instead of buying shares in a company.

> An index fund buys stocks of the top performing companies in a region/sector.

For example, the S&P 500 index fund buys shares in 500 big and reliable companies on the US market. If you buy 1 share in the S&P 500 index you, in essence, own a small portion of 500 companies.

> An index fund like the S&P 500 is basically like betting on the 500 companies that have proven to generate profits.

Why is this good? If one of the companies fails, the other 499 are still up and running. You spread your risk across many ventures without having to manage a complex share portfolio. Examples of an index 'market' are:

- Big US companies (S&P 500)
- Smaller companies that look like they will grow (Vanguard Global Small Cap)
- Sustainable companies (Sustainable Europe Index Fund)
- Companies in healthcare (Vanguard Health Care Index Fund)

Note that index funds too are not without risk and will certainly move up and down as market seasons change. They are however the easiest way to minimise your risk and make it very likely your money will grow considerably over the long-term. No investment is without risk, but as far as stocks go picking them individually is as risky and complex (if not more) as performing an open heart surgery and should be avoided by the vast majority of consumers (and in fact, many professionals should be shying away from it as well).

Bond index funds

You can also lend your money to governments and corporations. These loans are called bonds. You offer the bond issuer money right now and they promise to give you back a set amount later. Common bond issuers are governments and corporations.

> A government bond allows you to give a government money and at the end of the term (e.g., a year) they give you back more.

So what if a government can't pay you back? It has happened before (Greece, Iceland, etc.) and will certainly happen again. You can buffer against this by buying an index of bonds.

A share of a bond index means you are investing small amounts in many bonds at the same time. If you invest in a bond index you are at less risk of a government failing to pay their debts.

Do not pay humans to pick stocks

If you decide to look at the investment marketplace you will be confronted with mutual and hedge funds. In essence, these places have humans decide what investments to put money into. In theory, it sounds great. Give your money to a professional investor and they promise to do better than a passive index fund which makes no 'intelligent' decisions.

The problem is that funds that have humans do not beat index funds over time. Sure, some of them beat index funds in some years, but over time between 90% and 100% do not beat the market. There are plenty of studies done on this [204] that always come to the same conclusion. One of the issues is that even if such a fund would beat an index fund, they pay the humans that make decisions for the company a lot of money. This means that the fees they charge you are larger than the amount they can beat the market.

[204] *See for example, Does Past Performance Matter? The Persistence Scorecard (us.spindices.com) or the SPIVA scorecard*

(us.spindices.com) ↵

Interestingly, this issue is very much known about in investment circles. Consumers new to the market though tend to fall to the sales pitches of smart sounding people in suits. If this seems far-fetched, read Why Even Experienced Fund Managers Don't Beat The Market (businessinsider.com) or How Many Mutual Funds Routinely Rout the Market? Zero (nytimes.com).

Why the rich get richer

When you invest, your returns will be compounded. This year you get returns on your money, next year you get returns on the returns of last year as well! **This is way more powerful than you think.**

> €100 invested in the S&P 500 in 1928 would be €328,645.87 in 2016

One could argue that the above is an extreme example, but the concept holds true. Compound interest gives you more money the longer you have it invested.

Here are some demo calculations (assuming 4% returns):

Monthly investment	Years	Total invested	Outcome
€500	30	€180,000	€349,970
€500	40	€240,000	€592,959
€1000	30	€360,000	€699,940
€1000	40	€480,000	€1,185,918

The power of compound interest can hardly be overstated. You can see in the above example that 4% is already quite powerful, but from the previous chapter, we know that most countries perform between 5% and 8% over time. The difference between 4%, 5% and 8% may seem rather boring, but in reality it is life changing.

In the first few years you can see the difference start to develop:

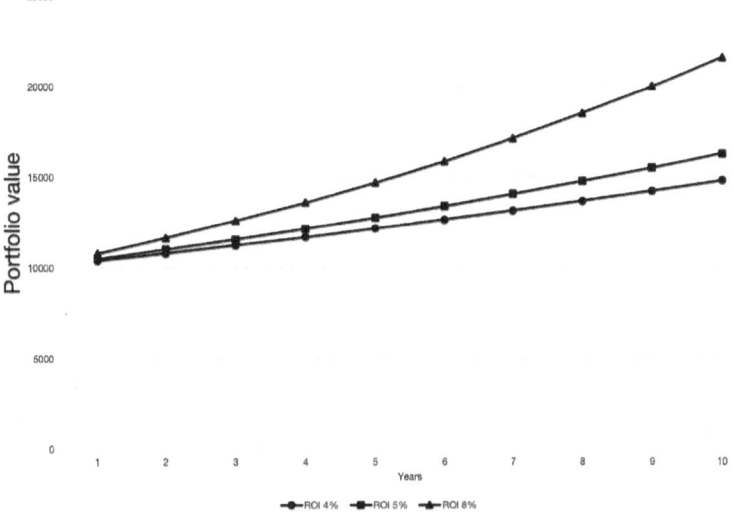

Development of 10,000 over 10 years

But when we zoom out we see that the above difference grows spectacularly big the more years pass:

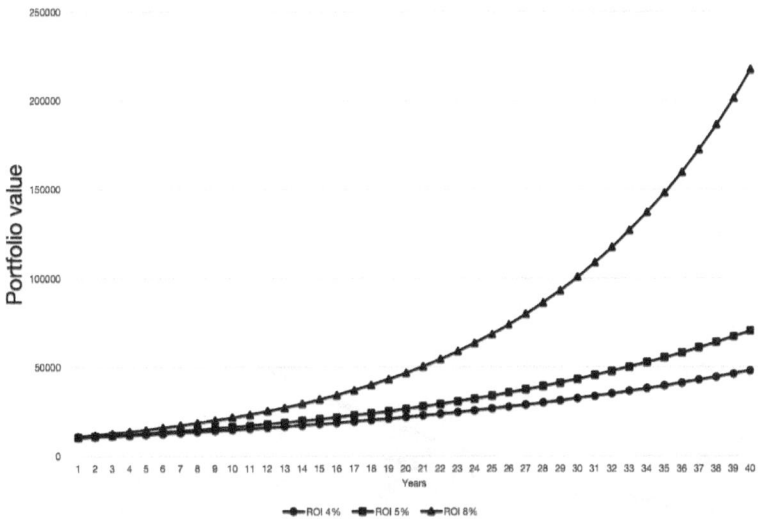

Development of 10,000 over 40 years

Compound interest is no joke. A well-invested portfolio will grow faster and faster over time.

Fees are dangerous!

Don't take your bank/broker fees for granted.

They have a huge impact. My fund provider charges me a yearly fee of 0.4% for example [205] . Have a look at the impact of fees if you invest €100,000 for 30 years with a 7% return rate.

> [205] *This is the cost of the actual fund. I also pay for financial advice, which puts my total expenses around 1%. As a rule of thumb a fund/ETF should not exceed 0.4%.* ↵

Invested	Fee	Outcome
€100,000	1%	€574,349
€100,000	2%	€432,194
€100,000	3%	€324,340

The difference between a fee of 1% and 3% is **over €250,000**! Take your time to find a good provider that charges low fees. it will pay off massively in the long term.

You can see the effect visually in the graph below. Note that similar to the compound return graphs, fees also compound. This means that over time they will have more and more impact.

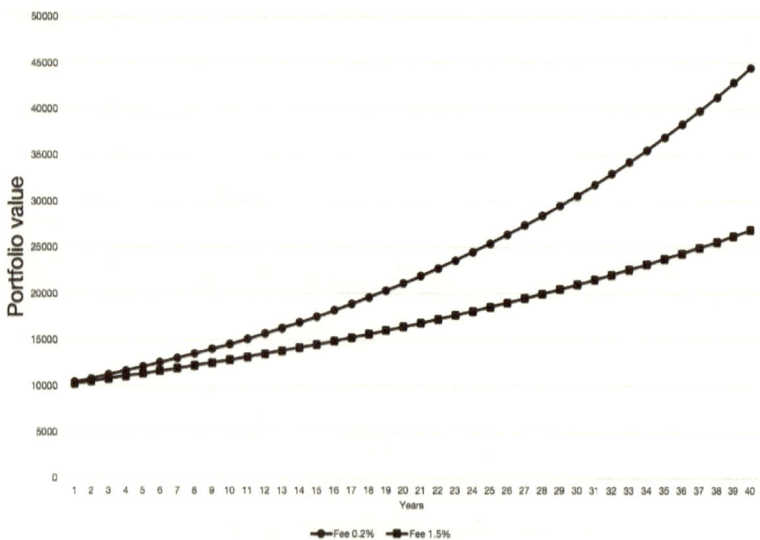

Development of 10,000 over 40 years with a normal ETF fee (0.2%) and a normal old-school brokerage fee (1.5%)

Age in bonds, rest in stocks

The rule of thumb for risk management is to have your age as a percentage invested in bond index funds and the rest in stock index funds. If you are 30 years old for example, you keep 30% of your investments in bond indexes and 70% in stock indexes. The reason for this is that bonds tend to be more predictable with lower returns and stocks tend to fluctuate more but offer higher potential returns.

The reasoning behind this is that when you are young you have more tolerance for fluctuations in your wealth portfolio. Historically we know recessions balance themselves out in the long run. The problem is that if you are 89 years old, you don't want to wait 10 years for the stock market to recover.

For that reason, this rule of thumb can be used to make your portfolio more predictable as you grow older.

Set up automated investing

Humans are not good at managing emotions when it comes to money. Since the stock market is bound to go up and down, you need to make sure you buffer against making bad decisions.

Decide on a strategy and stick to it

If, for example, there is a downturn in the financial market, you should not allow yourself to even consider selling any of your investments. Not if you set up a well-diversified strategy.

If you want to talk to a financial advisor, be sure to talk to a fiduciary, not just any financial advisor. A fiduciary is a registered professional who by law has to act in your best interest. Anyone can call themselves a financial advisor and often they get a commission on the financial products they sell you. They are basically salespeople who do not have your best interests at heart. A fiduciary on the other hand is required by law to be neutral (e.g. to not get a commission). Be sure to ask your fiduciary whether they have a dual registration as a broker as well, some of them try to circumvent the rules for fiduciaries that way.

Financial advisors can help you formulate a plan and keep you on track to implementing it, the data does bear out that the profession adds value [206] :

[206] *See How Financial Advice Can Boost Your Returns (investopedia.com)* ↵

> Vanguard ... estimates that clients who work with a good financial advisor will receive on average a **3% increase** in the value of their portfolios each year ... Morningstar ... computes the actual amount of improvement in investment returns at **1.82% per year** for those who use professional advice to make their financial decisions

Personally, I have created a 'Personal Investment Policy' with a number of rules. The point of such an approach is to make sure that you make investment decisions ahead of time so you don't make bad decisions in the heat of the moment.

Find a platform

In most cases, your bank will be way too expensive to use for investment purposes. It is important to realise that there is no high or low quality of the same financial product. A share in Google is a share in Google no matter where you buy it [207].

[207] *Of course there are types of shares, but so long as we are talking about the same asset the place you buy it has no impact* ↵

Most countries have a low-cost broker, also referred to as a discount broker. In Europe DEGIRO (degiro.eu") is active in many countries. Often you can find a list of platforms by searching the internet with the query "discount broker *country*" where *country* is the country or region you are in.

Automate your investing

You should be automating your finances as much as possible. Not only will this buffer your emotional reactions to stock market changes, but it will cause a cost averaging effect. This is sometimes called diversifying over time. The fact is that the stock market fluctuates a lot during any given year. If you invest your money once a year in one big chunk you run the risk that the time at which you bought was inopportune. By spreading out your investments you protect yourself from that scenario.

Make sure to have your investment platform deduct monthly chunks of money into your investment account. If you have no income but want to invest a chunk of savings you built over time you have two considerations.

The first being putting everything on your investment portfolio at once (lump sum investing) and the other being investing it over time (dollar cost averaging or DCA). When it comes to investing a large sum you already have available, the Vanguard study Invest now or temporarily hold your cash found that in two-thirds of the time lump sum investing beats dollar cost averaging. From their summary:

> We conclude that if an investor expects such trends to continue, is satisfied with his or her target asset allocation, and is comfortable with the risk/return characteristics of each strategy, the prudent action is investing the lump sum immediately to gain exposure to the markets as soon as possible.

They do add that if an investor is more risk-averse they may choose to dollar cost average instead, with the knowledge this will cost them returns:

> But if the investor is primarily concerned with minimising downside risk and potential feelings of regret (resulting from lump sum investing immediately before a market downturn), then DCA may be of use.

Rightfully so they remind us that making an emotion-based decision is likely to cause a reduction in returns:

> Of course, any emotionally based concerns should be weighed carefully against both (1) the lower expected long-run returns of cash compared with stocks and bonds, and (2) the fact that delaying investment is itself a form of market-timing, something few investors succeed at.

Balancing your risk

The first step is to find a low-cost provider of investment assets. Specifically, we are looking for parties offering index funds and ETFs (exchange-traded funds) of index funds, which are basically slices of assets. If you would buy a full chunk of an index fund you may have to pay hundreds or thousands for 1 unit. An ETF allows you to buy smaller chunks of an index. This means there is no big barrier to entry for small investors.

Since we are trying to maximally diversify our portfolio across the world's markets we are looking for 2 things:

1. A world index fund
2. A world bond index fund

There are those who will gravitate towards index funds of a specific region. Many US investors will, for example, have a larger element of their portfolio in the S&P 500 which tracks the US market. Likewise, a Japanese investor may decide to invest in the Nikkei index. This is called the "home bias", the tendency of investors to invest in their own country. The fact of the matter is that the largest level of diversification is investing in the whole planet instead of a specific country.

Based on your risk profile you can lean more towards the stock index (considered riskier but with higher payoff) or more towards the bond index (considered less risky but with lower returns).

The rule of thumb often used is:

> Invest your age in bonds and the rest in stock.

In other words, a 23-year-old would invest 23% of his/her money into a bond index fund and 77% into a stock market index fund. If you have a higher tolerance for risk you can decide to alter this ratio.

Make sure to rebalance your portfolio on a yearly basis. Meaning that if your stocks do very well and are now 90% of your portfolio, move some over into bonds to get back to the original ratio. Many investment platforms offer automated services for this.

Rules of thumb for trust

While not accurate in all cases, usually it pays off to assume:

- Mutual funds are not worth your money since they charge high fees
- Vanguard is a trustworthy player
- Don't take advice from someone who gains commissions from things they sell you

Getting started

In the previous chapters, you should have gotten a clear overview of how much money you want to accumulate in order to live the life you desire. This chapter should have given you a pretty clear idea of how to get started setting up your investment portfolio.

Your first step is to find a provider of low-cost index funds. This will depend greatly on the country that you reside in. The most important factors are that they 1) provide world index funds and 2) their fees are low. Low fees are generally well under 1% a year. My providers charge between 0.16% and 0.3% depending on the financial product. Take your time comparing providers, your decision will impact your trajectory greatly. Better to spend 2 weeks figuring out the best option rather than make an impulsive decision and find out years later you missed out on a lot of money because of fees.

Once you have established what provider of low-cost index funds (both bond and stock) you are going to be investing with, open an account with them. Some will allow you to do this online while others will require physical forms to be filled out. If you are confused about anything give them a call. Any provider worth their salt will have great service. If they don't they are probably no good. Once you open your account see if they offer an automatically rebalanced portfolio setup where you can specify a bond/stock ratio. If you can't find this option, call them and ask if this is possible. If not, ask their advice on how to rebalance your portfolio.

Now that your profile is set up, make sure to set a monthly automated investment amount. Be sure to balance this out with your budget. I personally have a number of automatic transfers in my budgeting software YNAB that reflect the automatic deductions my investment provider takes out of my account. I can't stress enough how important it is to automate this process. You want to set it up in such a way that you don't even notice it is happening. The only time you should be looking at it is at periodic reviews and when your income increases and you want to increase your monthly invested amount.

The idea of long-term investing is that you ride the wave of wealth generation the world's companies are producing. There will be plenty of ups and downs, just keep investing and riding that wave. Remember: you will encounter recessions. The winners will be those who calmly look at history and say 'this has happened before, and it will again'. The losers will be those that panic and deviate from their plan.

How I learned to put my money to work

I had just started university when the occupy movement gained traction. As I mentioned in the previous chapters, my years of university taught me a lot about money. The occupy movement popularised knowledge of all sorts of things like:

- The 1%
- The rich get richer
- Unfair banking practices

I understood very little about the underlying systems at the time. As I gradually learned more, I think I came to some conclusions that the occupy movement didn't intend.

The 1% richest in the world earn over €30,250 a year. Something a public school teacher can easily make in my country. I understood that the movement meant to point at difference within the US, but it lost some wind for me in the grand perspective of the world. I did learn that all happiness and health outcomes of a people are linked to income disparity. On all accounts, I'm happy to live in the Netherlands.

The rich get richer took me a while to internalise. It expresses that having money somehow gets you more money. It made no sense to me until I saw a graph of compound interest. Suddenly it made sense, based on basic math we can say that the more you have the more and faster you gain money. This felt like the best news ever! Who cares about the billionaires and aristocrats, you are telling me that as my life goes on I will progressively get more and more money? The race gets easier as I go along? Sign me up.

The unfairness of the banking and investing world did strike me as a fundamental disservice to humanity. As I found out about wonderful tools like low-cost index funds, I also found out most major Dutch banks charge a stupid and unfair amount of fees for you to buy financial products with them. I then discovered that this is a great time to be alive, there are multiple new players shaking up the industry with low cost and high-quality solutions (looking at you Brand New Day and Degiro).

All in all, the occupy movement firmly taught me one thing:

I need to learn the rules of the game called "money"

In the following years, I started looking at the game of money in more detail. Soon enough I found that things were not as bad as they seemed. There was a stark contrast between two camps, the people who:

- Achieved what I wanted to achieve had simple advice
- Wanted to sell me their financial products said investing is complicated

After reading a number of books I was sold on stock and bond index funds. I had read about a company called Vanguard that offered products structured in a fair way and was determined to get started with them. I did what I thought made sense: I called my bank to ask about the possibility to buy Vanguard ETFs.

The result was depressing. I was treated like an annoyance. As a twentysomething-year-old wanting to invest I had a few thousand euros available, which was a lot of money for me. The phone call went along the lines of this:

- Bank: "Hello, this is Bank"
- Me: "Hello, this is your customer Mentor. I would like to invest in Vanguard ETFs but can't seem to find the way to do this on your website."
- Bank: "We offer investment services through another department, how much are you wanting to invest?"
- Me: "I am just starting out and am looking to build up a solid portfolio for the coming 40 years."
- Bank: "Sigh. Well sir, I think for a person your age this is not the right avenue to explore. We like to deal with larger clients who let us manage their wealth."
- Me: "I get that and I intend to become one of those people. What are your fees?"
- Bank: "That really depends."
- Me: "Sir, I just want to know what your transaction and management fees are."
- Bank: "Sigh. That question is not so straightforward. There are many types of fees that differ per product and client."
- Me: "Can you give me an example?"
- Bank: Goes on to explain ridiculous fees.
- Me: "Thank you for your time, sir"
- Bank: Hangs up.

I was so utterly disappointed. Was this the kind of person I would have to deal with if I wanted to grow my wealth? Was the banking sector filled with dead-eyed snobbish 'advisors' that would not give me the light of day until I was a millionaire?

The day was still young, so I resolved to give the Vanguard corporation itself a call. Turns out they have an Amsterdam office. I expected to be talking to a receptionist who would connect me to an even worse banker. After all, this was the company behind the assets my bank would trade for me.

- Vanguard: "Hello this is X from Vanguard"
- Me: "Hello, my name is Mentor. I am looking to start a portfolio and have read many recommendations for Vanguard."
- Vanguard: "That is good to hear! It's always exciting when a person decides to start investing"
- Me: Confused. Is that enthusiasm? "So can I open an account with you directly?"
- Vanguard: "Ah sir, I'm afraid we don't do dealings with consumers directly in the Netherlands. We only do that in the US."
- Me: "Ok, thank you for your time"
- Vanguard: "But I'm happy to talk you through the types of products we have available in the Netherlands and their pros and cons if you would like?"
- Me: Astonished face. "Yes please."
- Vanguard: Takes a full half hour to talk me through all the options, answers all my questions in detail.
- Me: "So what company can I buy your products at?"
- Vanguard: "I'm afraid Vanguard doesn't recommend specific brokers."
- Me: "Any personal advice?"
- Vanguard: "Sure thing. I prefer working with broker Binck but have also heard good things about Brand New Day which was founded by some founders of Binck after they left. I have not heard good things about most traditional banks."
- Me: "Thank you very much for taking the time to help."
- Vanguard: "My pleasure, call back anytime."

I was astonished. This person just took 45 minutes out of his day to help a young guy who obviously is not a millionaire. That same day I called Binck and Brand New Day. Both took a great deal of time answering my questions. They gave me advice on diversification, tax structuring, lifetime cycles and all sorts of things I hadn't thought about. And neither of them tried to pressure me into buying anything.

That day I learned that there are kind and helpful people who are trying to do good in the banking industry. Sure, there are arrogant numbskulls who I imagine live up to the stereotypes the occupy movement put forth. But when I looked around, I found people doing their best to subvert the system to benefit regular people with regular incomes.

The helpful new companies did everything the advice I had received in the past years told me to do:

- Use low-cost index funds that reinvest dividends
- Have low transaction fees (a matter of looking for the lowest one)
- Automate the whole investment portfolio

The months following, I set up an automated portfolio and let my broker automatically deduct money from my account on a monthly basis. Of course, those transactions go into my budget as "present for future Mentor".

Chapter

Invest ethically

Principles for investing ethically

- Understand where your money goes
- Exclude things that are against your morals
- Be an activist shareholder

In this chapter

- where your money goes when you invest
- why keeping money in a bank is still investing
- incorporating your values in your investing

Understand where your money goes

If you have money, no matter how little, it is part of the monetary system. Both when you invest it and when you do not, you need to understand where the money goes it you want to call yourself ethical.

Investing in a company doesn't give it money

Let's say you go to the stock market and buy a share of Company A. That money goes to the person that held the share before you, not to the company.

The common path to becoming a public company (meaning you can buy it's shares on the stock market) is as follows:

Step	What happens	Company owners
Idea	Someone wants to start a business	Founder
Funding	Founder sells shares of the company (the promise of a % of future profit)	Founder, early investors like family/friends
Growth	Company makes money, maybe raises more money to grow faster	Founder, early investors
Initial Public Offering	Company makes new shares and offers them to the world	Founder, early investors, anyone who buys
Company is public	Anyone can buy/sell the share	Whoever buys it from someone who has it

Once a company is public, buying a share/stock doesn't mean you are paying them. It means you bought a piece of ownership. It means you have a right to their profits, and get to participate in shareholder decision making.

Your money only supports a company when you:

1. Buy it's product
2. Loan it money (buy it's bond)
3. Are an early investor or buy the IPO

If you have money, someone is investing it

Keeping money in a bank means you are loaning your money to that bank. As of 2019 there are few true 'deposit banks' where they keep your money in a vault. A true deposit bank (that only holds your money for you) will charge you money instead of paying you interest.

Instead, the money in your bank account is used by your bank to invest in all sorts of things [208] . And they have no incentive to tell you what exactly they do with it.

> [208] *Where did you think your interest came from? Magic?* ↵

Even 'green/responsible banks' that invest your money often obscure where exactly your money goes [209] .

> [209] *And for those that do not, the majority of their customers hasn't read the investment documents to can't claim to know anything other than a marketing message* ↵

If you are not investing your money yourself, someone else is doing it. And when someone else does it:

1. You have no control over (or insight into) what it goes in to
2. You do not get the profit, they do [210]

> [210] *Interest rates in 2019 are near 0%, a boring stock index returned near 10% this year* ↵

Unless you have cash money in a safe, not investing just means you are sticking your head in the sand.

Exclude things that are against your morals

Traditional index funds are *market cap* weighted, meaning they invest more in bigger companies and less in smaller ones [211] . If you buy such an index, you will be invested in everything from healthcare to tobacco companies.

> [211] *Or more specifically, more in companies with high valuations and less with those with low valuations* ↵

The companies in the index don't benefit from you owning them [212] , but you may not feel comfortable profiting from certain sectors.

For this reason there are *thematic indexes* like:

- ESG (environment, social, governance) indexes that only invest in companies that fit certain ESG criteria
- Religious indexes compatible with for example catholic or islamic values
- Exclusionary indexes that invest in everything except something controversial, like tobacco, coal, fossil fuels or weapons

To find out about all index types, go to the website of for example the MSCI (who formulates indexes) and find their current list of indexes.

To invest in such an index you will need to:

1. Find the name of the index you like, for example the "MSCI ACWI Low Carbon Target Index"
2. Now find available ETFs that implement that index. You can likely do so by going to your brokerage account and putting it in the search bar

Be an activist shareholder

Once you own stock in a company, you are one of its owners. You may be a small fish, but you do have a seat at the table and get to participate.

One example of this is the Dutch collective "Follow This", who buy shares in the Dutch oil giant Shell. From their website:

> Follow This is a group of responsible shareholders in oil and gas companies. We organise shareholder support for oil and gas companies to commit to the goal of the Paris Climate Agreement to limit global warming to well below 2 degrees C.

At the time of writing one share in the Shell oil company is €23. Buy one, and from that moment on you can come to the shareholder meetings and get a vote in the direction of the company.

Instead of blaming "those corporations" and achieving very little, consider sitting at the table and asking what "we the shareholders" are doing to address the issues you care about.

You will likely start as a lone voice, but hey start is how revolutions start.

Getting started

You have a limited amount of time, money and energy. Step one is deciding what impact you want to have and how you want to have it. If you want to be a shareholder activist, you likely only have time to be involved in one or a few companies for example.

I can't tell you what to care about, but I do recommend you start from there. Some guiding questions:

- What do I care about?
- What do I have time for? (e.g. do I have time for shareholder activism?)
- What can I change in my behaviour to have an impact (e.g. if you are thinking of investing without including oil but you drive an inefficient car, you are going about it the wrong way)

Going from the 99% to the 1%

Like many people I was enamoured by the Occupy Wallstreet movement and their slogan "we are the 99%". It spoke to this visceral feeling of being a cog in the machine, without a voice and without influence.

A few years later I found out that the top 1% of earners in the world make about €30,000/year. Which is firmly below the average yearly income in the Netherlands. My thoughts:

> Holy shit, my country is the 1%...

I later did learn that there is a serious and growing issue in wealth inequality, but these stats lead me to question my assumptions, a process that took years. Over that time I warmed up to the nuance involved in the financial system.

Learning to criticise better

I no longer blame the faceless 'corporations' for all the woes of the world. Instead I learned to understand the system better, leading to entirely different conclusions like:

- Central banks did more to create wealth inequality the past decade than corporations

- The rich are not a problem per se, the system in which they operate is. The billionaires I respect are all quoted saying they think they should be taxed more
- The extremes of any group are problematic. Crony capitalists do harm, but so do 'green' activists against nuclear energy [213]

> [213] Which is one of the most sustainable energy sources we have available, often far more feasible than wind and solar. ↵

Nuance complicates things, and I'm still learning. But I decided I didn't want to be an ignorant complainer.

A note on 'shareholder value'

A company must do what the shareholders demand, and most shareholders want money. So generally a company will try to make money and give it to the shareholders [214].

> [214] Either through dividends, share buybacks or investments in future profit and/or growth ↵

There is a lot of criticism on the idea of 'maximising shareholder value' as it implies doing things like:

- destroying the environment to make more profit
- treating workers badly
- lobbying politicians to favor the business/sector

But keep in mind that shareholder value is about "what shareholders value". To change a company, you don't need to change the company's mind about value, you have to convince it's owners: the shareholders.

There are rational arguments to be made in favor of many 'ethical' behaviours:

- 'green' techniques to save energy can save cost too
- treating workers well can make them more efficient
- gender/race/age balance in a company can benefit it's functioning

Whatever it is you care about, you care about it because you think it will make the world better for everyone [215]. Like any revolutionary it is your job to convince those around you that you are right, and that everyone will benefit from your suggested course of action.

> [215] If not, we are unlikely to become friends, sorry. ↵

In other words, it is up to you to change what those around you value. If those around you are the shareholders of a company, you are changing the meaning of 'shareholder value'.

A note on responsibility

It is an eternal frustration of mine that those who criticise investing, companies and shareholders are also those who are furthest removed from that world.

Is it any surprise that investors and activists don't like each other if they never meet on equal footing? If you don't interact it becomes easy to dismiss the 'other' if you spend no time exploring their ideas.

I am a born and raised Dutchman. Everybody in my country has cheap healthcare, universities cost ~€2000 a year by law and the upper income tax bracket is over 50%.

When I talk to investors about the benefit of such a system, they tend to warm up to it. Because instead of shouting at them I open up my reasoning to them.

Likewise, I learned to stop complaining about faceless enemies like 'the banks' and 'big business' by listening to those inside those systems. I now know *what* I don't like about certain banking practices and *why*. And when I talk to anyone in those sectors, I can speak to them in their language so that they listen.

In a conversation there is no need for 'us and them', just the 'us' will do just fine.

So if you see investors as money grabbing enemies, I challenge you to at least understand in general terms *what* it is they do and *why*.

Chapter

About me

I find writing about myself and what I do very challenging. A big part of it is that the way our society tells us to present ourselves tends to not give a good picture of a person. I'll attempt to give you a few different angles and hope that it gives you a little insight into the oddball behind this book.

Education

My primary school was a small establishment in the village right outside our city's border. My class had a size of 8 people, most of which were girls for the majority of the 8 years of Dutch primary school. In the last two years, two other boys joined, one of which became my best friend and the other my bully.

High school in the Netherlands is a very segmented system. From year one onwards you start either on a 4, 5 or 6-year track depending on what your teachers decide you are capable of. There are some standardised tests involved, but at least on paper, it is the judgement of the teacher that determines where you go. My mother asked me if I wanted to do a bilingual high school track geared towards teaching us English by having a large portion of our classes in English. I loved the idea so my mom signed me up. Later I learned this caused quite some drama in my primary school as the teachers there felt bypassed (we had to sign up before the teachers had given their advice on where to send me).

In year 4 of 6, we were required to choose between a number of 'profiles' for our continued education. Basically, it was a split between the hard sciences like math/physics and what they called 'social subjects' like economics and arts. Me and my friends came to the conclusion that with the science profiles we would be able to pursue any study/career, whereas choosing the social track would limit our options. Needless to say, we chose science over society.

Choosing what university to go to and what study to pursue was an interesting process. I was held back a grade in the 5th out of 6 years, mostly because of the strain of my parents divorcing that year. In the Netherlands there is no difference in university ranking like in the US or UK, and the majority of those studies didn't have a limit on applicants, meaning in practice you could just apply and get in (for most study programs the limits are set based on expected applications, but the spots are in most cases not scarce). When reaching the end of high school, a number of studies caught my eye, and obviously they were ones that had the most intense selection criteria. My Dutch equivalent of a guidance counsellor kept (in different words every time) telling me to set my sights lower. If anything, that made me more determined to get in. After visiting the University College in Maastricht (UCM) I had made my decision to go there. I resolved to apply until I got in. Even if it took a couple of times, which luckily it didn't.

University was a lot of fun. The structure of my degree meant I got to choose my courses every 8 weeks. Basically, there were level 1, 2 and 3 courses, where to take a level 2 you needed certain level 1's and to take a 3 you needed a number of 2's. The department was mostly social science and humanities, but they had a great selection of sciences. After I found out getting an exemption to prerequisite courses was easy to obtain if you could convince the course coordinator, I didn't take a single level 1 course in my time there. I spent most of my time learning about human biology like homeostasis, immunology and genetics. Aside from biology, I rekindled my interest in computer science with some programming and data mining courses. Due to the nature of the degree, it was mandatory to also take social science and humanities courses. I discovered I liked anthropology and spent a number of courses analysing the discourse of science and technology.

During my bachelor's degree, I learned a lot about nutrition, mostly through experimental science. I decided to do a 1-year course in nutrition on the side. I disagreed with a great part of the course but finished it anyway. At this point, I came to the conclusion that people with a degree in a certain field are not to be trusted if they can't back up their claims with solid references. At the same time, it made me more rigorous in finding solid references for the nutrition and health protocols like intermittent fasting I was reading about at the time.

After finishing my bachelor's degree, I worked for a while and decided to do a master's degree. Honestly, the primary reason I did it was because I felt like I would leave something unfinished if I didn't. I worked in Amsterdam at the time and basically filtered master's programs based on the criteria of being a science and taking max 1 year. The result was an information science degree in game studies. That year was very educational and a lot of fun. Learning about the psychology and prototyping of games was very educational, plus I got to play with toys like the latest VR headsets.

Trampolines and martial arts

I was a very active and mobile kid. One day when I was rolling on the floor, my mother asked me if I would like to try trampolining as a sport. It turns out she had done some classes when she was little with a guy that was still teaching. Obviously, I said yes. The result was that trampolining became one of the most impactful elements in my life.

Trampolining is a bit like gymnastics, only there is less stretching and more flipping. I was doing double flips by the time I finished primary school and developed a keen aerial body awareness. My coach did not believe in recreational sports so as soon as me and my fellow trampolinists were even remotely capable of competing he sent us to do competitions. The first few years were mostly me cracking under pressure and losing pretty much all the time. There were plenty of times the competition day ended in tears. The things I had practised in training never came out the way I had intended, and while I usually had a decent difficulty score my execution was pretty shitty. I learned to use this feeling as fuel to want to get better, and through a lot of ups and downs did so.

After a couple of years, I stopped losing everything and actually started winning here and there. At this point, my coach told me to participate in international competitions. Looking back, this was one of the most enjoyable aspects of doing trampolining. We travelled around Europe to Belgium, Germany, Denmark and the United Kingdom. The competitive trampolining scene is well-developed but not huge, so after a while there were a lot of familiar faces and friendships. By the time I was mid high school I had participated in two junior world championships, one in the Netherlands and one in Canada. I never won, but ended right about in the middle. Mostly it was exciting to perform amongst the next level performers at the event. Especially the Russians and Chinese were known to take things to the next level. Though my personal favourites were always the Australians who were doing well but were mostly having fun.

While I spent most of my time trampolining, my middle brother went down the martial arts rabbit hole. He started with judo, went on to jiujitsu and ended with competitive nunchuck fighting. The same way I drew my brothers to try trampolining (which they both did for some time) he drew me and the youngest brother to try martial arts. As little boys, we often engaged in physical fights, not because we were angry but just because it seemed like fun. I did jiujitsu for a while, once a week, next to trampolining and found I enjoyed it. Between high school and university, I would go on to spend a few months in China doing kung fu, which was physically taxing but not actually that useful in combat. I've since then continued to do martial arts on and off. Ninjutsu while in university and Shorinji Kempo for a shorter period while working in Amsterdam.

Things I get paid for

My first real job was being a waiter through a temp agency. Basically, my supplement habits at sports were cutting deep into my pocket money so I needed additional revenue. The only easy way for me to get a job was to register at a temp agency, who would send me here and there to be a waiter or to wash dishes in a restaurant. The work was not exactly fun and the hours often late, but I was proud to be generating my own money.

Towards the end of high school, I had resolved to do a gap year and was torn between kung fu in China or freediving in Thailand. I ended up going to China, which came with a price tag of about €3000. At the time this seemed like an impossible amount of money to make within a year. I couldn't say no to the challenge though and decided to go for it. I had since obtained my license to teach trampolining and gymnastics and was teaching gymnastics after school to primary school kids. It paid five times as much as my waitering jobs, though the hours I could work were limited.

What started as a once a week engagement grew to me managing three locations across three villages. In addition, I had found a company that paid €10 an hour for someone to clean houses. It was a solid three times as much as minimum wage, so I went for it. I started skipping a lot of classes in high school, but because I was above 18 and my grades were on the high end they gave me a bit more leeway. I did have a heated discussion with the department coordinator who was not happy with me. I found the school system to be ineffective and small-minded. I was juggling multiple jobs, competitive trampolining and school while this lady was threatening to expel me because I missed too many classes. I argued that my grades were better than the vast majority of the class, but she seemed to prefer the letter of the rules to their spirit (it ended up ok). In the end, I managed to get the money together, though it pushed my physical and mental limits.

In university, I decided that I preferred being paid money for my skill rather than my time. I registered as a freelancer and started selling websites and online stores. This was also the period of time where I started my funded company. Me and a friend participated in a program called 3

Day Startup where over a weekend we were challenged to think of an idea, prototype it and pitch it to investors. I had, for a while, been walking around with the idea of a USB stick that performed computer maintenance. It was born out of the fact that family members would constantly ask me to speed up their computers, and me being annoyed at doing such a repetitive task. I convinced some other attendees to work on it with me. This resulted in an investment that allowed us to launch CleanPC. It was not a commercial success, but one of the most educational experiences I've had. I made all the mistakes I now know beginners to make. The founders of the company were pretty much strangers I had met during a weekend, we had no vesting structure for our company shares and the skillset of the team was not balanced at all. This experience helped me avoid mistakes later in my career and I think back fondly to this time.

After graduating from my bachelor's degree I noticed that while I was trained in biology/anthropology, the job market seemed to value my programming skills more, so that is what I started developing more. I went from working for other people as a programmer and business consultant to freelancing as a teacher for programming boot camps and schools. I noticed that I very much enjoy teaching and figuring out how to help others understand things that I had taken a long time to learn. My first teaching engagement grew from "hey, can you come give a workshop?" to teaching for half a day 5 days a week. The other half of the day I was finishing up my master's. Looking back I seem to have a habit of periodically having a year where I do multiple full-time engagements. It again pushed my limits and taught me how to deal with getting up at 6 and getting home at 8 while still spending time on staying healthy and happy.

So what do you do?

By now I have no idea how to explain what I do. I was trained as a biologist, anthropologist and information scientist but make my money by teaching, coding and writing.

If a programmer asks me what I do I answer I'm a full stack developer who enjoys working with node.js and react.js. If an entrepreneur asks me what I do I tell them about my previous companies that include CleanPC and a number of VPN projects, some of which I sold and others I still run. If a scientist asks me what I do I tell them that I regularly read studies related to human disease, ageing and longevity. If I'm not sure who is asking, I tend to say I'm a programmer since they stop asking questions after that.

I honestly have no idea 'what I do' currently. I like to think I'm having fun building things I think should exist.

Chapter
My productivity habits

When reading the productivity chapters you may get the impression that I'm an always-on machine of perpetual concentration, motivation and productivity. This is not the case.

My habits and techniques allow me to get things done when I choose to do so. But often enough I choose to instead spend time travelling, gaming and reading. I am certainly not above binging a season of a Netflix series over the weekend (thank you, Marvel).

I know though that I can, within a reasonable margin of error, summon the productivity machine in me, regardless of place and time. The below habits are things that work for me.

The morning is my time of power

I have noticed I get my best work done while the sun is up. Morning and early afternoon are my best times. I'm very sensitive to light exposure, so on days I want to get things done I:

- Wake up using a wake-up light
- Do basic exercises within 10 minutes of getting up (when brain not yet awake)
- Have a shower (ending in cold)
- Meditate for 10 minutes
- Get dressed
- Have tea

The tea is usually a strong green Kabusecha/Gyokuro or high quality Matcha. Depending on the day, I drink the tea while staring out of the window or behind a computer screen. Having a tea ritual in the morning helps me feel like the day has properly started, the caffeine helps too.

Recently I've started to use bright light exposure in the morning through an obscenely bright LED light bulb (60W, not 60W equivalent) that lights my desk. Basically, it feels like it is a summer morning. It helps me stave off winter slowness.

Think in blocks of 10 minutes

I've observed in many people that they don't like doing any significant work unless they have at least 30 minutes to an hour to do it. I used to be like that as well and told myself "I can't get in a good flow in a few minutes" and "once I get started I will be annoyed at having to stop".

The reality is that working in small increments is a skill. And, like any skill, you can practice and master it. A few years ago I started to do work in any 10-minute increment in the day, mostly out of sheer necessity [216] . I noticed that within a week of practice it was almost effortless to:

> [216] *See How I Survive Multiple Full Time Engagements (skillcollector.com)* ↵

- Work for 10 minutes waiting for a train
- Pick up work I started earlier with nearly no startup time
- Gain hours of productive work this way

Of course, I had to facilitate my focus in odd environments. For me, that meant always carrying headphones to isolate myself from the bustle around me, as well as learning to sit with a decent computer posture on a chair, the ground or even standing.

You don't have to go all out like I did. But changing your perspective to see work in 10-minute increments will make you feel a lot more relaxed. Knowing that you can sneak in work here and there in a way that allows you to get things done, even if you don't have a 2-hour block of free time available, is liberating.

Set my goals and process in advance

Have you ever sat down to work only to realise that half an hour later you are reading a blog on some random thing that has nothing to do with your task? I certainly have.

My instinctive habit when getting behind my computer used to be:

- Crtl+t, press g, press enter
- Crtl+t, press f, press enter
- Crtl+t, press t, press enter
- Crtl+t, press r, press enter

Crtl+t would open a new tab and due to the browser autocomplete my successive keypresses would within the span of 5 seconds open:

- Gmail
- Facebook
- Twitter
- Reddit

One might argue the first still counts as productive (though by now I hold the view that it is not). I would go through this sequence every time I didn't know what to do next.

Luckily I grew to approach my productivity time in a different way:

1. Decide what I'm working on
2. Set parameters
3. Execute

For example:

- Write a blog post
- No social media, no messaging, 2 hours

If you have been conditioned for years to open time-sucking web pages, consider:

- Chrome Extension Work Mode - Block all social media (chrome.google.com)
- Rescuetime (rescuetime.com") activity tracker that shows how much time you spend doing what

Setting a timer for low-impact tasks

An empty inbox is nice. Spending 3 hours on emails is not. For tasks like email, cleaning etc that need to be done but are not life-alteringly important I like setting a timer. I'll decide on how much time I am willing to spend on this and then let the timer run.

Not only does it limit the amount of time I spend on it, but it also means I do these tasks faster. Remember, a task fills up the time allotted to it. So don't allot low impact tasks more time than they need.

Take naps

When I feel my energy levels are a bit low, I have a nap. Usually, that means setting an alarm for 20-60 minutes in bed with earplugs and an eye mask. Interestingly, I have found that spending an hour napping has never made my day feel an hour shorter. If anything the day seems longer due to my increased energy levels after the nap.

I have heard people say that they tend to wake up groggy from naps. If that is you, a potential solution could be the 'coffee nap'. Which basically means you drink coffee right before your nap (as in within a few minutes). The idea is that you have a nap and wake up once the caffeine kicks in.

Automate as much as possible

I love automation, every time a new task is automated I feel great satisfaction. My automations range from low-tech stuff to self-coded scripts and devices.

My favourite household automations

- Robot vacuum cleaner that runs an hour before I wake up (unless I have guests)
- Dishwasher. I despise doing dishes by hand. It is a waste of energy and an inefficient use of detergent. Not to mention the time you lose doing it
- Kitchen machines. Not strictly automation but rather an augmentation. I love my blender & food processor.
- Smart light bulbs allowing me to have only red light at night

Tech automations

- My entire computer backs up to Google Drive (I chose Drive due to its integration with Google Photos)
- At 2PM my Raspberry Pi server (a cheap €30 computer) downloads my Google Drive to an offline hard drive (so my data is on 3 media in 2 locations, in the server park at Google and on both my Pi and laptop)
- My photos always go to Google Photos where facial recognition compiles per person albums

- My phone sound settings also control power saving settings
  - Loud: overclock processor
  - Silent: regular processor, turn screen black & white, disable mobile internet when the screen is off, disable cell reception when connected to wifi
  - Vibrate: go into potato mode. Airplane mode, underclocked processor, forced Android doze (a built-in app freezer) on all apps
- My phone switches to a red filtered screen (night mode) after 22:00 and shuts off access to social media, email etc through the Tasker (play.google.com) app

Communication automations

- Keyboard shortcuts for information I type out often through aText (trankynam.com)
  - Bank accounts, credit card number, business VAT number
  - Email, signature, address
- Schedule calls with Calendly (calendly.com") which costs no time going back and forth
- Multi-people meetups are planned using Doodle (doodle.com)

Chapter
My health habits

This section details the habits and techniques I have chosen to implement in my life. These are of course subject to change.

It is important to point out that I:

- chose these habits to suit my personal lifestyle & goals
- regularly add and subtract habits & routines

Another very important thing to mention is that I consider none of my choices dogma. They are very strong guidelines. For example:

- if I want a blacklisted food for a specific reason (e.g., pizza in Croatia, because childhood memories) go for it
- if I have never tried a food (e.g., visiting a new country) ignore the rules

I do have to note that these scenarios only happen a handful of times a year. And even then I simply can't handle very sweet things like cake or candy. My body and taste have adjusted to not like it.

Food & fasting habits

The way I eat does not have a specific diet name. It is a blend of low GI diet, Paleo diet, longevity diet and personal preference.

Element 1: what I eat

In essence, I eat low GI/GL and have for about 10 years now.

Status	What	Notes
Never	Added sugar	Highest GI, unbuffered by fibre. No value.
Never	White grains, potato	High GI, have nothing I can't get elsewhere
Limited	Peanut, dark grains, legumes	I used to not eat these at all but changed based on the recent publication of Dr Longo's Longevity research.
Limited	Fruits	Preference for berries and less sweet ones
Limited	Meat	Terrible for the environment [217]. Fish and eggs are far better (though not perfect), I choose asc (scsglobalservices.com) label farmed wish when possible.
Unlimited	Vegetables	Low GI, nutrients
Unlimited	Fish	Studies so far seem to find a 'more is better' dose/benefit relationship. I prefer farmed fish with a good sustainability rating.
Unlimited	Nuts	Good for health, but easy to eat too much of [218].
Unlimited	Eggs, fermented dairy	Eggs are a great source of all sorts of things [219]. Milk poses a health risk to humans, but not when fermented [220].

[217] *Beef and lamb are terrible, pork is 5 times better (from the perspective of greenhouse gasses) and chicken/fish/eggs are even better than that. Dairy falls even lower on the harm scale. See this food versus impact chart (weforum.org)* ↵

[218] *I have a multi-kilogram bucket at home so eating multiple handfuls while working is easy. While not a direct health risk it can mess up caloric intake* ↵

[219] *And do not pose a risk to your cardiovascular health the way most people think. See my writeup on why we believe cholesterol to be bad (skillcollector.com)* ↵

[220] *Humans do not need cow's milk, and in fact, do worse health wise when drinking a lot of milk. Fermented milk products do not have this downside. See for example, this analysis on health risk based on fermented and raw milk consumption (naturalmedicinejournal.com)* ↵

In practice, I notice that there are certain foods I eat a lot:

- **High-quality olive oil** has great health benefits and seems to have a 'more is better' health impact in studies I've read so far. The key for me personally is using high quality only. That means that if it does not taste good when you drink it from a glass, it is not good enough. Good oil should be aromatic and leave a slight tingling sensation in your throat. You may be tempted to think of it as expensive, but on a cost per calorie basis, it is an incredibly cheap food (especially when bought in bulk). Average daily consumption: 50-100 grams.
- **Nut mix** of walnut, almond, cashew, hazelnut and brazil nuts. I buy this per 10 kilos from an online store that has a great unsalted nut mix product. Average daily consumption: 50-100 grams.
- **100% chocolate**, preferably raw chocolate. It's one of my favourite things to have together with a dose of mixed nuts.

Element 2: when I eat

I have an 8-10 hour eating window each day. Usually, I work backwards from when I will eat the latest that day:

- Alone? 12:00 to 20:00
- Friends? 14:00 to 22:00
- Party [221]? 16:00 to 02:00 (or make an exception)

> [221] *This doesn't happen very often, I don't like being up late, it's not my thing.* ↵

Consistency in your eating window really helps you maintain your discipline and routine, but after 6 years I have no lapses anymore.

Element 3: regular fasts

Every 3 months I fast for 5 days (100 hours minimum) non-stop. My goal here is to reach ketosis and maintain it in a fasted state for multiple days. See the hormesis chapter on the full health benefits of this, the short version is that it pushes the body into an extreme repair mode. Based on the fast mimicking diet research I supplement with MCT rich oil in the first days. Usually in the form of 2 teaspoons coconut oil.

An average fast looks like:

- Day 1-2: tea, 2-4 tsp coconut oil, salt
- Day 2-4: water, salt, 2 tsp coconut oil as needed
- Rest of the days: water

The purpose of tea in the first days is to keep my mind satisfied. I am aiming to eliminate this in the coming year.

The purpose of the salt is to compensate for the salt lost during fasting. This is for me personally compounded by the fact that I take saunas.

The purpose of the coconut oil is to give my body fuel to kick into ketosis. Also, it prevents me from being too cranky.

I measure my blood levels of ketones with the Abbott Optium Neo. My average statistics look like this:

Hours fasted	Ketone levels in mmol
24	0.5
48	1.5
72	3
96	2-4

The exact levels fluctuate based on how much I moved around and how much coconut oil I consumed on a given day.

Exercise

For me personally exercise needs to be:

- Location independent
- Equipment agnostic
- Intense but not debilitating

Based on the strength and muscle maintenance principles discussed earlier in this book my daily workout is a collection of the below depending on the equipment I have available:

- One-handed and one-legged push-ups
- Pistol squats
- Press handstands
- Kettlebell swings
- Pull-ups

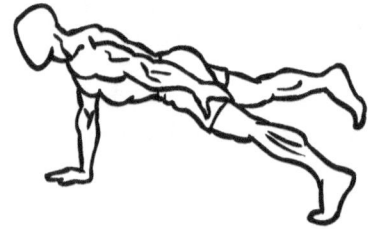

One handed push-up

Pistol squats

Press Handstand

Kettlebell swings

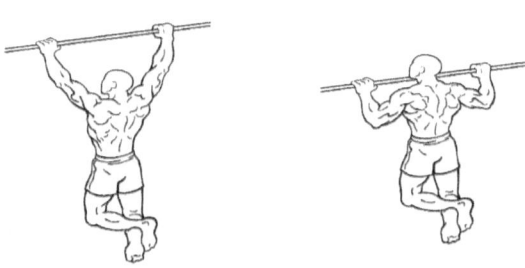

Pull ups

These exercises cover the strength angles most important to me and are mostly multi-muscle compound exercises.

This is complemented by the following stretch routine:

Exercise	Pulses
Pancakes	5
Nose to knee (in pancake)	2 x 5 per leg
Side stretch (in pancake)	5 per leg
Achilles stretch	5 per leg
Quad stretch	2 x 5 per leg
Glute stretch	5 per leg
Bridge (elevated feet)	10 pushes towards hands
Plow stretch	10

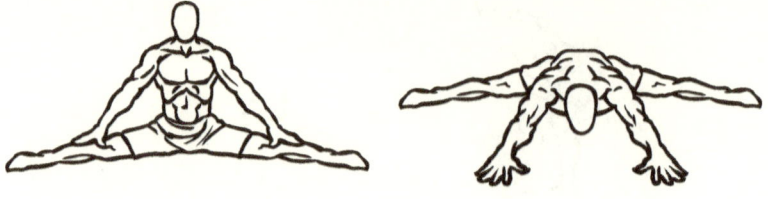

Forward Pancake

Side Pancake

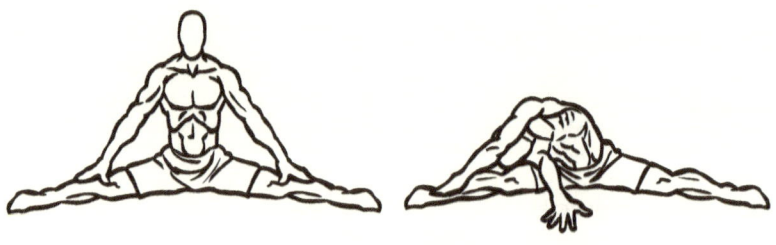

Straddle Side

Achilles Stretch

Reclined Quad

Glute Stretch

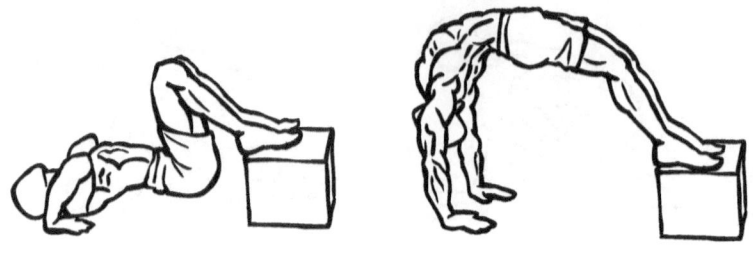

Elevated Bridge

Knees by ears

A pulse (see table above the images) is actively pushing down into a stretch while tensing the muscle until it is very uncomfortable but not painful. I hold this for 5-30 seconds depending on how tight I am that day.

While not entirely full body, this routine stretches the parts of my body that I know to get tense from my daily life. Ideally, this routine is preceded or followed by a sauna or other heat exposure.

Hormesis

Strictly, fasting is a form of hormesis so it would fall under this section. Aside from that, I use heat and cold regularly through:

- Cold showers
- Saunas
- Hot baths

I take cold showers in the morning to wake up. If I feel cold when waking up I'll start with a brief warm shower.

The saunas are a minimum of 20 minutes at the maximum temperature available. This is easier in infrared saunas, but I prefer the hotter Finnish variety. Ideally, I have one on a daily basis. When a sauna is not available usually a bath is (e.g., at a hotel). I don't consider sauna sessions a set part of my routine. It is nice to have, but contrary to exercise I am fine with a week without.

I regularly take a day to go to a spa with many saunas and cold plunge baths. I generally spend a full day there, preferably with a companion. Sauna establishments are very common in the Netherlands and other northern European countries. [222]

[222] *Fun fact, these places, as a rule, require you to go naked (mixed gender). It's hilarious to see my non-(northern)European friends freak out over this.* ↵

Blood values

I regularly visit my doctor for blood checks. This is an uncommon practice in the Netherlands and I had some explaining to do before they would let me do 'frivolous' tests. For me, it was as simple as explaining that I live an aberrant lifestyle and would like to make sure my body is responding well to it. I am required to pay what my insurance does not.

The things I usually have tested are:

- Lipid panel (LDL, HDL, Triglycerides)
- Hormonal
  - TSH (thyroid)
  - Testosterone
- Vitamins & minerals
  - Vitamin D
  - Vitamin B12
  - Iron
  - Magnesium
- Haematology panel
- Predictive/directional markers
  - Homocysteine
  - Hba1c
  - C Reactive protein
  - AST

Supplements

My primary philosophy for supplements is that they should be used for correcting deficiencies and not taken blindly. Taking supplements you don't need can lead to excesses. In some cases that is harmless, in others it is detrimental.

There are exceptions to this. Some supplements are quite harmless and can positively benefit health (or at least not impact it negatively). Personally, I take:

- Fish oil from Nordic Oils (from low food chain fish)
- Magnesium (citrate, bisglycinate, chelated)
- Lithium Orotate (just to emphasise, the 5mg dose I use is a mineral supplement, not a psychiatric drug)
- Collagen from Great Lakes (hydrolysed, flavourless)

The first has the potential to stave off declining vision (my 23andme and family history predict I will need glasses) as well as have a positive effect on mental function. The only thing to be aware of is that fish oil might be contaminated with toxins like heavy metals. Most supplements filter these out, but to be safe I tend to go with high-quality brands that preferably source the oil from smaller fish.

Magnesium is a common deficiency and many magnesium supplements are of low quality. I take different types that seem to have different effects due to the tissues they end up in. I keep a keen eye on my magnesium levels in my blood checks to make sure I don't overdo it.

Collagen is naturally found in skin and tendons. I started taking it as a way to support my tendons when I was developing my flexibility. It is not easy to measure the effect so this is the supplement that comes closest to me taking it 'blind'.

Based on my blood values, I periodically take other supplements. Mostly vitamin D since it goes a bit low in the darker months.

Take note that if a certain deficiency pops up without a clear reason (e.g., vitamin D in winter) you should have a look at your lifestyle to check if there is a clear cause.

Chapter
My financial structure

Let me start by saying that finances are very specific to a person's needs and situation. The needs of a programmer living and working in South Africa is different from the same job position in Sweden.

My current setup is geared towards a life in Amsterdam. These numbers are not meant to be a recommendation. They serve as an example of the applied principles.

My financials revolve around three elements:

1. Managing money for now (budget)
2. Planning money for later (calculate needs)
3. Managing money for later (investing)

While points 2 and 3 seem linked I consider them entirely separately.

Managing money (budget)

Human nature is part of us, so I designed my habits in such a way that it works with rather than against my nature.

3 bank accounts

- Wallet account
- Hub account
- Savings account

The wallet account's card is in my wallet (surprise). It never contains more than €100 or so. It should cover my daily needs of food and small sporadic spending. The key here is that anything out of the ordinary can't simply be paid from this card. If I have the impulse to buy a pair of shoes, this card should not cover that. Why? Well:

- The extra expense is now an extra hassle, making me reconsider
- I never make expenses based on money I shouldn't spend (like rent money)
- I see money as scarce since the card is not linked to my other money

It is, in essence, a self-protection measure.

The second account is the hub account. This is the account that manages bigger inflows and outflows. It takes in my income and spends regular expenses like:

- Rent
- Insurance
- Food (automatic transfer per week to my wallet card)
- Sports club membership

The key to this account is that the card is not in my wallet. It really never is. There is no expense that is too big for my limited wallet card that can't wait a few hours for me to manually transfer money from my centre to my hub account.

Another highlight is that as much as possible of my finances on this account are automated. There is no mandatory expense I have that I need to manually pay. If I drop off the map for 2 years I will never come back to a pile of checks and repo men. This has as advantages that:

- I never think about my expenses, they just happen
- I never miss a payment
- I don't feel any 'pain' paying mandatory expenses

Do note that I add all expenses in my budget and review them periodically to see if I can cut any of them down or out.

The third account is a savings account with a higher interest percentage than my hub account. The hub account holds 6 months of expenses, the rest goes into the savings account to garner some interest (even though it is quite low).

Budgeting

I love budgeting. When I started I thought I would hate it, but it has turned into a source of pleasure for me. At no point am I in any doubt as to what I can and cannot afford, and I know exactly how long my money will last me.

I personally use You Need A Budget (YNAB) to manage my expenses. It is a very good tool for managing the week by week operation of your budget.

The YNAB principle that had the most impact on me was "give every euro a job". In other words, when money comes in I give it a category, even if that category is 'buffer'. What that means is that I started adding more money than I needed to categories like rent and food. After a few months of using it, I noticed I had 'aged my money'. I was spending the money that came in 2 months ago because the system had helped me plan ahead.

I have three sections in YNAB:

1. Obligations & survival
2. Desires
3. Investable wealth

The first contains things like rent, food, insurances and a buffer for unexpected expenses. The second (desired) was all the things I want out of life. I have chosen to include the categories:

- Wellbeing (money for massages, wellness etc)
- Guilt-free (spend on whatever, no strings)
- Sharing the love (money I can only spend on others)
- Saving goals (snowboard)
- Getaway fund (travel money)

The last category has a number of categories for different types of investments I allow myself to make (for which there are rules I have set).

Planning money for later

This section is essential. If you don't know where you are going, you will never get there. The assumptions I work with are a 4% safe withdrawal rate [223] which translates to needing 25 times your desired yearly income invested.

[223] *which should according to the creator of the 4% rule be fine to live off of it indefinitely* ↵

Based on the prices in Amsterdam I have set up the following goals currently:

Stage	Monthly	Yearly	4% nest egg
Survival (rent, food, insurance)	800 + 400 + 200 = 1400	16.8k	420k
Joyful (wellness, toys, travel)	1400 + 300 + 300 + 200 = 2200	26.4k	660k
The Life (megatravel, megatoys, megahouse)	2200 + 500 + 500 + 1000 = 4200	50.4k	1.26m
Me +1 [224]	8200	100.8k	2.52m

Me plus a partner I can sustain entirely to join my adventures
↵

Investing money

My investment philosophy is quite straightforward and basically a copy of Warren Buffett's advice: invest your age in bonds and the rest in stocks. Of course, you should spread the risk by buying index funds of bonds and stocks instead of individual ones.

Operationally I invest with 2 parties:

- Brand New Day (pension account [225], index funds)
- Degiro (index funds, individual stocks)

> [225] *The Netherlands has special retirement accounts with special rules.* ↵

The reason I also use stockbrokers that offer individual stocks is that I can't help myself. Like all human beings I think I have some sort of unique understanding that will help me predict the future slightly better than my neighbour. To satisfy this urge I have a small amount of play money that I am allowed to put into stocks. I consider this money lost. It's more like gambling than a long-term plan.

Brand New Day, on the other hand, is my favourite broker in the Netherlands. They offer a limited selection of index funds at exceptionally low fees. I have three accounts with them:

- World index (age in bonds rest in stocks)
- High-risk small cap and developing nation index (small amount)
- Tax-advantaged account specific to the Netherlands

Every month a set amount of my income is automatically transferred to these low-cost accounts which will keep on growing over the coming decades.

www.ingramcontent.com/pod-product-compliance
Lightning Source LLC
Chambersburg PA
CBHW030611220526
45463CB00004B/1253